*America's economic joyride
is coming to an end . . .*

Thus far, we have met each new piece of bad news with disbelief and sometimes outrage. There has been a lot of talk about "who is to blame," and some groups have taken the position that they have been singled out for unfair treatment . . . charges and counter-charges fill the air, clog the media, and do nothing at all to hasten an adjustment to new ways of life.

The overall assumption is that each scarcity is temporary—*an assumption typified by the rapid move back toward larger automobiles, the pressure to raise speed limits from an energy (and life) saving 55 mph, and the desertion of mass transportation when gasoline supplies increased in the spring of 1974.*

# THE END
# OF AFFLUENCE

A Blueprint for Your Future

**Paul R. Ehrlich**
and
**Anne H. Ehrlich**

BALLANTINE BOOKS • NEW YORK

**To David Brower**

whose single-minded pursuit of environmental quality sets an example
for us all.

SBN 345-24376-5-195

First Printing: November, 1974

Design by Frederic Dodnick

Printed in the United States of America


BALLANTINE BOOKS
A Division of Random House, Inc.
201 East 50th Street, New York, N.Y. 10022
Simultaneously published by
Ballantine Books, Ltd., Toronto, Canada

# CONTENTS

# Acknowledgments

WE ARE INDEBTED to the following colleagues who were kind enough to read and criticize the entire manuscript: D. L. Bilderback (Department of History, Fresno State College), John P. Holdren (Energy and Environment Program, University of California, Berkeley), Richard W. Holm (Department of Biology, Stanford), and Johnson C. Montgomery (attorney, Palo Alto, California). John W. Gofman (Cardiodynamics—Vida Medical Systems, Dublin, California) and Jim Harding (Friends of the Earth) were kind enough to review the section on nuclear energy. In many cases their advice was followed, and it greatly improved the manuscript. As Richard Nixon would say, we must accept the responsibility for all errors of fact and opinion, but any guilt associated with the errors must rest with others.

Reid A. Bryson (Department of Meteorology, University of Wisconsin) and Lester R. Brown (Overseas Development Council) have been most helpful in keeping us up-to-date on the world weather and food situations. William Kaufmann (Kaufmann Associates) wielded his fine editorial pen over our efforts; his comments were enormously helpful. Jane Lawson Bavelas, Ann Duffield, and Darryl Wheye handled the typing and proofreading chores with their usual excellence and dispatch. Ms. Bavelas also assisted with the editing and made many helpful suggestions on the content. Julia Kennedy and Paul Growald helped with proofreading the final manuscript. And once again, Margaret Craig and her assistants in the Stanford Biology Library were most helpful in running down sources.

# Approaching the Future

---

"A calamity is a time of great opportunity"
—Chinese Proverb

WORRIED ABOUT INFLATION? Unsure whether you'll be able to purchase the food or clothing you need next year? Uncertain whether you will be able to get enough gas to drive to work in the future? Disturbed about the incompetence and dishonesty of American political leaders? Distressed about the kind of environment our children will have to live in when they grow up? If you are, you share the concerns of many millions of Americans. Things are going badly for them, too, and they sense—without knowing why—that conditions may well worsen rapidly.

Perhaps they don't know why because they believe in a great many of the fallacies and fairy stories that pervade our society—nonsense based on history that will not repeat itself, ignorance of environmental systems, or just plain wishful thinking. You are doubtless familiar with some of these notions, such as:

1. The United States will always have abundant food.
2. Economists and politicians know how to end inflation.

3. Our problems will end if we can supply ourselves with superabundant energy, and the Government will adopt policies that will ensure energy independence for the United States by 1980.
4. Nuclear fission plants are a clean, safe, desirable source of energy.
5. Economic growth will end poverty.
6. Most members of Congress are well-informed and working hard on cures for the problems of society.
7. The twenty-first century will be the Century of Japan.
8. The Amazon Basin is a vast, untapped resource base for mankind.
9. Our children will live even more affluent lives than we have.
10. There is nothing you can do to change the future, the government must and will take care of us.

Many other bits of nonsense could be added to this Alice-in-Wonderland array, but these should be enough to give you the idea. This book is especially aimed at those who *do not* believe item 10—people who would like to depend more on themselves than on the government to shape their futures.

What are the prospects for the future? We are facing, within the next three decades, the disintegration of an unstable world of nation-states infected with growthmania. The game of unlimited growth is ending, like it or not. We are approaching the limits, and this will have profound consequences for the rest of our lives; some of them indeed have already begun to appear. This is what underlies the sudden, seemingly mysterious shortages and the widespread inflation that have plagued the world. In addition, changing physical conditions on the planet have exacerbated the economic problems we face. Yet most American citizens, and their leaders, have little understanding of the root causes of their escalating problems—a major obstacle to solving them.

But there is a brighter side. When *The Population Bomb* was written six years ago, few people were deeply concerned about the population-resource-environment crisis the world was entering. Today we might take heart because people *are* worried; getting people concerned about a problem is half the battle. And concerned people have taken action. Since *The Population Bomb* was published, millions of Americans have made responsible personal decisions to limit the size of their families to at most two children. They did this at least partly because they were apprehensive about the impact of overpopulation on the future quality of their lives and their children's lives. The individual actions of millions of Americans brought the fertility rate down to the replacement level—the point at which each generation just replaces itself. If fertility remains at that level, natural population growth will stop well before there are 300 million Americans. If the fertility rate were to go even lower, we could halt growth before there are 250 million Americans.

*The Population Bomb* was directed primarily at people under thirty, whose direct action could influence population growth. This time the battle involves everyone, not just a particular age-group. There is no adult who cannot actively affect what happens in his or her personal life if he or she chooses to do so. But now the choices are far more complex than simply deciding not to have a large family. Population growth is just one of the three key factors that, multiplied together, threaten the quality of life for all of us by threatening the integrity of the environmental systems that sustain us. The other factors—increasing affluence and the use of faulty technologies to support that affluence—cannot so easily be affected by individual action. The entire society is locked into a way of life that will take decades to change, just as it took decades to develop.

For instance, since World War II, people have been persuaded that driving cars everywhere is "better" than using mass transit, that air conditioning is the way to make things more comfortable in the summer, that disposable everything is better than durable anything, and that embalmed foods are more convenient and just as nutritious as fresh foods. That kind of "affluence" a decade or two ago seemed desirable, wasteful as it was. It has only been recognized as undesirable by a few people who have added up its real costs in reduced health, environmental degradation, and resource depletion and then realized that there are viable and often more pleasant alternatives.

But even those who realized that commuting by train is more fun and healthier than commuting by car, or that a well-insulated house can be more comfortable and cheaper than an air-conditioned one, or that convenience foods are often not only more costly but also less healthful and tasty than other foods, could do little about it. Society, rather than the individual, had to act before mass transit could be available in many areas. Most people either rent or buy a home that is already constructed, and therefore adequate insulation is difficult or impossible to provide. And buying from the array of foods in supermarkets requires considerable attention if one is to get adequate nutrition without overloading with calories and undesirable additives. To get wholesome foods, it is often necessary to pay a premium at a "health food" store. In short, the individual who wants these alternatives has generally been forced either to resort to political action, to put up with considerable inconvenience, or to pay much higher prices in order to gain them.

Our extremely complex, interdependent society would have to undergo radical changes if it is to be made ecologically sane. In the 1960s an attempt was made to initiate a reorganization. Ecologists and others concerned with overpopulation, declining resources, and a deteriorating environment tried to alert voters to the perils of an approaching age of scarcity. During that period, it became more and more apparent to concerned observers that mankind was rushing toward disaster, although the precise form of that disaster, the time of its occurrence, and the pattern of socio-political response to it were still far from clear. But it was all too clear that the political system was not generating the rational, planned change required to avert catastrophe.

In the early 1970s, the leading edge of the age of scarcity arrived. With it came a clearer look at the future, revealing more of the nature of the dark age to come. But more importantly, it exposed the hopeless inadequacy of society's response to a diffuse and slowly evolving crisis. The time for warning is now past, and it appears that a coordinated social response to humanity's peril may never come at all. In view of the latter probability, it behooves each individual to introduce into his or her personal planning the recognition that a period of environmental and social decay has begun.

This book is not, as *Bomb* was, directed primarily at the younger set. It is addressed to *all Americans* in an attempt to provide individuals with help, both in evaluating the developing state of the system and in making appropriate personal and political decisions. It is our great hope, of course, that an adequate organized social change of the sort outlined by Pirages and Ehrlich in *Ark II: Social Response to Environmental Imperatives* (Viking, 1974) will take place. But in the absence of any indication that such general and massive social change is possible (let alone likely), all of us should consider the alternatives, however grim.

In short, it is *up to you*. You cannot count on "society" or the government to help you solve your problems. On the contrary, every effort will probably be made to continue in the same old growthmanic ways—business attempting to maximize consumption and profits, the government printing money and manipulating complex tax laws to disguise its redistribution of wealth (all too often from the poor and middle class to the rich). Although the physical, ecological, social, and political situations that permitted these economic practices during the past few decades no longer exist, the fact will be ignored. The US government-industrial establishment will continue to act as if it can go on increasing its resource gluttony, raping the world's ecosystems, and tromping on many American citizens and those of other nations with impunity.

All of this will inevitably lead to a period of great turmoil. What happens to you during that period will be in part a function of how well you read the signs that tell what is going to happen, how well you prepare for it on the basis of that reading, and how good your luck is. People who become involved in their own futures *now* can help to change them. If you face what's coming squarely, you may be able to ride the crest of the tidal wave that will engulf society, rather than be crushed beneath it. Whatever your position in society, there are a great many things you can do to improve your own chances for survival—things that will reduce your dependence on a sagging social system. You must evaluate information on your own, rather than blindly accept other people's interpretations. You must make contingency plans on the basis of your analysis and be prepared to act on them.

This book is a guide for such personal planning. In it we attempt to tell you what portents to look for and give suggestions on how to respond to them. First, you must understand how the world system is behaving and how our society is functioning. Then you will be able to place yourself in the big picture. The suggestions in the latter part of the book will, we hope, give you some help in formulating a flexible personal plan of action.

Before taking a hard look at the world, you should carefully examine your own attitudes and beliefs for they must supply the basic framework for your future action. You will have to answer difficult questions, particularly about your relationship to the rest of society, and only your own views, morality, and goals can provide guidance. For instance, does the knowledge that President Nixon and many other people have cheated on their taxes, or that the tax system favors certain groups, relieve you of the obligation to pay your taxes in full? Are you duty bound to obey if the government urges you to consume in order to keep the economy growing? Is it irresponsible for you not to vote when you are constantly presented a choice between bad and worse? Should you forego extra salary or profits to help fight inflation? If the nation is hell-bent on destroying itself, are you ethically committed to making a maximum effort to change its course? Or may you ethically ignore society's plight entirely?

Suppose you have been an "ant" and worked diligently and saved to insure the future of your family while the "grasshoppers" have loafed and spent all their earnings. You have built up a stock of food, water, and other articles against the day when the distribution systems of the country break down. When the crunch comes, are you obliged to share with the grasshoppers? This is a version of the "would you let your neighbors into your fallout shelter" question that caused so much controversy in the past. For many the question remains unresolved—in spite of the great interdependence of our society, most questions about individuals' responsibilities to one another are rarely even posed, let alone answered.

These queries are closely related to philosophical questions that have long puzzled mankind—the most fundamental of which is probably "what is the value (or purpose) of human life?" Some people think that human life is intrinsically valuable and desire to see the world filled with the maximum number of people. A Brazilian economist at a recent UN meeting we attended said quite explicitly that his goal was to have the maximum number of people existing at the minimum standard of living. His reason? "Because I was glad to be born." Since our personal view is that it would be better to have one-half billion people living a comfortable and secure life rather than twenty billion living at the fringes of existence, we immediately asked him if he would have been sorry if he had not been born!

But our view, that human life has whatever value people give to it, is no more defensible "scientifically" than his view. Society could attempt to maximize the number of people, or it could attempt to maximize the standard of living of each individual. Both cannot be maximized simultaneously, however, and attempting to maximize either in one generation would have profound consequences for future generations.

The genetic, social, political, and economic diversity of mankind make these problems more complex. How much social and personal effort should go into equalizing incomes, opportunities, and attitudes within and among nations? Would the world be better off if everyone were the same height, color, personality, and had the same income and social status? Some say yes, because they think it would do away with racism and war. We think not, because we feel that biological and cultural diversity, in addition to adding interest to human life, provide mankind with the flexibility necessary to avoid disaster. But diversity of income is easy for the affluent to espouse, and extolling genetic diversity can be an excuse for maintaining a supply of underdogs to do menial tasks. Can a satisfactory balance be struck between equality and diversity?

An informed person today faces very serious choices. This is nothing new, however. Plato wrote about similar choices, as did St. Augustine. One of these deals with how to behave when the interests of the individual and society are not congruent because the body politic is intent on suicide. For instance, it is prudent, we suggest, to stash a few cases of tuna in your basement (if you're lucky enough to have a basement and the money for the tuna) because periodic protein shortages (or at least sky-high prices) seem certain to occur within the ten-to-twenty-year shelf-life of the cans. But if everyone suddenly became aware of the possibility of food shortage, a hoarding spree could start that would create a food shortage even if one hadn't been in the cards.

In April, 1973, when President Nixon was assuring the nation that there would be no energy crisis, what might have happened if everyone had realized he was lying? A lot of resources might have been wasted sinking back-yard fuel tanks for which there would soon have been no gasoline anyway. It is, of course, standard operating procedure for a government to conceal the size of vital stocks in order to prevent hoarding—the Indian government has been periodically deceiving the Indian people on this score for more than a decade. In this context, the energy story could be considered one of the few constructive lies told by Nixon.

Thus, each of us must decide how much effort to put

into trying to save society, how much into personally preparing for the crises ahead, and how much into doing things that are pleasant while they still can be done. This is a choice that each individual must make for herself or himself, and the choice will vary greatly with circumstances—such considerations as finances, family, health, and location will mix with personal bent. For instance, if it were certain that governments and industry will continue to do very nearly the worst possible thing at every juncture, everyone could concentrate on enjoying himself, since social collapse would be inevitable, and no set of personal preparations will allow anyone to enjoy that!

As you prepare for the most difficult period ever faced by industrial society, you will be presented with many such choices that involve your attitudes toward your fellow human beings. As you read this book, consider in particular the question of whether to put society's or your own interest first; it is a conscious choice everyone will soon have to make. We are unimpressed by those who say, "why bother to make plans? If society breaks down, life will not be worth living." Human beings seem to be genetically and culturally programmed to struggle on in the face of extreme adversity—as the record of wars, slavery, death camps, and the like testifies. Almost all will struggle to stay afloat in a sea of troubles, but those who are mentally and physically prepared are most likely to succeed.

Undoubtedly, you will see this book criticized because we take such a "pessimistic" view of the future. It seems to be part of American popular culture to consider optimism, in itself, to be good. In the face of disasters, our political and social leaders frequently castigate the "prophets of doom" who fail to accentuate the positive and who want the lifeboats manned merely because the ship is sinking. Our entire society seems to suffer from a sort of mental block and may refuse to take action to correct its fatal course until it has passed the point of no return. This book is only "pessimistic" in the sense that recognizing a severe problem and recommending action to solve it are "pessimistic."

In giving a prognosis for a sick society, we have inevitably been highly critical of various people and institutions. Unpleasant as these may be, however, the criticisms are accurate to the best of our ability. While such negative comments are necessary to illuminate the kinds of personal and institutional behavior that make it impossible for society to respond adaptively to its plight, they have been made without malice. We recognize that even "the worst and the dullest" usually have good intentions and believe they are behaving responsibly.

We think our diagnosis of the ills of society is substantially correct, even though the exact pattern of future decline remains obscure. Nevertheless, our suggestions for "cures" must be taken with caution, since among other things, no one, including ourselves, has had any prior experience with the disease. After all, industrial society has never been threatened with total collapse before! We are willing to make suggestions because we and a small group of colleagues have devoted much of our time over the past fifteen years to seeking ways to meet the problems of the period humankind is now entering.

But no one knows enough to chart the future with great precision. You must evaluate our suggestions carefully, listen to others, compare and contrast ideas, and make your own decisions. Now is not a time for the blind following of "authorities"—be they politicians, economists, priests, or ecologists. If enough citizens take the time and trouble first to learn what is going on and then to take political and personal action to deflect society from its suicidal course, then we can all become "optimists" about the future of humanity.

But whether or not that happens, the course of your own future is largely up to you. Your personal survival plan is going to depend on two broad areas of action:

1. To prevent the development of circumstances that could destroy you (the construction of a nuclear plant near your home, for example); and
2. To create circumstances that can maintain the quality of your life (sources of food and water,

friends, community support, things to add interest to life, such as books and hobbies).

It is only fair that we end this introduction with a comment about our personal choices. We have chosen to divide our own efforts between doing the things we like to do and trying to change the system. We live in a crowded suburban area in a moderate-sized house without a basement. Our only child is an adult. We enjoy our friends and our work too much to move to a remote spot and start farming and hoarding—although we think that may be a very intelligent choice for some people. If society goes, we will go with it—which makes our efforts to change its course anything but altruistic. Yet, dark as the future may seem, the struggle to prevent disaster is to us still worth while. If we only manage to reduce the chance of catastrophe by a percentage point or two, we won't be sorry that we tried.

# 1

# The Edge of the Crisis

"Many millions of people in the poor countries are going to starve to death before our eyes . . . upon our television sets. . . ."

—C. P. Snow, 1968

". . . there is an absolute limit to the ability of the earth to support or tolerate the process of industrial activity, and there is reason to believe that we are now moving toward the limit very rapidly."

—Robert L. Heilbroner, 1974 [1]

TOO MANY PEOPLE using too many resources: we have been talking and writing about that for almost a quarter of a century—but as Americans, we hadn't experienced any severe shortages either at home or abroad until we were in Costa Rica in early December of 1973. Then we had our first direct confrontation with the future. World oil scarcity combined with a local political foul-up had led to a severe gasoline shortage; the usually bustling traffic of San José had been reduced to a trickle. We were there to conduct research on how tropical grasses protect themselves from insects, hoping to discover useful methods for reducing the impact of pests on grain crops. The ingenuity and connections of Jorge Campabadal, the local research coordinator for the Organization of Tropical Studies (OTS), had produced enough gasoline for our Land Rover to carry out field work around the capital city during the first weekend we were in Costa Rica, and on Monday more was promised to carry us from the cool plateau on which San José is located to the steaming rain forest of the Sarapiquí region on the Atlantic lowlands.

17

Early Monday morning we were at OTS headquarters for instructions on where to get our gas, only to learn that the promised shipment had not  arrived at the gas station patronized by OTS. "No matter," said Jorge, conscious of our limited time and our need to get to the forest field site, "We'll siphon gas from the other OTS vehicles for you." But we were too late—someone had already siphoned the others dry. All we could do was hope that some gas would arrive that afternoon; at least one of five precious days for research was down the drain.

Then, as we chugged back from our unsuccessful siphoning expedition, a miracle occurred; we spotted a gasoline tanker pulling into a service station. A line of automobiles was already forming, and by the time we found our way to the end of it through a maze of one-way streets, the queue was several blocks long. It took about an hour and a half to reach the pumps, because a large number of cars had already been parked in the station for days waiting for fuel, and those were cleared out first. The jeep in front of us ran out of gas at the end of the first half hour, and we pushed it along for the last hour.

Perhaps the strangest part of the experience was not knowing whether the station's fuel would last or how much we could get. Our colleague, Dr. Michael Singer, who spoke more fluent Spanish than we did, walked ahead to the station to see if we could get a full tank. The station owner was king for the day, deciding who would get what, and limiting most customers to a few gallons. He refused to commit himself, so we waited, not knowing whether we waited in vain (anything less than a full tank would not permit us to go to the boondocks and return). Apparently we looked pathetic enough, however, for when we finally reached the pump he topped our tank, permitting us to leave on the four-hour drive to the Sarapiquí. During that trip we saw three or four other vehicles on the road and no open gas stations.

Most Costa Ricans seemed to be making the best of a grim situation. It was encouraging that a service station would take pity on three foreigners and fill their tank

while limiting many regular customers. The gas crisis
had a darker side, however. Virtually all Costa Ricans had
locks on their gas tanks—to be without one was to be
siphoned dry. And the government had forbidden gas
stations to fill gas cans.

In California three months after our Costa Rican experience, our car was in line for four hours to get ten gallons
of gas, even though there was *no* severe shortage of gasoline. A small cutback in supplies and a large amount of
bureaucratic bungling had produced a maximum of inconvenience for the public. Price gouging and line-jumping
became commonplace, and there was even occasional
mayhem at the gas pumps. Various groups pleaded for
special allotments of petroleum, and states squabbled with
the federal government over what was their "fair share."
Lacking leadership from Washington, states, counties, and
municipalities initiated various distribution plans, some
voluntary, some mandatory. In Hawaii, the state "gasplan"
was attacked in the courts. The mayor of a small town
without gas in West Virginia threatened to hijack any
gasoline truck that came through.

In reality, the US in 1973–74 faced two energy crises.
One was a mini-crisis of supply: a shortage of gasoline and heating oil for the consumer. It caused enormous
hoopla in the media, unending speculation at cocktail
parties, inconvenience for almost everyone, and considerable suffering (and some deaths) among the poor. The
other was a maxi-crisis of demand—*of too much energy
use*—that went relatively unnoticed.

The causes of the mini-crisis are complex and somewhat
obscure; the cause of the maxi-crisis is simple and obvious.
In the last decade or two, growth in worldwide use of
energy has averaged between 4 and 5 percent per year.
This means consumption has been doubling about every
sixteen years. The US, which consumes 30 percent of
the energy used in the world each year, has tripled its
petroleum consumption since World War II. Some countries such as Japan have increased their consumption even
faster. (Petroleum and natural gas now supply three-
quarters of America's energy; our use of coal—which is

domestically more abundant—has not kept pace.) By 1973, the US consumed nearly eighteen million barrels (a barrel equals 42 gallons) of oil *a day*—a stupendous amount. As the more accessible reserves of fossil fuel have been drained, it is not surprising that production should begin to fall behind this soaring demand.

Given the chaos that resulted from a minor reduction in gasoline supplies in the mini-crisis, one wonders what would happen if the US had been faced with an extreme shortage like that in Costa Rica or if our gasoline shortage hadn't been considered temporary. How would Americans behave if faced with permanent severe shortages, not just of gasoline, but of electric power, food, clothing, paper products, plastics, and many other goods? Has the US learned anything from the "energy crisis"?

These questions are not just academic. Since 1972, besides the gasoline shortage, Americans have experienced relatively minor shortages and rising prices for everything from newsprint to bicycles. Many of the shortages—plastics, paints, fertilizers, drugs, antifreeze, synthetic fabrics and clothing made from them—were a direct result of the energy shortage, because these products are made from petroleum and/or natural gas. Many others were indirect results of the energy shortage, sometimes combined with unexpectedly high demand. Among these are chlorine, lumber, roofing tiles, and food. Production of all of these—and myriad other things—was hindered by lack of fuel. Shortages in transport facilities and steel scrap caused a shortage in steel; poor harvests have caused shortages in cotton, canned salmon, and some other foods; short supplies of synthetic fabrics and plastics put pressure on natural fabrics, leather, paper, and wood as substitutes. The meat shortage of 1973 caused price rises for fish and beans, and a shortage in home freezers. Many shortages can be traced to world trade—Japan's buying up of supplies of cotton and wool, for example.

Nor are shortages limited to the US; they are worldwide. And they will become more frequent and more severe. In the near future millions of people will experience—perhaps for the first time in their lives—not occasional inconvenience but real hardship. In our opinion, the last decades of the twentieth century will initiate a worldwide age of scarcity. Moreover, unless human institutions and ways of doing things undergo radical change, this new age could continue indefinitely.

## The Food Crunch

Although the minor gas shortage in 1973 and 1974 was the first instance of the age of scarcity to be perceived by the average citizen in the overdeveloped countries ODCs),* scarcity has been all too real for hundreds of millions of people in the underdeveloped countries (UDCs) for decades. For many of them, reductions in the supply of gasoline and electric power would be unnoticed, since they have never had access to either. The most serious shortage they have faced has been a food shortage—a shortage so severe that in the decade of the 1960s, between ten and twenty million people died prematurely each year because they had inadequate diets.[2]

This vast tragedy, however, is nothing compared to the nutritional disaster that seems likely to overtake humanity in the 1970s (or, at the latest, the 1980s). Due to a combination of ignorance, greed, and callousness, a situation has been created that could lead to a *billion or more people starving to death*. Although many things can still be done to lessen the scale of this coming disaster, it seems most unlikely that sensible action will be taken, for reasons elaborated in the following chapters.

* Overdeveloped countries are those in which population levels and per capita resource demands are so high that it will be impossible to maintain their present living standards without making exorbitant demands on global resources and ecosystems. Underdeveloped countries (UDCs) are those that are unable to provide even the basic necessities of life—food, clothing, shelter, and health care—for the majority of their citizens.

The world food situation can be discussed in terms of three interrelated factors: supply, demand, and distribution. In the past decade, food supply per capita has increased in the developed countries, which were already well fed. The per capita supply has remained essentially constant in the underdeveloped countries, where a significant portion of the population constantly suffers from hunger. The populations of UDCs have been increasing rapidly, and in the past ten years an estimated one-half billion people have been added to the ranks of those with inadequate diets. Thus, while the *proportion* of people in UDCs suffering from undernutrition and malnutrition* probably remained about the same during the last decade, there are now *many millions more* hungry people than there were ten years ago.

In underdeveloped countries, there has been little increase in per capita income and therefore little increase in the per capita demand for food—that is, the desire and ability of the average person to *buy* food. Thus the growth in total demand for food in the UDCs has been chiefly due to population growth. Since the early 1950s, most of these populations have been growing at between 2 and 3 percent per year—rates that would double the number of people in twenty-four to thirty-five years. In the ODCs, on the other hand, where population growth has been considerably slower (one percent or less per year),[3] much of the rise in total demand for food has been a result of increased affluence, leading to rising per capita demand.

We can see how affluence affects what happens to the world's supply of food by looking at both direct and indirect consumption of grains—the most important of man's foodstuffs. In UDCs the average person consumes slightly over a pound of grain a day, nearly all of it directly. The average American, by contrast, consumes

---

* Undernutrition results from lack of calories; malnutrition results from an inadequately balanced diet—most often shortage of protein.

nearly five times as much grain, though less than half a pound directly (mostly in bakery products and breakfast cereals). The remainder is consumed indirectly—that is, it is fed to farm animals and then eaten secondhand as steaks, pork chops, fried chicken, eggs, milk, and so on. In recent years, increases in food consumption in ODCs have mostly been caused by increased indirect consumption of grain. People in ODCs, especially the United States, aren't eating more *food*; they are eating more meat, poultry, and dairy products. Americans (6 percent of the world's population) not only consume about 30 percent of the world's natural resources, they also consume 30 percent of the world's meat.

The protein-rich, highly varied diet of the average American requires nearly *five times* the agricultural resources (such as land, water, fertilizers, and pesticides) that are needed to feed a citizen in a UDC.[4] In the process of feeding himself, as in almost all other areas of activity, the gluttonous American thus has a disproportionate impact on the ecosphere.

This brings us to the third major factor in the food problem—distribution. Food scientist Georg Borgstrom has stated that if every human being received his or her precise "share" of the world's food supplies, everyone would have enough calories and everyone would be slightly protein-deficient. Although there are many uncertainties involved in making such a statement, two related assertions can be made with confidence. First, total world food production clearly is not much greater than that required to provide an adequate diet for some four billion people, and may be somewhat less. Second, most of today's hunger can be traced to problems of distribution.

The most obvious distributional problem with food is what Borgstrom has called the "protein swindle": the trade system by which large amounts of protein are moved from the malnourished poor nations to the overfed rich. In the late 1960s, for instance, fish exported to developed countries by Peru alone would have been enough to make up the protein deficit of all Latin Americans. Poor nations all too often export food that is needed at home in a world where money, not need, determines international flows of goods. For example, a recent 40 percent rise in meat production in Guatemala was accompanied by a 6 percent decline in Guatemalan per capita meat consumption.[5]

Maldistribution among nations is, however, only part of the story. There is maldistribution *within* nations as well. In both ODCs and UDCs, some people are well fed while others go hungry. Millions in the US still do not have adequate diets; many of the poorest people in countries like Mexico and Brazil do not share in what income improvement there has been and continue to subsist underfed and malnourished.

Even within families, food may be inequitably distributed, with infants and young children (precisely those most in need of abundant protein and other nutrients) often receiving the poorest diets. Among the causes are superstition, ignorance of nutrition, and a rapid abandonment of breast-feeding in UDCs. The latter is a special bit of insanity, since mother's milk is by far the best diet for infants, all the more so in UDCs where water for making formulas may be polluted and proper bottle sterilization may be difficult or impossible. The sources of the trend seem to be advertising by baby-food manufacturers and imitation (among urban women) of ODC fads. Better-educated women in ODCs, on the other hand, are now returning to breast-feeding. The trend away from breast-feeding in the UDCs is a tragic example of repetition of ODC mistakes—mistakes that in some cases the ODCs are now trying to correct.

Described in these bland terms, the world food problem, although serious, seems soluble. After all, what appears to be needed is simply some combination of dampening demand among the affluent, increasing the total supply, and modifying distribution patterns. This may sound simple, but in practice the necessary changes may be impossible to achieve. Indeed, we think the chances of maintaining even present nutritional levels are extremely slight, and that a great increase in the death rate due to starvation will occur well before the end of the century, quite possibly before 1980.

## The New Famines

While middle- and upper-income Americans and Europeans are still eating high on the hog, consider what is happening in other areas of the world. In 1973, public attention was called to a large-scale famine in the sub-Saharan region of Africa, where the nations of Mauritania, Mali, Niger, Chad, Upper Volta, and Senegal had undergone six consecutive years of drought. Newspapers reported that "untold thousands"[6] had died of starvation in the famine. There were even rumors that this was a vast underestimate and that perhaps 1.5 million people had perished. In Ethiopia,[7] which also suffered from drought, as many as 100,000 more people died of starvation. Statistics are difficult to come by because many deaths in Africa occurred among nomads in very poor countries and because, at least in Ethiopia, deliberate attempts were made by local government officials to conceal the famines.[8] What seems certain is that the loss of livestock has destroyed the way of life of some proud nomadic peoples, such as the Tuareg, forcing them to become hangers-on around the fringes of poverty-stricken towns. Even though 1973 rains were better than those of the previous five years (but not normal), the region remained in deep trouble because of a lack of breeding animals and seed stocks from which to start again. In short, the perennial optimists, who a few years ago were laughing at predictions of major famines in the 1970s,[9] have already been proven wrong.

But, "What the hell," you say, "the world has always had famines and probably will continue to have—what has this got to do with me?" It seems an all-too-common human ability to bear other people's suffering stoically. But even those who don't care about other people dying far away should not take the sub-Saharan drought lightly. Events there are symptomatic of far more universal food problems that have already had a dramatic effect on American pocketbooks and stomachs. (These problems will be dealt with further in the chapters on the international situation and on food.)

In 1972 there were also serious crop failures in India, Pakistan, Bangladesh, Afghanistan, Nepal, Ceylon, Indonesia, the Philippines, the USSR, China, and parts of tropical America. In May, 1973, Dr. Addeke Boerma, director of FAO (United Nations Food and Agriculture Organization) announced that world reserves of grains were at their lowest level since 1952, the equivalent of what the world consumes in less than seven weeks. The world population in 1952 was some 2.5 billion people; in 1973 it was almost 4 billion. Therefore, in early 1973 the world's *per capita* reserves were far lower than they had been at the previous low, twenty-one years earlier.

Although 1973 generally produced bumper crops, they were still not enough to compensate for the previous year's shortfall. Spring 1974 crops were hampered by the energy shortage and the return of adverse weather in many areas. In June, 1974, world grain reserves were even lower than in 1973: enough to feed the world population for only twenty-seven days. By midsummer 1974, crops in the US and much of the world had been severely damaged by poor weather, and the world food picture looked darker than ever.

For Americans and Europeans, tight food supplies in 1973 and 1974 led to some shortages and rising food prices. But for UDCs, after a quarter of a century of agriculturalists' assurances that they could feed an ever-increasing population indefinitely,[10] and after six years of a "green revolution" that many uninformed optimists promised would solve the world food problem, a very large portion of the human population was once again threatened with massive famines.

## Agriculture and Climatic Change

The argument is sometimes heard that "bad weather," not mankind, has caused escalating food shortages. This is a preposterous evasion. "Bad" weather is a characteristic and well-known feature of the planet Earth. Climatic change has occurred naturally throughout the past, caused by such things as solar cycles, changing positions of continents, and cycles of volcanic activity. Today these natural changes are continuing and interacting with other changes induced by human activities. Industrial societies produce air pollution, cut down forests, and build heat-producing cities. Overpopulated farming societies not only cut down forests, but also expose land to wind erosion, leading to the injection of large amounts of dust into the atmosphere and forming agricultural hazes. All these human activities may be contributing to recent unfavorable shifts in the climate—especially the monsoon failures that are responsible for the sub-Saharan droughts and that have intensified already severe food problems in southern Asia.

The factors that control the climate are still not thoroughly understood. Small changes in such things as the dustiness of the atmosphere may cause shifts in the colossal interacting forces that create planetary weather patterns. One of the scientists most knowledgeable about these weather patterns and their relationship to food supply is Professor Reid Bryson of the University of Wisconsin. He has a new theory about the climatic effects of adding carbon dioxide ($CO_2$) and dust to the atmosphere. It has long been realized that, as far as global average temperature is concerned, these should have opposing effects: additional $CO_2$ should tend to warm the planet, additional dust to cool it.[11]

Bryson has concluded that, in addition to these effects, both dust and $CO_2$ operate together to change atmospheric patterns so as to make the monsoons in Africa and southern Asia less dependable. Monsoon rains come from moisture-rich air masses that normally move north from the South Atlantic and Indian oceans each summer. These rains provide the moisture on which perhaps half a billion people depend for growing their crops. According to Bryson, carbon dioxide and dust pollution from human activities and the injection of fine dust into the atmosphere by renewed volcanic activity are combining to block the northern movement of the monsoons. *He doubts that the monsoons will return to India with regularity in this century.*[12]

If Bryson is correct about the monsoons, the human death rate will increase greatly in the near future, with hundreds of millions of additional people perishing. But a potentially far more ominous conclusion about future food supplies can be drawn from meteorological data. By convention among meteorologists, "normal" weather is that which occurred between 1930 and 1960. Careful reconstruction of past climate, however, shows that this period was *the most extreme weather pattern to occur in a thousand years*. Those thirty years were on the average the warmest since the days of Viking exploration. Since 1960, the average temperature worldwide has been dropping to levels more typical of earlier times (Figure 1). But practically all of mankind's high-yield crops are genetic strains selected to give maximum productivity under a narrow set of environmental conditions—those that prevailed during a once-in-a-millennium period of freakish weather!

Of course, it should be possible to select new crop strains that will give their maximum response under a different set of climatic conditions. Two very important factors are required to do this successfully: time and genetic variability in the crops. Time might be available if climatic changes were slow enough, their recognition prompt, and the human response rapid. But climatic change is not necessarily slow (as we have seen in the sub-Saharan region); it is extremely difficult to distinguish short-term fluctuations from long-term trends; and agri-

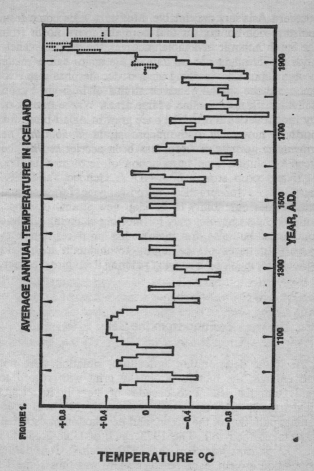

FIGURE 4.

**AVERAGE ANNUAL TEMPERATURE IN ICELAND**

**YEAR, A.D.**

**TEMPERATURE °C**

Mean annual temperature in Iceland over the past millennium (after Bergthorsson). The dashed line indicates the rate of temperature decline in the 1961-1971 period, and the dotted line shows the variation of Northern Hemisphere mean temperature plotted to the same scale.

*from* CLIMATIC MODIFICATION BY AIR POLLUTION, II: *The Sahelian Effect by Reid Bryson, August 1973, Report No. 9, Institute for Environmental Studies, University of Wisconsin.*

cultural scientists have, for the most part, failed to recognize the evolutionary dimension of their business.[13]

Even if time were available, however, the required genetic variability might not be. One of the major errors made by agriculturalists in the last two decades has been to encourage the spread of single strains of high-yield crop plants, which now dominate large areas. Where dozens of traditional varieties of wheat once grew in Asia Minor, for instance, now only one modern strain is found. The growing uniformity of crops has been accelerated by the green revolution—the introduction of fertilizer-sensitive, high-yield crop strains into UDCs. Genetic variability, once lost, is for practical purposes gone forever—and with it goes our ability to develop new strains of crops, critically necessary not only for meeting changing climatic conditions, but also for maintaining crop resistance to pests.[14] In terms of the ability to maintain high-yield agriculture, mankind is quickly painting itself into a corner.

## Food from the Sea

As if the deteriorating agricultural situation were not bad enough, the picture is equally grim with regard to food from the sea. Two decades of steadily increasing yields of fish came to an end in the early 1970s as overfishing, pollution of the ocean, and destruction of estuaries have taken their toll. The 1973 catch of table-grade fish was *12 percent less* than the 1970 catch.[15] Considering population growth, each person's share was thus some 18 percent less than it had been three years before.

Marine biologists seem to agree that the global catch is now about at its maximum. Therefore, as the population continues to grow, the amount of protein from the sea available for each individual will continue to shrink. In theory, mankind could partially compensate for this by eating fish that are now used as livestock feed. By feeding the fish to farm animals and then eating the animals, 50 percent or more of their food value to man is lost, since at best a pound of fish produces one-half pound of animal —and most conversions are far less efficient than this. In practice, there are serious technical and cultural problems, and it seems highly unlikely that the economic system would even permit such a shift, at least as long as the demand for meat remains high in ODCs.

## The Global Prospect

What is the future likely to hold for the world's food supply? In the global situation, *the* major factor will be the weather. Two places to watch are the monsoon lands and midwestern North America. If monsoon failures continue in the sub-Saharan region, that area will require massive imports of food to prevent the deaths of perhaps six million people. Although the region involved is large, it is relatively sparsely populated. Only about 25 million people live in the six countries most hard-hit in the sub-Saharan region, and just slightly more than that in Ethiopia. Assuming the food situation doesn't deteriorate badly elsewhere, emergency supplies could probably be provided for a long time. If, however, the climatic change and its effects are semipermanent (as seems probable), something will have to give, since the populations in these nations are doubling in size every twenty-five to thirty-five years. They face in microcosm the major dilemma of humanity: either birthrates must decline or death rates will rise.

Should monsoon failures persist in south Asia, however, no solution is possible. Well over one billion people live in countries affected by the Asian monsoon, and no conceivable transfer of food could make up for the inevitable shortages. A soaring death rate in this area alone could bring the world population explosion to a halt—for a few years.

One way or another, the human population explosion will probably come to an end well before it reaches the

often-discussed UN projection of some 6.5 billion people
in the year 2000.[16] It would be a miracle if the halt were
caused by a precipitous decline in family sizes to below
replacement level all over the world. Lacking miracles,
the halt will occur in the only other way possible—
*through the drastic shortening of the lives of enormous
numbers of human beings.*

## The Prospect for the United States

The midwestern regions of North America are the last
granary of mankind with the capacity to produce substantial and dependable surpluses (food for which there is
no domestic economic demand). But unhappily this area
is subject to a twenty-year drought cycle, and dry periods
occurred in both the 1930s and 1950s.[17] During the spring
and summer of 1974, drought conditions once again developed, starting in the Texas and Oklahoma panhandle
areas and spreading by midsummer as far as southwestern
Iowa. There were reports of severe damage to the corn
crops of Nebraska and Iowa in July, while the wheat-crop
estimates had already been reduced about 12 percent from
earlier projections. It looked as if the drought cycle had
recurred on schedule. If it persists for several years, as it
did in earlier decades, the food situation in the US could
abruptly move from marginal to critical. Needless to say,
our ability to assist other nations would accordingly disappear.

In the early 1970s, the major questions about food
in the US still concerned prices and amounts for export.
The Soviet Union leaned on the North American granary
to supplement the yield of the perennially incompetent
Soviet agriculture. The ability in years past to send huge
shipments to other countries has given Americans a false
sense of their own nutritional security. A lasting midwestern drought, difficulty in importing what we need, and

the increased demand created by foreign purchases could combine to make food shortages a reality in the US.

To Americans, therefore, the age of scarcity could mean much more than empty gas tanks—at best it will mean radical changes in diet, at worst widespread hunger. Obviously, if you're interested in maintaining the quality of your life in hard times, the first thing you can do is inform yourself and your children about what constitutes good nutrition and how you can protect your health on a less affluent diet. This is not a minor matter, and it will be discussed in some detail in Chapter 6.

Not only are Americans largely unaware of the precariousness of the food situation, many also believe that the energy shortage of winter 1973–74 was merely a temporary economic imbalance. After all, President Nixon outlined a plan for energy self-sufficiency by 1980, and no less a genius than Henry Kissinger pronounced that the same knowhow that America used in the space program can be turned to solving the energy crisis.

Nevertheless, although there may be temporary improvements, it seems certain that energy shortages will be with us for the rest of the century, and that before 1985 mankind will enter a genuine age of scarcity in which many things besides energy will be in short supply. Shortages of many items have already begun to appear, but they are destined to become much more severe. During the next decade, in the US and most of the rest of the world, such diverse commodities as food, fresh water, copper, and paper will become increasingly difficult to obtain and thus much more expensive. The accessible supplies of many key minerals will be nearing depletion—and "revolutionary" attempts to extend those supplies by expending greater amounts of energy (which will also be scarce) to mine low-grade ores or reconcentrate scattered "scrap" will not come close to meeting demand at prices most people can pay. Furthermore, for what is made available, a high cost will be exacted from the environment. Starvation among people will be accompanied by starvation of industries for the materials they require.

Our growthmanic economy, failing some adjustment to

the age of scarcity, could plunge into a production depression, accompanied by either a monetary deflation or a runaway inflation. We would then reach a no-growth (or a negative-growth) economy in the worst possible way. Indeed, in our thrashing around, we might even manage to accelerate destruction of the environment while reducing per capita energy consumption—no easy trick!

The exact timetable of society's decline and the sequence of steps on the down staircase are impossible to predict, *but they are relatively unimportant*. What you need to know is that in ten or fifteen years—twenty or twenty-five at most—you will be living in a world *extremely different* from that of today—one that, if you are unprepared for it, will prove extraordinarily unpleasant. This gloomy forecast is not based entirely on America's resource position. It is a conclusion drawn in large part from the response by this society in 1974 to the energy crisis—a pussycat crisis compared to the tigers lurking around the corner. For the energy mini-crisis illuminated once and for all the hopeless incompetence of our political and business leaders and our institutions when it comes to coping with fundamental change. Clearly, any initiatives for meeting the future crunch in energy, food, and other essentials of life will have to come from individuals.

## Be Prepared

The first and most essential thing that you can do to protect yourself from unpleasant surprises is to keep informed about the state of the world. This is not an easy assignment, but your reward will be a deeper understanding of what may happen and an increased ability to prepare for it. Part of the difficulty is the multiplicity of subjects to monitor. We have already introduced two vitally important ones—the state of food supplies and energy resources. In later chapters, we will expand on these and go into many others—the economic and political systems, the international situation, and mineral resources, among others. All of them are interrelated, and all will have profound influence on the future course of our lives. Those chapters will give you specific suggestions as to which aspects of each subject are significant and which aren't.

How can you keep track? The first place to start is with news reports. Pay attention to television and radio broadcasts, perhaps even taking notes on important items. If you can afford them, subscriptions to a first-rate newspaper, such as the *New York Times* or the *Washington Post,* and a newsmagazine, *Time* or *Newsweek,* are useful. The back pages of the *Times* are an especially rich source of information on the topics dealt with in this book. In this respect, it is generally superior to the *Post* except in the area of political reporting. For economic trends, the *Wall Street Journal* and the business sections of the *Times* are helpful. We find a mail subscription to the *Times* quite satisfactory. It arrives about a week late here in California, but that matters little for the in-depth stories we're interested in. Our local paper is quite adequate, in combination with radio and TV, to let us know if the world has come to an end. Unfortunately, most news sources pay disproportionate attention to relatively unimportant political or other happenings (i.e., the Patty Hearst affair) at the expense of vastly more important events, such as the success or failure of the Indian monsoon—threatening you with a case of information overload. It may take a little practice to cull the useful from the useless, but it's worth the effort.

For digging out facts or checking statements, access to basic reference books such as the *World Almanac,*[18] the *Statistical Abstract of the US,*[19] and the *UN Statistical Yearbook* [20] is essential. Further information and clues to vulnerable aspects of the world system can be gleaned from many of the references cited in each chapter (they are listed together following Chapter 7) and from the reading list at the end of the book. If you cannot afford many books or subscriptions, most of these sources of information are available in public libraries.

Keeping track can—perhaps should—be a family activity. Specialization may be the key to handling the information flood. It seems only logical that the family cook and/or food shopper be the specialist in food and nutrition, or the family handyperson be the expert on energy consumption, or the person who handles family finances be in charge of economics. Even a fifth- or sixth-grade child can become aware of the events that will influence his or her life and help in collecting information.

Your children should have it impressed upon them that their adult life-style will bear very little resemblance to yours and that they should now be acquiring knowledge, skills, values, and tastes that will sustain them in less materially affluent circumstances. On the other hand, the fresh insights and imaginations of your children may help you find a viable future while there's still time.

# 2

# The Worst
# and the Dullest

---

"Neither a reduction nor a cessation of energy growth in the US is necessary . . . such suggestions come only from a noisy minority of rabid environmentalists."

—prominent American
utility executive, 1973 [1]

"The decisive conflict of today is not between capitalists and communists, not between rich and poor, but between the mass producers of plutonium and us who merely wish to survive."

—Hannes Alfvén,
Address at 24th Pugwash Conference
on Science and World Affairs,
Baden, Austria, August-September, 1974.

WHILE PUBLIC ATTENTION in early 1974 was focused on the gasoline shortage as mainly an economic and political phenomenon, there was awareness in some quarters that supplies of fossil fuels are not limitless and someday may run out. Yet, amid lively proposals for developing alternative sources of energy, Americans were repeatedly assured that, once the crisis was over, they could continue to escalate their profligate use of energy just as before.

Most people still are not aware that the real limits on energy consumption are posed by physical and environmental conditions, not mankind's ability to discover and mobilize sources of useful energy. The ultimate limit is set by the amount of heat that humanity can afford to dissipate in the global environment. All human activities produce heat as a consequence of the second law of thermodynamics, and no technological gimmickry can prevent humanity from heating up the world as human energy use increases. If worldwide energy consumption continued to increase at the rate that prevailed during the 1960s, it would probably be less than a century before the heat produced caused unacceptable climatic changes.[2] Of course, other environmental impacts probably would halt growth of energy use before global overheating did, but if all these other threats were somehow averted, heat would ultimately bring things to a stop.

Anything that tends to reduce the excessive energy consumption of the overdeveloped countries works to benefit mankind. Even if the "heat limit" is not considered, the level of energy consumption is probably the best index of the amount of damage that an individual or a society is doing to the environment.[3] Indeed, energy use is central to nearly every kind of environmental impact from human activities. Destruction accompanies the extraction of all fossil fuels—especially by strip mining—and the building of hydroelectric projects. Transportation of petroleum pollutes the oceans through oil spills. The burning of fuels, whether in factories or vehicles, causes most of the air pollution, at least in developed countries. Energy-intensive industry, "development," and agriculture generate a wide variety of assaults upon ecological systems, overloading them, poisoning them, paving them over, and plowing them under. Environmental deterioration and energy consumption go hand-in-hand.

Humanity is utterly dependent on natural ecological systems for a wide range of vital services, including the production of food from the sea, maintaining the quality of the atmosphere, the control of most agricultural pests, and the recycling of wastes. There is no way that societies can perform these ecological services for themselves. Therefore anything that tends to lessen the assault mounted by *Homo sapiens* on those systems is beneficial. However, attempts to increase energy supplies in foolish ways in response to energy shortages may inflict damage on ecological systems that will more than cancel out any benefits derived from the energy obtained.

## Why Shortages Now?

Unfortunately, the mini-crisis did not serve to stimulate conversion of the US (and other overdeveloped countries) to sensible energy policies—policies that emphasize conservation. Government and industry seem incapable of reacting intelligently to the crisis of too much energy use, just as they were paralyzed in the face of the approaching mini-crisis. After all, the petroleum shortage of 1973–74 was not only foreseeable, it was foreseen. In 1952 the basic energy situation of the US was outlined in the Paley Report,[4] which analyzed the situation statistically and among other things discussed the possibility of fuel conservation through increasing the number of passengers per car.[5] The coming of a petroleum shortage was forecast by M. King Hubbert, Shell Oil Company research geologist, in 1956, almost two decades before the crisis hit.[6] Hubbert predicted that petroleum production in the US would peak between 1960 and 1970, and it did peak shortly before 1970.

Dr. Hubbert points out jokingly that his 1956 paper was responsible for the greatest increase (on paper) ever seen in US petroleum reserves. After its publication, self-serving petroleum industry spokesmen hastily produced reports with much more optimistic estimates (the most extreme based on ludicrous assumptions). The growth-minded oil industry and its friends in government simply couldn't face the truth.

As gasoline, electricity, and heating oil became scarce in 1973–74, it became popular to blame "all of us" for the shortages. After all, don't all Americans *want* to drive big cars, heat and air-condition their homes electrically, and gawk at enormous displays of Christmas lights? The answer is, Hell, no! Many millions of Americans would be delighted to enjoy the economy of small cars and the accompanying reductions in driving congestion and smog. Many also would prefer the comfort of a well-insulated house without the drying effects of air-conditioning in the summer and heavy heating in the winter, not to mention the lower costs. The much lower utility bills resulting from the efficient direct use of gas for heating (rather than the extreme inefficiency of electrical resistive heating) would also be welcomed.[7] And fewer garish commercial Christmas displays would doubtless please true Christians and atheists alike.

The notion that government and industry are only giving people what they want is just one more falsehood promoted by government and industry. Industry spends enormous sums of money to create demand for a myriad unnecessary products ranging from Cadillacs and Continentals to useless patent medicines and nutritionless foods.

The most grandiose falsehoods, however, have appeared in the form of eco-pornography—oil companies lying about their concern for fishes, electric utilities lying about the safety of nuclear power plants, and so on. In addition, governments and politicians spend huge amounts to create the illusion that they are looking after the public welfare, when in large part they are well paid to look after the profits of industry and are earning their pay.[8]

During the 1950s and 1960s, when both government and industry could have been taking action to avoid the energy mini-crisis, both were taking action to ensure its occurrence. The oil industry has long held special advantages in taxes, beginning with the oil depletion allowance, which went into effect in the 1920s and was reduced from 27.5 percent to 22 percent a few years ago. (As this was written, an attempt was being made in Congress to repeal it altogether—we hope it will be successful.)

Beginning in 1950, oil companies that invested in foreign countries were allowed to write off the "taxes" (a euphemism for royalties) they paid to those countries as a credit against their US income taxes. The effect of this policy, besides inflating the oil companies' profits, has been to encourage drilling abroad at the expense of developing domestic reserves. Consequently, as domestic production fell behind rising demand, the US imported an increasing proportion of its oil from abroad. By 1971, 28 percent of our oil came from elsewhere, about 10 percent from the Middle East. In 1959, the oil-import quota system was begun as a device to encourage domestic production by keeping prices up in the face of a potential flood of cheap foreign crude oil. The system was revised by the Kennedy administration in 1962 in ways that further benefited domestic oil producers.

By building the $50 billion Interstate Highway System, beginning in 1956 and still underway, the government also indirectly subsidized the mushrooming growth of gasoline consumption in automobiles and trucks. Airlines have also been generously subsidized. However, no such encouragement was provided for railroad passenger service, which is *twelve times* more energy-efficient than moving people in automobiles. The number of people using trains declined by 83 percent between 1945 and 1974. Since 1947, with the full encouragement of the government, the consumption of petroleum products in the US has all but tripled, and per capita consumption of electricity (much of which is generated by burning natural gas or oil) has more than quadrupled.

Thus, by the early 1970s, the US had become dependent upon petroleum for nearly all of its transportation and most of its power needs, with very little flexibility in the system other than emergency conservation measures such as lower thermostat settings and highway speed limits. And we were dependent for more than a quarter of that petroleum on outside sources, including the Arab states. We were already due for an energy shortage; the Arab embargo only put frosting on the cake.[9]

As recently as the early 1970s, electric utilities in California were still trying to *increase* demand for electricity, when simple arithmetic showed that blackouts in that state were a certainty before 1980, *even if the rate of growth in demand were reduced*. In April, 1973, less than two months before serious gasoline shortages hit Colorado drivers, President Nixon delivered an incompetent "Energy Message" to Congress. He abolished the oil-import quota and said, in essence, that the US should go full speed ahead to find new sources of energy while relaxing environmental safeguards. No serious moves toward energy conservation were proposed. If any effort at all had been made toward reducing demand at that relatively early stage, much of the inconvenience and confusion of later mandatory programs might have been avoided, and the quality of American life might even have improved.

Who was responsible for these inept performances? For the government's role, the blame rests primarily with voters, who decade after decade have paid little attention to the fumbling and filching of the men they have elected to public office.

The utilities can be blamed for their unenlightened fixation on growth as an ultimate good. The electric utilities have always had pathetically weak research and development operations, due in part to public utility commission rate-setting policies which made such operations financially unattractive. Perhaps they simply lacked anyone able to put two and two together. Or maybe they believed that a few blackouts would serve to extinguish public resistance to the building of nuclear power stations.

As for the oil companies, there is no question that greed lay behind their behavior. They embody perfectly economist Milton Friedman's notion that the sole social responsibility of American business is to maximize profits. While a genuine world shortage of pumpable petroleum appears certain by the turn of the century *if* demand continues to grow as it did in the 1960s,[10] there was no such shortage in the early 1970s. But there certainly was a shortage of gasoline and heating oil for the American consumer, and there *may* have been a basic shortage of supply in the US, since domestic production had passed its peak a year or two before. (We must say "may" because there is no independent source of petroleum statistics—the government depends on statistics supplied by the oil industry. And when a notoriously avaricious liar tells you that he *cannot* sell you something which it is to his advantage *not* to sell to you, some skepticism is in order.)[11]

How much of the energy mini-crisis can be attributed to genuine shortfall, how much to industry conniving, and how much to government bungling? At this writing it is impossible to judge accurately, but the best guess is a combination of all three. The oil industry appears to have prolonged the shortage in the US during the embargo in order to increase its profits.[12] The profit picture was further enhanced by Nixon's energy "czar," William Simon, who, with a staff of ex-oilmen and businessmen with connections in the oil industry, encouraged gasoline price hikes. (Although one element in a long-term cure to our energy problems *should* be increases in the cost of energy, these increases should be imposed gradually and designed so that the poor do not suffer disproportionately. They certainly *should not* end up as sky-high profits for energy producers. Needless to say, the Nixon-Simon approach most hurt the poorest wage-earners who must commute to their jobs by car.)

And, finally, Congress contributed with its usual combination of inaction and bumbling, including some especially stupid legislation (from the viewpoint of its typically short-range goal—making more fuel available immediately) discouraging refineries from importing as much crude oil as they could.

## Petroleum Shortfalls and Profit Longfalls

Whatever its causes, the oil shortage proved of great advantage to the giants of the petroleum industry. They were able to raise gasoline prices while pushing many of the independent dealers out of business. They made such huge windfall profits that even the cleverest accounting tricks were unable to hide them from the public. Six huge oil companies reported 1973 fourth-quarter profits up an average of 57.1 percent over 1972.[13]

A high executive in one of the largest companies explained away his company's 85 percent profit increase on a network television interview: "Only twenty percent of that was increase in our domestic operations; the rest was on foreign operations, and that percentage increase was from a very small base."[14] This remark is typical of the contempt with which industry and government treat the public. The official obviously assumed that the people would not realize his statement was at best misleading. If the company as a whole enjoyed a profit increase of 85 percent and only 20 percent came from domestic operations, then profits in the foreign operations (which had previously been low) must have increased many hundred percent.[15]

In the first quarter of 1974, oil companies reported further profit gains (over first quarter 1973) ranging from 39% for Exxon to 718% for Occidental. Shell upped its profits 52%, Mobil 66%, Gulf 76%, Standard of California 92%, Texaco 123%, and Continental 130%. How did Exxon, the giant among them all, manage to show the least profit increase? Easily—they concealed $400 million in profits by stashing it away in a "reserve fund." [16] The oil industry uses a series of tricky accounting practices, permitting profits to be moved easily from the "foreign" to the "domestic" column and concealed in various ways. In this respect, they represent only an extreme of normal business practice. In spite of repeated efforts by the organization of professional accountants to establish ethical reporting standards, it is still possible for corporations to mislead the public legally about their profits.

Besides getting rid of competition and raising prices, the oil profit-seekers took advantage of the energy crisis to strike a body blow at the movement toward environmental sanity. Aided by their hirelings in the executive and legislative branches of the government, they got restrictions eased on offshore drilling and the burning of high-sulfur fuels, and finalized the Alaskan pipeline fraud. The latter was an especially ominous portent, since it showed the power of public relations and lobbying activities to push even the most ridiculous measures through the government.

It is difficult to say whether the environmental costs of putting in the pipeline will be balanced by its purported benefits. These are difficult value judgments for society to make, even when it has all the pertinent information. But the public has been badly misled about the benefits of the pipeline. Industry propaganda has promoted the idea that the pipeline will be a panacea for America's petroleum problems, while giving the impression that environmentalists would let the wheels of industry grind to a halt to avoid inconveniencing a few caribou. In other words, the industry's liars are still on the job.

The known recoverable reserves in the Alaskan oil field are 8 to 9 billion barrels, and the estimated recoverable reserves are 45 billion barrels. In 1973 the annual oil consumption of the United States was about 6 billion barrels.[17] Thus the *known* reserves of the Alaskan field could supply the US at its 1973 level of usage for only about one and a half years! Even if the *estimated* reserves actually exist, the field could supply the country for less than eight years—hardly a panacea for our petroleum woes.

Remember, the above figures are based on 1973 demand. Prior to the energy mini-crisis of 1973–74, demand for petroleum in the US was growing at a rate of 4.2 to 4.3 percent annually (doubling every 16.5 years). Such growth in demand is considered desirable in the confused minds of many economists and industrialists. These people showed no hesitation in encouraging a resumption of growth in rates of consumption once the mini-crisis seemed to be over. Should growth in demand return to the previous rate, America would require 24 billion barrels of petroleum annually by shortly after the turn of the century. This would use up the equivalent of the known Alaskan reserves in about *twenty weeks*. If the estimated reserves are there and the Alaskan field were used as the sole source of supply for the US, the field would be sucked dry in *less than two years*.[18] So at best, the Alaskan reserves could supplement our supplies for a few decades, providing perhaps 5 percent of the total, depending on demand and the actual contents of the field.

And when those reserves are exhausted, what will those who understand only expanding supplies (as opposed to reducing demand) suggest for an encore? Can we expect to discover and develop the equivalent of a new Alaskan field every two years by the turn of the century? One every year by 2020? The final joke is that the US may never see much of the Alaskan oil. There is good reason to believe that the oil giants intend to sell it to Japan.[19] If it is really meant for the US, it should be piped across Canada to Chicago, where the need is.

Even the proven oil reserves of the Middle East, slightly over 350 billion barrels,[20] are only enough to supply the 1973 level of American demand for less than sixty years (with nothing left over for the rest of the world). Proven reserves for the entire world are estimated (perhaps conservatively) at about 640 billion barrels.[21] At the 1973 world consumption rate of some 18 billion barrels per year—*with no further increase in total demand*—proven world reserves of petroleum would last just slightly more than *thirty-five years*.

Continuing to increase our dependency on petroleum consumption is clearly a suicidal course of action. The only intelligent alternative is to begin *reducing* energy consumption and finding alternative energy sources to substitute for petroleum. So far, America's leaders have emphasized only the latter recommendation while ignoring the former.

Short-term "solutions" to the petroleum shortage should include breaking up the major oil companies and possibly setting up a Federal Oil and Gas Company analogous to the TVA (but without subsidizing energy consumption). This would allow assessment of reasonable profit levels for the rest of the industry. Many of the conservation measures temporarily undertaken when the mini-crisis was in its acute stage—lowered speed limits, car pools, reset thermostats, etc.—should be instituted on a permanent basis.

But there is *no* long-term solution that does not involve dramatic social changes designed to limit our profligate use of energy. In the long run, energy should be made *expensive,* especially for large users, as an incentive to conservation. We must take positive action to reduce our dependency on energy-intensive modes of transportation and ways of living. How our society can do this and how you can do it for yourself will be discussed in detail later in this book. Compared to what will occur if we do not start seriously conserving energy—and compared to the food, environmental, and economic crises soon to come

—the 1973–74 energy shortage was truly only a mini-crisis.

## What Will We Do When the Pumps Run Dry?

Assuming no serious attempt is made to reduce world-wide consumption, how long will mankind's liquid petroleum supplies last? For you, the individual consumer, the answer to this question is crucial to understanding the *real* long-term energy problem and which energy alternatives can and should be developed during the next few decades. The answer depends on a combination of how much there actually is in the ground and what the future rate of consumption will be. And both of these factors will vary with economic factors—cost of recovery and ability of consumers to pay.

But some points are clear. The US is now using a third of all the world's petroleum extracted each year. Our energy *wastage* is enormous—each American uses *three times* as much energy as the average person in western Europe. Furthermore, some projections indicate that by shortly after the turn of the century, Americans alone will "demand" each year more than today's annual *world production*. No reasonable supply-demand scenario can be created that will meet such demand. The figures presented in the previous section clearly show that by early in the twenty-first century, the era of pumping "black gold" out of the ground to fuel industrial societies will be coming to an end.

We can be reasonably sure, then, that within the next quarter of a century mankind will be looking elsewhere than in oil wells for its main source of energy. Considering the time-lag that will inevitably accompany efforts to deploy new energy technologies and the almost total lack of planning to date, we can also be reasonably sure that the search for alternatives will be a frantic one. Furthermore, mobilizing many of the alternative sources

of energy may create extremely grave environmental
effects which, judging from American behavior during
the 1973–74 mini-crisis, will be vastly underrated and
the efforts to deal with them will be inadequate.

One of the most abundant sources of energy available
to the US is coal, which can be burned directly in power
plants and furnaces or used for conversion to gas or liquid
fuel. Many US coal deposits are so situated that strip-
mining is economically possible, and it seems likely that
the proportion of coal recovered by strip-mining will increase.[22] But the environmental disruption caused by strip-
mining is even more serious than that produced by under-
ground mining. The scale of the damage can perhaps best
be appreciated by flying low in a light plane over ravaged
areas in, say, Kentucky. Although executives of coal companies talk a good line about restoring strip-mined land,
very little has actually ever been restored. Furthermore,
restoration may be very difficult and expensive in steep
terrain, and the original productivity of farming or grazing
land may be impossible to restore. Some of the strip-
minable deposits lie under our richest farmland in Illinois
and Iowa,[23] and huge tracts of grazing land in western
states are already slated to be strip-mined in the near
future. Besides the damage to the land, rainfall often
leaches poisonous substances from the debris left from
strip-mining, creating a water-pollution problem. Thus,
strip-mining in search of scarce energy is likely to worsen
growing scarcities of both food and fresh water.

Oil shales (and to a lesser degree, tar sands), found in
abundance in the western US and Canada, are another
relatively rich source of fossil energy. Theoretically,
enough liquid fossil fuels could be extracted from them to
supply mankind's energy needs for centuries, the major
constraints being, in all likelihood, environmental. In mining and processing oil shales, for instance, the volume of
waste rock produced is even greater than the amount
mined (shale expands during the extraction of the oil).
While it may be feasible to dispose of huge amounts of
waste rock without severe environmental effects (water
pollution, creation of dust bowls, destruction of aesthetic

values), judging by past performance of the energy industry, it seems unlikely.

In addition to the environmental side-effects of obtaining either coal or oil shales, there are serious problems associated with their use. Coal is a much dirtier fuel than oil or natural gas, especially coal that contains a high proportion of sulfur. If it is converted to liquid or gaseous fuel, the process will lose a fourth to a third of the energy in the coal and will generate further pollution. Processing oil shales will also require large inputs of energy and water (which tends to be scarce in areas where shales are common). It will also cause considerable pollution of air and water in addition to that associated with landscape defacement and waste rock disposal. Whether sufficient energy "profit" can be made in these processes to balance the financial and environmental cost is problematical.

These are only two of the possible alternative sources of energy being considered by economists and politicians, whose main concerns still are to keep the economy growing, the factories producing ever more, and the commuters rolling. Let's look more closely at the role of the federal government in energy policies. If you understand the plans and motives of government agencies and legislators, you'll have a better idea how to influence those plans for your own protection—or how to protect yourself from the results of bad decisions.

## Government by Incompetents

Unfortunately for Americans, the leading edge of the age of scarcity, the energy mini-crisis, did not arrive while the "best and brightest" were in the government. It arrived during an administration unparalleled for its dishonesty and stupidity, one that even more than most was bought and paid for by industry. It is not surprising that leaders who were busy fighting to stay out of jail failed to deal effectively with the energy mini-crisis. Furthermore, the

Nixon administration was in an especially poor position to take action against the profiteering oil industry—oil interests had chipped in more than $5 million to Nixon's 1972 campaign.[24]

Having an administration made up of the worst and the dullest helped prevent an appropriate response to the energy mini-crisis. Because of the Watergate scandal, the administration's credibility with the public was so damaged by the time the crunch came that its belated efforts were met mainly with suspicion. Many people refused to believe that there was a shortage at all, even when confronted with closed gas stations and long waiting lines.

It is tempting to conclude that if someone else had been in office, things might have been very different, but we doubt it. The track record of earlier administrations at anticipating crises was also lousy, nor were they noted for taking the long view. The blame for failing to establish energy conservation programs goes at least as far back as the Eisenhower administration. Dwight Eisenhower did not urge Americans to reduce their sky-high birthrate; during his administration, the multi-billion-dollar Federal Highway Program was launched. Jack Kennedy did not recommend legislation to tax large cars out of existence, stop highway construction, rejuvenate railroads, or create a nationwide program to build mass-transit systems. Lyndon Johnson did not call for a reduction of GNP or a restructuring of energy prices so that the biggest energy users would pay the most per unit of energy rather than the least. But he did carry on an insane war that wasted hundreds of thousands of lives in addition to huge amounts of energy. Richard Nixon was only the latest in a dreary parade of presidents surrounded by advisors who take a purely political view of history and by economists who do not realize that the basic assumptions of their system no longer hold.

Even a competent and relatively honest president, moreover, must deal with Congress, where dishonesty and incompetence have long been endemic.[25] Few Americans are aware of how bad their legislature is, even though in 1973 one of the best senators (Hughes of Iowa) decided not to run again because he felt helpless and frustrated. Few indeed know the names of the political dinosaurs who help control their destinies—men like Wayne Hays of Ohio and Jamie Whitten of Mississippi, who wield enormous power behind the scenes. Through the years, the power in Congress has tended to rest with men owned and operated by special interests—such as the late Senators Robert Kerr of Oklahoma (oil) and Everett Dirksen of Illinois (the drug, gas and oil, insurance, and banking industries)—or with men who ensured their reelection by wasting taxpayers' money on military bases in their own districts in the name of national security (as did superhawk Representative Mendel Rivers of South Carolina before his death ended the threat he posed to human welfare).

Nowhere is the incompetence of the government more manifest than in its lopsided promotion of nuclear power. The impetus for this promotion has come from a variety of sources, including the corporations that build reactors (such as Westinghouse and General Electric) and the power companies, all of which intend to profit from a nuclear-power technology. Other advocates are politicians like Representatives Chet Holifield and Craig Hosmer (both of California and, mercifully, retiring) of the Congressional Joint Committee on Atomic Energy (JCAE). These men built reputations by their irresponsible pushing of nuclear power. Then there are those scientists who have an unfounded faith in the ability of technology to find solutions for all environmental problems. Sadly, many of the major promoters of nuclear energy are clearly suffering from guilt complexes because of their involvement in atomic-weapons programs. These people are determined to solve the problems of humanity with nuclear power as a sop to their consciences for bringing all of us to the brink of destruction. As a result, they tend to turn a blind eye to the catastrophic risks of current fission technology.

Perhaps the biggest villains in the nuclear-power scandal are a government agency, the Atomic Energy Commission (AEC) and its overseers on the JCAE. The AEC was set up with the incongruous charges both of promoting and of regulating the peaceful uses of atomic energy. As is usual with government regulatory agencies, the AEC quickly became cozy with those whom it was supposed to be regulating. This does not necessarily mean the AEC people were dishonest; it just means that when an industry is regulated by an agency, close contacts are necessary. Government employees become friendly with industry leaders at conferences and at cocktail parties. The government often must rely on industry-owned technologists for advice, and may end up dependent on industry data (as the government depends on the oil industry).

It was thus a natural process by which the AEC became a first-class promoter and a tenth-class regulator. And the more it became a promoter, the more dishonesty became standard operating procedure. It soon became a secretive, lying agency that put its own bureaucratic interests and those of its industrial partners far ahead of the public interest. Such a transformation is serious enough when it occurs in an agency like the Interstate Commerce Commission or the Department of Agriculture. But with the AEC, the consequence could be *an irreversible and catastrophic course for the US—turning to dependence on nuclear fission to fulfill our future power demands.*

## Nuclear Benefits and Risks

Why are we and so many other scientists opposed to the use of the current and proposed nuclear technology? To understand why, you must know a little bit about the technical aspects of the issue. The struggle to prevent the spread of nuclear power plants will in our opinion be the most critical environmental battle of the next decade. We hope that this introduction to the problem will convince you to join the battle and give you some of the basic knowledge required to fight effectively.

The potential benefits of obtaining energy from "splitting" atoms—nuclear fission—seem great indeed. There is no air pollution of the sort produced by fossil-fuel plants, nor is there the property damage, aesthetic blight, sickness, and death associated with such pollution. The power plants themselves occupy less space than conventional plants and can be made considerably more attractive.

In a nuclear plant a compact, self-contained hot reactor core (rather than large, dirty fossil-fueled fires) is used to produce steam to drive turbines which turn generators. The core consists of bundles of rodlike fuel elements that produce heat through a nuclear "chain reaction," which is regulated by control rods. The environmental damage associated with mining uranium for nuclear reactors is minuscule today compared to that produced in the course of obtaining fossil fuels, and if the entire power grid could be made up of breeder reactors (reactors that change nonfuel materials into their own fuel), the amount of mining necessary to obtain nuclear fuel would be very much reduced.

With such great benefits potentially available, why do we oppose the building of fission power plants? Simply because, at the present stage of their development, fission power plants pose an extreme hazard to mankind and many other forms of life; and since safe alternatives are available, we do not feel that the benefits of today's nuclear power technology even begin to justify the risks. Those risks include:

1. Thermal (heat) pollution;
2. Low-level routine releases of radioactivity from power plants and subsidiary fuel-processing plants;
3. Radiation exposure of people involved in the mining of uranium, the primary fuel for nuclear fission power plants;
4. The possible contamination of the environment by large amounts of highly radioactive wastes, which must be flawlessly contained in storage for many thousands of years if such contamination is to be avoided;
5. The chance that a catastrophic accident might re-

lease the enormous inventory of highly radioactive materials in a reactor core;

6. The possibility that terrorists may sabotage facilities or steal sufficient fissile material to make a nuclear bomb.

If you wish to understand these risks thoroughly, you should know something about the process by which nuclear fission (and its potentially safer and more potent complement, nuclear fusion) yields energy, about how the energy is tapped in power plants that use up their nuclear fuel ("burners") or manufacture more fuel than they use ("breeders"), and about the nature and hazards of radiation. Appendix I at the end of the book gives a brief description of these things in layman's language, and excellent longer treatments can be found in books by physicists.[26] So if you are interested in the technical side of the nuclear-power controversy, turn now to the Appendix; if your interest stops at the social side, read on.

As we shall see, the first three risks listed above do not seem to justify opposition to nuclear power, but the last three certainly do.

**Thermal Pollution.** In nuclear power plants, thermal pollution does not present a novel problem, but like such pollution from conventional power plants, it may have extremely harmful environmental effects. Today's nuclear plants are less thermally efficient than fossil-fueled plants (they produce more waste heat per kilowatt of electricity generated). Most of their waste heat is added to bodies of water while much of that produced by conventional plants goes up smokestacks into the atmosphere. Thus, heavy heat burdens are imposed on lakes and streams that receive discharged cooling water, and much of the life in the water may be destroyed. But thermal pollution problems alone would not justify across-the-board opposition to fission power plants. Engineering advances can increase their thermal efficiency, and where necessary, utilities and their customers can bear the additional expense of cooling towers that transfer the heat to the atmosphere. Basically, the ultimate thermal constraint on the use of nuclear power is the same as that of fossil fuel plants—weather modification by waste heat (discussed at the beginning of this chapter).

## Radiation Hazards

Among other hazards inherent in nuclear power plants are those associated with the radioactivity of their fuels and by-products. The danger depends on the kind of radiation produced, the amount of exposure, and who (or what) is exposed. Depending on the circumstances, exposure of people to radiation can lead to immediate illness or death, to cancers that show up many months or years after exposure, and to genetic damage that results in death or disability for people in future generations. The delayed effects make radiation an especially insidious hazard.[27]

All of us are continually exposed to radiation, however, whether or not more nuclear power plants are produced. Cosmic rays and naturally occurring radioactive substances give us a constant low-level exposure to radiation, but the amount of exposure in a year is less than one five-thousandth of the dose that would be lethal if delivered in a short time.[28] This natural radiation made up about 60 percent of the average American's exposure in the mid-1960s. Of the remaining 40 percent, diagnostic X-rays accounted for three-quarters, and therapeutic X-rays and radioactive fallout accounted for nearly all of the other quarter. Releases from nuclear power plants were negligible—as late as 1970 they contributed only one-half of one percent of the average person's exposure.

**Low-level Emissions.** Why, then, should there be concern about low-level, routine emissions from nuclear plants? First of all, an enormous increase in the number of nuclear power plants is planned. Only sixteen were operating in 1970, while fifty-four more were being built, many of them larger. An additional thirty-five were far enough into the planning stage that the reactors had been ordered.[29] By the year 2000, roughly a thousand reactors are "expected" to be in service.[30] Considering expansions in size, this is likely to mean about a 200-fold increase in power generated[31] and could mean a comparable rise in routine emissions—that is, radioactive isotopes that are released into air and water during the normal operations of a plant.

This potential increase has led to a bitter controversy over the significance of routine emissions. The issue is complex, but some major points can be summarized. First, the AEC, as it did in the bad old days when it was claiming that radioactive fallout from atomic tests was harmless, took the position that routine emissions were not a significant hazard. In 1970, D. Theos Thompson, an Atomic Energy commissioner, stated, "To date, in spite of many careful studies, no one has been able to detect an effect from these low levels of radiation and it is unlikely that studies of literally millions of cases would show such effects." [32]

This is a characteristic AEC statement. No "careful studies" of such effects exist—moreover, they would be very impractical (if not impossible) to design. On the other hand, a considerable body of both theory and evidence supports the view that no level of exposure to radiation is so low as to be harmless.[33] Even the very small amounts of radioactivity released by the nuclear industry up to 1970 have almost certainly been responsible for some deaths and will be responsible for more.

Before 1970, the AEC had established guidelines for the permissible amount of routine emissions from nuclear power plants. These guidelines were attacked by biologists and others who thought they were set unacceptably high. In an attempt to discredit Dr. Ernest J. Sternglass, one of its severest critics, the AEC requested two of its most distinguished health physicists, Dr. John W. Gofman and Dr. Arthur R. Tamplin of the AEC's Lawrence Radiation Laboratory, to look into the matter. Gofman and Tamplin concluded that Sternglass' estimates of risks were too high. They also concluded, however, that if nuclear reactors released the maximum amount of radiation permitted under AEC guidelines, there would be some 32,000 additional deaths annually from cancer and leukemia. These results were in line with estimates by other qualified scientists. One might think that the AEC would have welcomed Gofman and Tamplin's results, which would help them to insure against the possibility of an enormous tragedy, and that they would have revised their guidelines accordingly.

Hardly. After unsuccessfully trying to suppress Gofman and Tamplin's conclusions, the AEC launched an unprecedented campaign of lies and obfuscations, attempting to discredit these two outstanding scientists. They failed totally, but they did manage to subject Gofman and Tamplin to enough continual harassment to drive them out of the Lawrence Laboratory.[84] Finally, when the AEC discovered that falsehoods and character assassination could not overcome Gofman and Tamplin's facts, they agreed to lower the permissible emissions for one major type of burner reactor by 100-fold.

The routine-emissions battle is far from over, but in one sense it is not critical to the question of whether it is wise to go full speed ahead with a nuclear-fission technology. Although it might be expensive, it seems to be technologically feasible to reduce routine emissions to an acceptable level. While reduction to "zero emissions" is not possible, nuclear engineers should be able to lower routine emissions to less than one percent of the "natural background" radiation.[85] The main requirement is responsible regulation—but can we expect this from the AEC?

**The Hazards of Uranium Mining.** Risks to uranium miners are another drawback of fission power. The miners inhale radioactive dust and become highly susceptible to lung cancer. Dr. Gofman states, "In the late 1960s, we appreciated the fact that we'd created an epidemic of lung cancer in the uranium miner. More than 125 are now dead, and another 500 to 600 will die no matter what is done for them. That's a fantastic epidemic." [86]

Of course, everyone dies eventually, but these miners will die many years before they would have if they had been in a less hazardous occupation. But, as with the low-level-emissions problem, technological change (dust control, respirators, automated mining) can probably provide substantial protection for the miners. And unlike the case of routine emissions, the population at risk is relatively small. Risks to uranium miners should not alone halt the use of fission power, any more than the serious risks run by coal miners have halted the use of coal. (It is a revealing commentary on our society, however, that little has been done to reduce the latter risks.)

**Waste Disposal.** An intractable problem created by generating fission power concerns the disposal of the long-lived radioactive wastes that are produced. Fuel elements that have been in reactors for a long time (a year or so) become loaded with waste products which interfere with the energy-yielding process. In a fuel reprocessing plant, the valuable remaining uranium 235 and newly created plutonium (both of which can be used as reactor fuel) are extracted from the elements, leaving a residue that boils continuously because of the heat released by its radioactivity. This waste material contains long-lived forms (isotopes) of elements. These isotopes are extremely toxic because of the radiation they emit and must be kept perfectly isolated from the environment for many thousands of years.[37]

A wide variety of proposals for storing these wastes has been put forward, but no acceptable solution has yet been found because of the time scale involved, which may be up to half a million years. The quantities are not extraordinary —hundreds of tons a year—so temporary storage in guarded concrete mausolea is feasible. One AEC official has testified that that agency would guard the wastes for the full 500,000 years![38] This of course means 500,000 years *after the last reactor is shut down*. His testimony was a tribute to what Ralph Nader has called the "professional insanity" that afflicts scientists involved in promoting nuclear power. There is good reason to doubt that the AEC could do *anything* flawlessly for fifty years, let alone 10,000 times that long. This is more than *100 times* the length of recorded history, a period during which several ice ages might be expected. The same AEC has been guarding high-level wastes from weapons programs at its Hanford facility in Washington for over twenty years. In that time there have been numerous leaks of those wastes, and in 1973 alone, 150,000 gallons escaped through leaks. One major escape came at the climax of an atomic-power public-relations extravaganza, the Nuclear Industry Meetings in San Francisco in December, 1973.

It is clear that no storage system that depends on continuous human vigilance would be satisfactory, even if the group in charge of storage were competent and honest. The most workable plan may well be to solidify the wastes and bury them in impermeable geological formations such as deep salt beds, or in the sea bed where they would be drawn into the Earth's core by the same processes that cause continents to drift. Unfortunately, we don't understand such things as earthquakes and volcanic activity enough to guarantee the integrity of such sites for hundreds of thousands of years. The effects on geological formations of heat from the wastes are another important unknown.

One suggestion that seems plausible to laymen is shooting the wastes into outer space (or even into the sun) in rockets. But even if the costs weren't prohibitive, the risks would be. Consider NASA's capability for bungling, and picture the consequences of a rocket containing tons of radioactive waste blowing up on the launch pad or within the Earth's atmosphere after it is airborne. We cannot, however, guarantee that it won't be attempted.

The potential performance of the AEC coupled to NASA can be judged by the Space Nuclear Auxiliary Power (SNAP) Program. The nuclear power systems designed for this program use heat from radioactive plutonium to create electrical energy. A SNAP rocket disintegrated over the Indian Ocean in 1964, scattered fine particles over a wide area, and thereby doomed many human beings to death from lung cancer. It is estimated that this single accident will deliver to the lungs of adults a cumulative dose of radioactivity over fifty years' time equal to about one-third of the yearly "background radiation."[39] Subsequent studies indicated that, under certain circumstances, as many as 40,000 lung-cancer deaths could follow the burn-up of a SNAP reactor in the atmosphere. After the 1964 accident, a committee of AEC's Division of Biological Medicine was charged with investigating the safety of subsequent SNAP launches. The committee was assured that the chances of an accident in another launch were "about one in a thousand." Dr. Arthur Tamplin, who served on the committee, felt that a judgment should be made on the "downside risks"—the worst that would happen *if* an accident occurred. The committee, in classic AEC fashion, ignored Tamplin's advice and wrote a report pooh-poohing the estimate of risk contained in a safety study done by the Martin-Marietta Company. Another launch was made, and that "one in a thousand" chance showed up: the rocket blew up, and the reactor fell into California coastal waters.[40]

One of the most unusual "waste storage" problems is what to do with the nuclear plant once it has ended its useful life of thirty to forty years. The internal reactor structure is unavoidably bombarded during operation with neutrons from the fission chain reaction, making the structure itself radioactive. One approach to this problem is to permit the landscape to become dotted with run-out, abandoned power plants, walled off to prevent the unwary from entering—monuments to humanity's error in following the Judas-goat of fission power. It may be possible, however, to dismantle the plants and add their components to the overall long-lived waste problem. New plants could then be built on the same sites.

Is the lack of a solution to the long-term waste-disposal problem a reason to turn away from fission power? We do not think it wise to embark on a project in which mankind may be grabbing the tail of an immortal tiger. Sooner or later humanity's grip would weaken, with lethal results.

A recent technical review concludes: "If nuclear power is to resolve our energy needs in the coming decades, its benefits should not be delayed for lack of a viable management program for high-level wastes." [41] We strongly disagree.

**Catastrophic Accident.** Both fossil-fueled and nuclear power plants are subject to sudden accidents caused by structural failures and human errors. This is not surprising, considering the multiplicity of pumps, valves, and pipes carrying superheated steam (or molten sodium), the nature of the fuels, the high-speed turbines, etc. Accidents in conventional power plants take the lives of plant employees, and so could accidents in nuclear plants—but these could kill hundreds of thousands or even millions of people outside the boundaries of the plant if they should occur near population centers. [42]

To understand the nature of this threat, one point is essential to remember. When a large burner reactor has been running for a year or so after refueling, it contains radioactivity equivalent to the fallout from *several thousand Hiroshima-sized atomic bombs*. [43] This enormous accumulation is due to the buildup of radioactive fission products as a result of the continuing chain reaction. Any accident that allowed the escape of any significant portion of this radioactive inventory would be a catastrophe.

Several barriers guard against such a disaster. In burner reactors of the kind widely used in the US, most of the radioactive materials are bound up in the metal-clad fuel rods, which in turn are contained in a pressure vessel of six-inch-thick steel. The pressure vessel, in turn, is housed in a containment building made of thick concrete reinforced with steel. As impressive as these multiple barriers are, however, there are conceivable events that could breach all of them at once. A jet aircraft crashing into a reactor could penetrate the containment building and damage the innards so badly that a mammoth release of radioactivity ensues, as could an atomic bomb exploding nearby, or a major earthquake. Moreover, converting our electric power system to nuclear energy would greatly increase the military vulnerability of the US, since the wrecking of reactors in an attack could greatly add to the deaths caused by radioactive fallout from a nuclear attack. Interestingly enough, it appears that the Soviets are even more irresponsible than the AEC in controlling their nuclear program. Reportedly, many Soviet reactors do not have containment buildings, and are thus even more vulnerable to catastrophic rupture.

If a nuclear war does not occur, and if the nuclear-power industry can be persuaded to stop siting plants in active earthquake zones, then rupture of a containment building from within would be more likely than from without. Such a rupture could be caused by a malfunction (such as the breaking of a major pipe), a human error, or deliberate sabotage that resulted in a reduction or interruption in the flow of coolant around the hot fuel elements of the reactor core—a "loss-of-coolant" accident. If such an event occurred, the reactor would be "scrammed" (shut down by full insertion of the control rods, stopping the chain reaction). That, however, would not necessarily end the problem. In a reactor that had been running awhile and thus had a high waste load, the radioactivity of those wastes would cause the uncooled core to heat up rapidly. Unless emergency coolant could be supplied *within a minute,* the core would melt, and hundreds of tons of molten steel and uranium at a temperature of 5000° Fahrenheit would flow to the bottom of the containment building.

This would be the start of the "China Syndrome." No man-made structure could contain such a white-hot mass, and it would melt through the containment structure and proceed on toward the center of the Earth. Although it obviously would not reach China (in spite of the name), it would penetrate a mile or so into the Earth. At the same time, the gaseous components of the radioactive wastes, amounting to some 20 percent of the accumulation, would be released. In a 1000-megawatt plant that had been refueled one year previously, this would amount to the equivalent of the fallout from some two hundred Hiroshima-sized bombs.[44]

The AEC admits that such a release is worth taking some trouble to avoid, since it could kill millions of people and make a substantial portion of the United States uninhabitable. The AEC therefore has required that all reactors have emergency core-cooling systems (ECCS). Meanwhile, of course, they continue to insist that reactors are so well designed that the emergency system will probably never be needed.

Some outside groups have raised questions about the efficiency of the emergency systems. Two men in the Union of Concerned Scientists, MIT physics professor Henry W. Kendall and Daniel F. Ford, a brilliant young economist and staff member of the organization, quickly became *the* experts on ECCS. In a series of hearings, they made mincemeat of the AEC's professional liars, aided this time by the scientists within the AEC who were most knowledgeable about the emergency systems. These AEC scientists, in the tradition of Gofman and Tamplin, risked their jobs to express their doubts as to whether the emergency core-cooling systems will work.

Ford and Kendall recently stated:

> It is a reasonable conclusion . . . that, within ten years or so, there may be a catastrophic release of radioactivity from an operating nuclear power reactor. This conclusion is based only on the AEC's own stated probability of a pipe break. This estimated accident rate neglects other possible initiating events, such as pressure-vessel rupture, operator error, and other presently undefined events.[45]

This statement may substantially underestimate the actual accident rate. Extensive defects in the construction of existing nuclear power plants increase the probability of accidental radioactive release. The RAND Corporation, well known for its work for the US Department of Defense, recently commented on "[the] increasing reports of poor quality control and documented carelessness in the manufacture, operation, and maintenance of these complex nuclear machines." [46]

If a catastrophic release occurred, what would the consequences be? In 1957 the AEC did an analysis of a hypothetical accident occurring in a small (200-megawatt) nuclear plant sited about thirty miles from a city. The results were published in a now-famous document, WASH-740, *Theoretical Possibilities and Consequences of Major Accidents in Large Nuclear Power Plants,* sometimes called the Brookhaven Report.

WASH-740 estimated that such an accident could cause 3000 to 4000 deaths from acute radiation exposure, an additional 50,000 subsequent deaths from cancer, and $7 billion in property damage. An area equivalent to fifteen Maryland-sized states could be contaminated from fallout, rendering water supplies unusable and making it necessary to forbid or restrict agriculture. Perhaps 500,000 people would have to be evacuated rapidly, and resettlement for them might be difficult because people elsewhere feared radioactivity in the refugees. Some 3.5 million people might be restricted in their outdoor activities in order to keep their radiation doses within acceptable limits. Finally, the public would probably demand that all nuclear power plants be shut down, bringing on the ultimate electric-energy crisis and worsening the economic chaos caused by the direct effects of the accident.

In 1964–65, the AEC ordered an update of the horrifying WASH-740 report, believing that a more refined study would show WASH-740 to be too pessimistic. In addition, the update was to deal with the reactors then under design, which were five times the size of that analyzed in WASH-740. The results, which assumed the plant was located in a city, were not released by the AEC, possibly because full disclosure to the public might well have brought the nuclear-power industry to a grinding halt. In June, 1973, the Union of Concerned Scientists gained access to the files on the 1964–65 study by threatening to sue the AEC.

This new study projected an even grimmer scenario, with 45,000 fatalities, between $17 billion and $280 billion in damage, and contamination of an area the size of Pennsylvania. At the time of this writing, the information was still being assessed, and further details were not available.[48]

Using the available AEC data, another group, the Committee for Nuclear Responsibility, has estimated the following potential for destruction if 10 percent of the radioactive inventory were released from a plant of the size being built in the early 1970s (rather than 50 percent from a small plant as in WASH-740; otherwise the postulated conditions were the same):

Required evacuation of cities, industrial complexes, defense installations, and large sections of the countryside, perhaps for years;

Outdoor activities restricted for millions of Americans.

Agriculture and water supplies ruined in an area as big as the state of California (150,000 square miles); food and water shortages;

Massive unemployment and business chaos overnight; panic near other nuclear plants;

*Un*insured property damage and income losses over $20 billion; possible bankruptcy for several health- and life-insurance companies;

Between 4000 and 500,000 people killed by acute radiation exposure, depending on the difficulty in evacuating radiation refugees;[49]

Thousands more people killed by radiation-induced cancer or leukemia years later (excluding plutonium casualties over the following quarter-million years),[50] plus more birth defects and mental retardation in children of irradiated parents.

Horrible as these projections are, they are well within the bounds considered "acceptable" by the technological optimists. The AEC continues its public-relations campaign, scoffing at the risks, implying that the projections are extreme, and declaring that such accidents are highly unlikely. For instance, in December, 1973, the new chairperson of the AEC, Dixie Lee Ray, a marine biologist, went on nationwide television in an attempt to lull Americans into accepting nuclear power as a solution to the energy mini-crisis. She implied that the risks of catastrophic accident were exaggerated because in the projections the reactors were situated in cities (not true in WASH-740). She further claimed that emergency core-cooling engineering safeguards were "fail-safe as far as we know"

—which can be most charitably described as an extremely misleading statement.[51]

In late 1974 the AEC made one more attempt to mislead the public about the safety of nuclear power plants. It released WASH-1400 (also known as the *Rasmussen Report*), a 2500-page technical document purporting to show that the probable consequences of nuclear reactor accidents are much smaller than a whole array of risks to which society is already exposed: chemical explosions, airline crashes, automobile accidents, tornados, etc. In fact the entire document is based on a logically questionable investigative technique known as "fault tree" analysis, backed up by preposterous assumptions. Basically, the fault tree analysis consists of estimating failure rates of individual components from laboratory or other data and then calculating the chances of a system breakdown as if each component would perform on-line and in combination with all the others exactly as it did in its individual tests. One assumption of the report is that people will be quickly and readily evacuated from major urban areas after there have been large releases of radioactivity (an assumption any commuter can easily judge for himself). Another incredible assumption is that sabotage will not occur. Dr. Rasmussen covered most of the flaws of the study in the fine print, but the AEC of course trumpeted the conclusions without pointing out its shortcomings —safe in the knowledge that few laymen could digest or criticize the monster report itself. More accurately, this document should have been entitled "WHITEWASH 1400".

## How the Public Is "Protected"

You don't have to know the technical details to see clearly that AEC spokesmen lie about reactor safety. All you need to know is that insurance companies refuse to give coverage to nuclear power plants for more than one percent of the potential liability. Similarly, if you read the fine print in your homeowner's policy, you will find that damages from radioactivity are *specifically excluded.*

As Insurance Commissioner of Pennsylvania, Herbert S. Denenberg gained an enviable reputation as perhaps the only insurance commissioner in the US who actively served the interests of the public rather than of insurance companies. His pamphlet listing the true values of life-insurance policies was a landmark in the struggle to protect consumers from the unarmed robbery practiced by many American insurance companies. In August of 1973, Commissioner Denenberg stated,[52] "It may be that nobody but God could write the insurance policy we need on nuclear power plants. . . . The only adequate insurance against catastrophic loss from nuclear accident is to stop building more nuclear plants and to begin closing down the ones we have now. It's that simple."

His office has also issued a "Consumers' Guide to Nuclear Non-Insurance." It contains eight points:

1. If your home is destroyed, DON'T COUNT ON YOUR HOME-OWNER'S COVERAGE—it has a total exclusion against damage from a nuclear accident.

2. If your auto is destroyed or contaminated, DON'T COUNT ON YOUR AUTOMOBILE POLICY—it may have the same type of exclusion as does your home-owner's policy.

3. If you need cash, DON'T COUNT ON YOUR CASH-VALUE LIFE INSURANCE POLICY as a source of income. Your life insurance company may go bankrupt as claims mount up and up and up.

4. If you're injured, DON'T COUNT ON YOUR HEALTH INSURANCE POLICY to pay the bill. Your health insurance policy covers your loss, but your health insurance company may be in no better shape than your life insurance company.

5. DON'T COUNT ON SUING THE UTILITY COMPANY which owns the reactor that caused the damage. Under the Price-Anderson Act, total compensation for all victims of a nuclear accident is limited to $560 million, and most of that is paid by the federal gov-

ernment. You might get back no more than a few cents for every dollar of your loss.

6. DON'T COUNT ON SUING THE COMPANY WHICH BUILT THE REACTOR which caused the damage. The same Price-Anderson Act lets the manufacturers of reactors off scot-free.

7. DON'T COUNT ON THE ASSURANCES OF THE NUCLEAR ESTABLISHMENT that you will be able to recover all losses above Price-Anderson limits. The nuclear establishment says that you can go to Congress and ask for help for any such losses, as can the victims of natural disasters. But you'll have to get in line behind the past flood-and-earthquake victims, who are still waiting for such payments.

8. DON'T TAKE THE ADVICE OF THE NUCLEAR ESTABLISHMENT ON THE ISSUE OF NUCLEAR SAFETY. The people who make and run nuclear power plants have assured us that there will never be a major catastrophe. But some manufacturers of nuclear reactors also make toasters, dryers, washers, television sets, and other household appliances. Are nuclear reactors that much more perfect and dependable?

Do you suppose our giant insurance companies know something that Dixie Lee Ray doesn't? Why would these profit-hungry corporations, even as a coalition, refuse the gigantic profits that would come their way if, as the AEC claimed, the chances of catastrophic accident were virtually zero? After all, it would be just like insuring concrete airplanes against midair collisions. Think of it—all those juicy premiums and no possibility of a claim to pay!

In the mid-1950s, while the AEC and its Congressional "watchdog" accomplices in the Joint Committee on Atomic Energy (JCAE) were claiming publicly that fission power plants were perfectly safe, the insurance companies were telling them behind the scenes that the risks were so great that they would not insure against them. This led in 1957 to the notorious Price-Anderson Act mentioned above. Since no insurance company would write complete liability coverage on a nuclear power plant,

Congress assumed its accustomed role as a prostitute for big business and decided that the taxpayers would bear more than 80 percent of the burden. This was accomplished in two ways. The first limits the liability of companies owning nuclear power plants to $560 million, a tiny percentage of the many billions for which the companies could be liable. They would, of course, be liable not just for property damage but also for personal injury and death. Suppose a million people were killed, with $7 billion in property damage. If the liability for each life were set conservatively at a mere $10,000, the total liability would be $17 billion. The Price-Anderson Act limits liability to 3 percent of that amount, so injured taxpayers would be compensated for their losses at three cents on the dollar.

But Congressional-AEC-JCAE fleecing of the taxpayer doesn't stop there. Of the $560 million in damages that would be paid out, only the first $110 million would be paid by insurance companies. The remaining $450 million would come from the public treasury, from the taxpayers themselves.

Congress not only passed the Price-Anderson Act in 1957, they renewed it in 1965 and again in 1974. It is, of course, another example of the American system of "capitalism for the poor and socialism for the rich"—an enormous hidden subsidy for industrial giants like Consolidated Edison, Pacific Gas and Electric, Westinghouse, and General Electric—a subsidy required because their nuclear products are so shoddy and dangerous that private insurance companies will insure them for only a tiny fraction of the potential damages.

The above discussion of catastrophic reactor accidents is based on burner reactors of standard design. Breeder reactors present even more serious problems. They have very compact cores in relation to the power they produce, which presents difficult engineering problems, such as finding an appropriate coolant to carry away the heat produced, since water (used in burners) won't do. The coolant used in the best-known breeder design is molten sodium—a substance that explodes violently on contact with air or water. Breeders also contain large quantities of plutonium, the most dangerous material known to man. The combination makes them enormously more hazardous than burners at their present stage of development. Plutonium for instance, is subject to possible "criticality accidents," small nuclear explosions that could blow open any conceivable containment building.

The nuclear industry's vaunted "safety record" with burners consists of a long, but largely unpublicized, string of errors, flaws, and blunders (as noted in the RAND statement), none of which so far has caused a catastrophic release. Its record with breeders is even more frightening. Together with an industry coalition, the AEC built a "demonstration" breeder power station, the Fermi Fast Breeder, near Detroit. It "demonstrated," all right. In 1966 it suffered an accident that exceeded the "maximum credible accident" previously defined for this particular reactor by the AEC.[53] This accident occurred when the reactor had been in full service for less than one year, and was caused by a manufacturing goof—a piece of metal added to the reactor as an afterthought (and which did not appear on the blueprints) had torn loose and blocked the flow of molten sodium, causing a melt-down.

At the time, there was great fear that the melt-down would proceed until the reactor blew up and breached the containment vessel. If that had happened under the worst possible weather conditions (the wind in the right direction and a persistent thermal inversion to keep the radioactive cloud near the ground), millions of people would have died and an enormous chunk of North America would have been made uninhabitable.[54] To everyone's relief, this did not happen. After four years of being shut down for repairs, the Fermi plant was restarted in 1970, but it was soon closed down again because of continuing malfunctions. People in Detroit could sleep at night when it was operating only because they were *unaware* of the nature of the radiation bomb the AEC had planted a mere thirty miles from them.

In late 1973, Dixie Lee Ray was touting the breeder

reactor as a great cure for the energy problem. The lady was confused—it promises to be a much more effective cure for the population problem! And just as contraceptives are the preferred method of population limitation, there are many superior alternatives to the breeder for supplying us with energy. Even burners are better!

The argument that we must rush ahead with current breeder technology because we will soon run short of uranium has been exposed as nonsense in a detailed analysis of uranium availability by physicist John Holdren.[55] It turns out that the uranium "shortage" is more AEC propaganda and that increases in the price of uranium (constituting a minuscule fraction of the cost of electricity generated) will guarantee enough uranium for at least half a century. *So there clearly is time for at least twenty-five more years of research into breeders to see if there is some way of building one that is reasonably safe before adding breeder stations to the power network.*

The risk of catastrophic accident is, by itself, a more than adequate reason for a complete moratorium on the building of nuclear power plants. It will remain so until private insurance companies are willing to give full liability insurance to power companies and to insure you and your home against damage by radioactivity. You don't have to guess whether the AEC and the nuclear-power industry are suddenly starting to tell the truth about safety; just let the insurance industry be your guide. But even here you must be careful. Rumor has it that the AEC–nuclear-industry lobbyists will attempt to get Congress to declare reactor accidents "acts of God." If this were done, the revealing nuclear exclusion *clauses* could be removed from insurance policies while the *exclusions themselves* would remain.

## Diversion and Sabotage

So far we have been discussing nuclear safety. Now we turn to an aspect of safety that conventionally has been segregated under the name of "nuclear safeguards." Some technologists feel that foolproof safety systems for nuclear plants can be contrived, although it is a well-known law of technology (often credited to Edward Teller, "father of the H-bomb") that a fool of sufficient magnitude can always be found to circumvent any such system. Both the technologists who favor nuclear power plants and those who oppose them agree that there is no certain way to safeguard fissile materials (those capable of sustaining the chain reactions required for either A-bombs or nuclear reactors) from being directed to clandestine uses. Nor is it possible to safeguard reactors completely against sabotage.

What kind of clandestine use could fissile material be put to? The answer is simple—*it can be made into atomic bombs*. Who could do it? Any determined person or group with some intelligence and a willingness to learn. Some background in physics, chemistry, or nuclear engineering would help speed the process, but would not be essential. Information on where and how to steal the materials is freely available, as is the necessary technical information on how to make the bomb itself. A three-part *New Yorker* "Profile" of physicist Theodore B. Taylor, published in December, 1973,[56] contains almost everything the amateur nuclear demolitions man needs to know. In the unclassified pages of that magazine, he can find everything from where to purchase a centrifuge for use in turning uranium 235 oxide into uranium 235 to step-by-step instructions for the construction of a home-made gun-type or implosion-type atomic bomb. Suitable targets for terrorists are discussed, including the timing, position, and kiloton yield required to kill virtually everyone in the US government, to make a crater where the Pentagon now stands, or to fell the World Trade Center like a gigantic tree.

Dr. Taylor had serious reservations about assembling all of this information in a single article, even though it is openly available to the general public scattered in other publications. His alarm over the problems of safeguarding nuclear material was so great, however, that he thought the benefits of alerting the public outweighed the risk of starting someone on the path to a bomb.

There are substantial amounts of fissile materials available to anyone who wishes to steal them.[57] Both in transit and at rest, these materials are not guarded with anything like the care allotted to money, for example. Shipments, moving like ordinary freight by common carrier, have more than once gone astray, only to be recovered later.

Investigators for the General Accounting Office (charged with checking on the performance of other government agencies) found that plants handling "SNM" —special nuclear materials—had laughable security precautions. At one it was possible to enter a room containing raw materials for bombs merely by pulling off flimsy metal louvers covering vent-holes in a wall. The guards at another plant had inadequate patrol procedures, "watched" from a station where they could not see 80 percent of the plant, and lacked the required proficiency with their revolvers. Another plant had a sophisticated alarm system and a plan to telephone the local police every hour to confirm that all was well. A test of the telephone system produced a prompt reaction from the police. When the call didn't arrive, they roared off to another plant fourteen miles away from the one with the nuclear materials.

One of the most serious aspects of the safeguards situation is that, if the AEC gets its way, first tons and eventually hundreds of tons of plutonium will be produced annually.[58] Not only is this material entirely suitable for making bombs,[59] it is also one of the most dangerous materials known to man. Plutonium has an extraordinary capacity to cause lung cancer—about one-thousandth of a gram of inhaled plutonium dust will kill you in two days at the most, and one-millionth of a gram is probably lethal over the long term (for comparison, a penny weighs about three grams). Some scientists think that significant cancer hazards exist with even lower doses. Furthermore, because of its long half-life, a speck of plutonium can last for tens of thousands of years, killing more than one person.

Knowing this, it is not comforting to realize that the AEC and the nuclear industry already have lost a great deal of potential bomb-making material. For example,

the Nuclear Materials Enrichment Corporation could not
account for 6 percent of the materials it handled over a
six-year period.[60]

Considering the projected scale of power-plant operations, it seems inevitable that fissile material will remain
available to clever and determined thieves or terrorists
even if the AEC and the industry tightened up their security system. Raids and hijacking may not even be
necessary. There is inevitable attrition in any material
that is being handled, machined, hammered, heated, and
so on. In 1971 the AEC could not account for one percent of the plutonium it handles, although fortunately
there is no reason to believe this amount has either been
stolen or lost to the environment. If they immediately improved their accounting procedures fourfold (unlikely, if
not impossible), by the year 2000 they would still be
unable to account for enough plutonium to construct 250
Nagasaki-sized bombs.[61] There are many ways that a
clever person on the inside of the nuclear industry could
steal small amounts of plutonium or uranium little by
little until enough was accumulated for a bomb, while
staying within the statistical bounds of "normal loss."

In the early 1970s, plutonium was worth something like
$10 million per ton, roughly twice the market value of
gold.[62] It is not unlikely that a black-market price a
hundred times as high would prevail (the markup on illegal
drugs such as heroin is very many times higher), so the
financial rewards for a little illegal "diversion" would be
great indeed. A thief might be able to fence twenty pounds
of plutonium, enough for a dandy bomb, for around $10
million. Few crimes in our society would be easier and
more fiancially rewarding—if a buyer could be found.

Who might such a buyer be? It seems unlikely that a
terrorist group would have the funds, although organized
crime might. But either of those groups would be more
likely to take the required fissile material in a simple
armed robbery. The most likely buyer would be a small
nation interested in joining the nuclear club. For instance,
an underdeveloped nation might want nuclear weapons in
order to prevent an overdeveloped country from threat-

ening to recolonize it in a resource crisis. The potential of this sort of situation could easily be perceived during the 1973–74 energy mini-crisis. Early in 1973, there were announcements that US Marines were practicing desert maneuvers,[63] and later in the year there was discussion in the American media of possible military action to break the Arab oil embargo. In early January, 1974, it was reported[64] that the Saudis had wired their oil wells for demolition in case of invasion.

The only countries that would need to buy fissile material on the black market would be those nations that have no nuclear reactors. In past years one often heard silly debate about whether the Israelis have nuclear weapons. But they have long had reactors and are one of the most technologically advanced nations, so the real questions are what kind of delivery system they have developed and what targets are programmed. With their backs against the wall, would they demolish the Aswan Dam and flush Egypt into the sea? Would they hit Arab capitals? Or have they secretly put together a system capable of hitting Odessa or other southern cities in the Soviet Union? Tempting targets there are only twelve hundred miles from Israel, within easy reach of Israeli Phantom fighter-bombers or intermediate-range ballistic missiles.

India abruptly ended the speculations about her nuclear capability by exploding a nuclear device derived from reactor materials in May, 1974. This led to a new discussion of the suitability of spreading nuclear-power technology to nations outside the nuclear club, fanned by President Nixon's promise to build nuclear power plants in Egypt and Israel. The US government, surprised by the public outcry, defended itself by pointing out that it had already made similar agreements with twenty-nine other countries!

It has been argued that biological or radiological agents would make a more potent blackmail weapon than the bomb for both terrorists and small nations. While this may be true if measured in terms of lives threatened per unit effort, it ignores a central point—the psychological impact of threatening someone with an atomic bomb.

Neither terrorists nor small nations would intend to win wars; their goals essentially would be blackmail—to gain something by making a credible threat. For this purpose, atomic bombs are ideal. Orlando, Florida has already been presented with such a threat in the form of a diagram of a workable bomb and a demand for money. The terrorist was caught and was found to have a small quantity of uranium 238—a non-fissile isotope of uranium— with which he planned to make his last threat (he had purchased it from a scientific supply house and correctly assumed the police would not quickly be able to distinguish it from uranium 235, the fissile isotope that is used in bombs). This "terrorist," incidentally, was a fourteen-year-old boy! [65]

Besides providing the crucial materials for homemade fission bombs, nuclear plants can support antisocial activities in another way. Terrorists already realize the public apprehension about nuclear reactors and are likely to use them increasingly as targets of threats. Already in one incident, hijackers threatened to crash an airliner into an AEC reactor at Oak Ridge, Tennessee. If the countryside becomes dotted with nuclear power plants, criminal incidents involving them might become commonplace. And credible threats of radiation atrocities could be made by psychotics possessing only a few grams of lethal plutonium.

The technologists who push nuclear power are aware of the magnitude of the diversion and blackmail threats. Why, then, do they continue to push the program? The answer is that they are willing to accept the possibility of the millions of deaths in the name of their kind of progress. Some typical comments by nuclear engineers and the like include: [66]

"I think we have to live with the expectation that once every four or five years a nuclear explosion will take place and kill a lot of people."

"The largest bomb that has ever exploded anywhere was sixty megatons, and that is one-thousandth the force of a hurricane. We have lived with earthquakes and hurricanes for a long time."

"After a bomb goes off, and the fire ends, quiet descends again, and life continues."

These are the statements of people suffering from professional insanity. They represent the kind of minds that will control the destiny of humanity if we proceed much further toward getting our electricity from the "peaceful atom."

The safeguards problem alone, in our opinion, is reason enough to halt the growth of nuclear power, phase out the plants now in service, and "burn" as much as possible of today's inventory of fissile material in reactors designed to dispose of it. Combined with the threats of catastrophic release and the unsolved (and perhaps insoluble) problem of long-term waste disposal, the case for turning away from fission power—at least temporarily—is persuasive to any sane person *who is aware of the alternatives*.

## Power Alternatives

One of our greatest problems, however, is that the President, the Joint Committee on Atomic Energy, the AEC, and the nuclear industry have made a determined effort, first, to keep Americans unaware that there are viable alternatives to fission power other than returning to the Stone Age and, second, to retard the development of such alternatives. In addition to rapidly reducing our wastage of energy, the short- and medium-term alternatives consist largely of developing new sources of fossil fuels and more efficient ways of handling them. Some of these have already been discussed. In the longer term, however, there are several additional possibilities.

**Fusion.** Nuclear fusion was mentioned earlier as a second way to obtain nuclear energy. In *fission,* heavy nuclei are split to form medium-weight nuclei, with an accompanying release of energy. On the other hand, two very light nuclei can be forced together until they *fuse* into a medium-weight nucleus with a release of surplus energy.

(For further details, see Appendix I.) Thus, in theory an energy bonus can be gained either by splitting heavy atoms or by fusing light ones.

The sun, a giant power generator which operates by fusing hydrogen and other light nuclei, testifies to the amount of energy obtainable if small nuclei can be made to travel fast enough to fuse when they collide. The way to speed them up is to heat appropriate materials to extraordinary temperatures.[67] This means using large amounts of energy to begin with—you have to use energy in order to produce energy through fusion. So far, the only energy "profit" from fusion has been with thermonuclear (hydrogen) bombs. In these devices, the enormous initial heat required is provided by conventional fission bombs employed as triggers. The temperature at the center of a fission bomb can build to several hundred million degrees—higher than the temperature in the center of the sun—in a hundred-millionth of a second.[68]

The problems of creating and maintaining fusion-level temperatures under controlled conditions remain to be solved. The basic difficulty is to contain the mixture of atoms while it is heated, since the hot fuel gas would be instantaneously cooled by contact with any physical material from which a container might be made. Several promising leads exist, however, including the use of magnetic fields to form "bottles" containing the superheated gases, or pulsed blasts of energy from lasers to heat and compress pellets of fusion fuel (lithium, deuterium, tritium). Controlled fusions have been obtained, but so far the energy injected into the system exceeds that coming out—energy loss instead of profit. There is no certainty as yet that a profitable fusion reactor can be created, although knowledgeable scientists think it probably can.[69]

If practical fusion machines can be developed, they are almost certain to replace fission reactors in power plants. The fuels for them will be much cheaper, since they consist of various isotopes of the light elements of hydrogen, helium, and lithium, which are either superabundant or could easily be "bred" in a fusion reactor. More important, the environmental threats from fusion could be small compared to those of fission. The amounts of radio-activity produced would be at least an order of magnitude smaller and theoretically could be made several orders of magnitude smaller.[70] Moreover, fissile material can be created in a fusion reactor only with a very special effort—the material is not automatically produced as it is with burners or breeders. Finally, while a fission reactor is always on the verge of "getting away"—that is, of having the chain reaction proceed too rapidly—a fusion reactor would always be on the verge of "going out." The type of catastrophic accident that will always threaten burners and breeders would be impossible with fusion power generators.

For years, fusion research has been a poor stepchild for the AEC. The money has gone into fission, because the nuclear industry wanted to plow ahead without regard to environmental threats, and because so many in the AEC wanted to soothe their consciences by turning the process that destroyed Hiroshima and Nagasaki into a benefit for mankind. The energy mini-crisis finally resulted in more funds going toward fusion research, and with luck it will yield results. But, we repeat, this is only a hope for the long run. It is unlikely that fusion power will be delivering significant quantities of energy to consumers in less than forty years.

**Solar Power.** Even if fusion power never becomes practical, there is no need to panic. *Indeed, we may be better off without it, considering the kind of ecological damage produced by human beings when supplied with superabundant energy.* Enough energy to provide a reasonable lifestyle for, say, an eventual equilibrium population of 100 million Americans, *could* be supplied by solar energy technology—supplemented where feasible by geothermal energy, wind power, and other sources—with little environmental damage. Such energy sources may be potentially capable of serving a larger population than we now have, but the desirability of having a smaller ultimate population if an energy-intensive way of life is to be maintained is obvious.[71]

According to solar-energy experts Aden and Marjorie

Meinel of the University of Arizona at Tucson, a solar plant with a collector covering about three square miles would produce power equivalent to that coming from a large nuclear power plant (one million kilowatts, which is the same as 1000 megawatts). To replace the entire installed nuclear and fossil-fueled power capacity of the US in 1970 (slightly over 300 million kilowatts) would require collectors covering about nine hundred square miles.[72] Such a thirty-by-thirty mile area would be a tiny portion of the area of the American Southwest now wasted on air-force gunnery and missile ranges.

Because of inevitable losses in transmission, it would not be feasible to place all of our solar-generating capacity in the Southwest. Fortunately, however, solar energy can provide useful energy in localities much less sunny than Arizona. Individual solar-energy units to heat homes reportedly will be on the market before the end of 1974.[73]

## Meeting Energy Needs in the Near Future

Whatever the eventual solution to the long-term energy problem, two things are crystal clear.

First, there is no need to rush the deployment of present-day incompetent fission-power technology. Conservation measures and fossil fuels can see us to the end of the century while crash programs to develop and perfect new technologies are carried out. During that period, we can both investigate the feasibility of alternatives to fission power and perhaps find ways to reduce the risks associated with fission to an acceptable level. Then around the year 2000, society can decide which way to go— unless, of course, the success of solar (or fusion) energy has already made the decision unnecessary.

Second, it is clear that we should begin planning for extensive changes in our overall energy technology. Most of the energy used by Americans (in transportation, for example) is not used as electricity. Yet electricity will be the useful output of nuclear, geothermal, and wind-driven power plants (hot water from fission plants might in some cases be used for local heating). Solar power plants may also produce electricity. Therefore research and development on such things as improved batteries, electric vehicles, flywheel vehicles, and so on should be greatly accelerated. Beyond that, plans must be formulated for using electricity to produce portable fuels (hydrogen, methane) for uses such as powering airplanes, where electricity simply will not do, or for building solar plants that can produce hydrogen.[74]

It is sometimes claimed by the technologists that environmentalists and others opposed to fission power are "antitechnology." On the contrary, they are optimistic that technological solutions *other than* the mindless proliferation of unsafe fission power plants can see us through the coming *real* energy crisis. In fact, the technologies for solar, geothermal, and wind power are better understood than is the technology for breeder reactors. Therefore, given comparable effort, they could be more quickly put into operation. And each of them would be infinitely safer.

But, although we may be optimistic with regard to technological possibilities, there are many social and political reasons for pessimism about future energy supplies. The AEC and its supporters in Congress are completely in league with an increasingly monopolistic nuclear industry in promoting nuclear power. It is a classic case of the fox guarding the henhouse. For example, the 1954 Atomic Energy Act contained provisions for antitrust review of each planned commercial reactor operation before the AEC could grant a license. The AEC swindled the public out of this protection by granting *no* commercial licenses. Up to the end of 1970, all functioning power reactors were operating under "experimental" licenses, granted under a part of the act dealing with medical and research use![75] In summary, the public can expect *no* protection of either its financial or safety interests from the AEC.

Also, there is no effective lobby—other than environmental and antinuclear citizens' groups—promoting the development of the best alternatives to fossil fuels and

nuclear energy. Except for investments of oil companies
in geothermal power (and their goals conceivably may
have been largely to *retard* development), there are no
corporations with vested interests in alternatives. Rather,
many corporations see them as dangerous competition.[76]
Our main hope therefore lies in the actions of an alerted
citizenry. Public opposition to nuclear power plants has
been effective in the past, is growing,[77] and could become
widespread enough to turn the situation totally around.
Much will depend on how skillful the AEC and its accomplices are at using energy shortages to bamboozle the
public. A good indicator in the near future will be the
vote on a nuclear-safety initiative in California, if one
should get on the ballot. The governor of that state,
notorious for his ignorance of environmental matters, recently supported coating the Golden State with nuclear
reactors. His reason: "People are part of the ecology,
too." Ronald Reagan apparently doesn't know that people
are precisely the part of "the ecology" that is *most vulnerable* to radiation injury.

Our guess is that, in the absence of a catastrophic accident or terrorist incident in the next decade, the US
government and much of the rest of the world will attempt
to dig itself deep into the hole of fission power. Much of
the public will accept the guarantees of the nuclear engineers and their supporters that the reactors are designed
so that accidents cannot happen, forgetting that men of
the same mentality designed the "earthquake-proof" over-
passes that collapsed in Los Angeles in a rather small
earthquake in 1971. They have already forgotten that the
*Titanic* was guaranteed by its designers to be unsinkable.


## What You Can Do


Faced with this, what can you do about it? Citizen
action, especially aimed at getting many of our worst
politicians out of office, may help, but there is hardly an
army of competent replacements waiting in the wings.

The most successful group actions can be fought at the community level. You can oppose the construction of a nuclear power plant anywhere near where you live, and there are organizations that will help you.[78] If you are faced with this problem, find and read Richard Lewis's fine book, *The Nuclear Power Rebellion*. It will show you how other citizens have successfully fought having their lives and property threatened by the AEC and its accomplices.[79] As an individual citizen, you can bombard your senators and representatives with demands that they support funding for development of solar, geothermal, wind, and fusion power, and that they keep asking hard questions before funding fission programs. You can also join one of the antinuclear-power citizens' groups. For example, the Environment Coalition on Nuclear Energy is a collection of some thirty-five groups from eastern Pennsylvania, New Jersey, and Delaware that fights AEC efforts to build plants in their area.

The congruence of your own and society's interest is rarely as clear as it is on this issue of nuclear power. There is no need in this case to wonder whether dropping out or attempting to change society is preferable: even the most isolated hermit will be in danger by the year 2000 if the nuclear-power establishment has its way. Helping to push the country toward a sensible energy policy is in everyone's self-interest.

This doesn't mean that there is nothing you can do to enhance your future security besides joining the battle against the spread of nuclear power plants. You can also attempt to minimize your own energy consumption and to make yourself as independent as possible from the power system. Then, if the government and utilities blow it without killing you, you will suffer less from power breakdowns. We'll give some concrete suggestions for doing this later in the book. Another thing you can do is not live within a hundred miles downwind of a nuclear power plant. The accompanying map (Figure 2) will help you locate them. With a little effort, you should be able to avoid living near one over the next two decades, and you'll sleep better as a result.

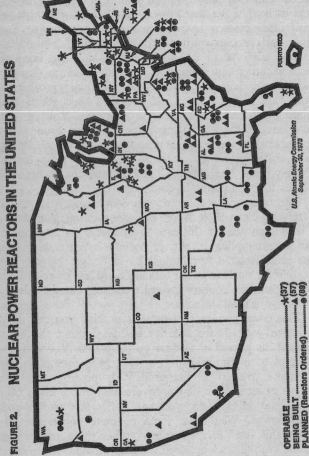

FIGURE 2.    NUCLEAR POWER REACTORS IN THE UNITED STATES

U.S. Atomic Energy Commission
September 30, 1973

OPERABLE ......................... ★ (37)
BEING BUILT ..................... ▲ (57)
PLANNED (Reactors Ordered) ...... ● (99)

We fully expect that politicians will continue to miss the critical point that the environmental safeguards must be paramount precisely *because* "people are part of the ecology." They will continue to take the short-range view and grope for panaceas to increase energy supplies rather than making an all-out effort to limit demand. Most politicians are all too aware that they will be dead long before future grateful generations reach the polls.

The story of the energy mess underlines the utter incompetence of our institutions and leaders at dealing with dislocations that, compared with the coming food–environment–economic–human-relations problems, were easy to foresee and avert. It would be nice to hope that these institutions can be revised so that the response of society to crisis will not forever be determined by greed and stupidity. It would be splendid if intelligent, humane, forward-looking politicians appeared to lead us out of the wilderness. But we must conclude that, for the moment at least, personal plans should be made on the assumption that we're stuck with the worst and the dullest.

# 3

# We Are Not Alone

---

"In individuals, insanity is rare, but in groups, parties, nations, and epochs it is the rule."
—Nietzsche, *Beyond Good and Evil*, 1886

"History shows that men and nations behave reasonably only when they have exhausted all other alternatives."

—Abba Eban,
Foreign Minister of Israel, 1970 [1]

THE ENERGY MINI-CRISIS in the United States brought home to all Americans how international politics can affect their daily affairs. They believed that the Arab oil embargo was a major cause of the petroleum shortage, whether or not it really was. Suddenly the foreign-policy objectives of Arab sheiks needed to be considered when one decided, for instance, whether to buy a Volkswagen or a Cadillac or whether or not to spend extra money on home insulation or a solar swimming-pool heater. That our nation of superconsumers is not a resource-rich, self-supporting entity came as a surprise to many—but it may be the most important fact of American life in the last quarter of the twentieth century.

Like the energy mini-crisis, the food "crisis" of 1972–73 also came as a surprise to the American people. Its causes, despite reams of newspaper explanations, were largely misunderstood. The public assumed that American farmers and middlemen were somehow cheating consumers, although many of them were caught in a squeeze between rising costs and controlled retail prices. The result was rapidly rising prices on uncontrolled foods and temporary shortages of controlled ones.[2]

These disconcerting, but still minor, disruptions in what Americans have come to regard as their dependable food supplies were largely part of a ripple effect caused by the far more serious food problems in other parts of the world. In 1972, reduced harvests in some temperate areas such as the USSR, together with inadequate monsoons and consequent crop failures in India and parts of Southeastern Asia, created enormous pressure on what grain was available for sale in the international market. Most of this grain came from the US and Canada. In 1973, the US exported a staggering 75 percent of its 1972 wheat crop, over 50 percent of its soybean crop, and 15 percent of its feedgrain.[3] Such extraordinary depletion of domestic stocks was bound to produce shortages.

The way of life of every American is intimately tied to the functioning of the international trade system. This is so for two reasons. First, the US depends on imports of a great variety of things, including petroleum, tin, chromium, nickel, manganese, newsprint, and shrimp. Second, American prosperity depends on the prosperity of other nations that buy American goods—goods like airbuses (such as the Lockheed L-1011 and Douglas DC-10), automobiles, and home appliances. In some cases, domestic markets for such products are nearly saturated. The economic prosperity of the US is inextricably interwoven with that of the world, and thus Americans, along with everyone else, will suffer if the world trade system and international monetary managements collapse. The first signs of the onset of a full-scale depression in the US may be, not a gigantic "bust" on the New York stock market, but, for example, a steady deterioration of Japan's economic position or a rash of English bank failures.

To put it simply, mankind has blown its chance for a smooth transition to an equilibrium society. The general economic trend is going to be downhill from now on. There may be temporary reversals—renewed flows of oil, bumper harvests, partial recoveries—but as the end of the century approaches, each decade will be worse than the preceding one for the average American, to say nothing of the average human being.

How can we be so sure, especially since there are so many things that could be done to ameliorate the coming crises? One reason is that many important trends have a built-in momentum that would make reversal difficult, even if the effort were made. As one example there is a momentum to population growth built into the age structure of growing populations. Even when fertility is reduced to the replacement level—when each couple only replaces itself in the next generation—a population will continue to grow for more than half a century. The US and a very few other industrialized nations have reached the point of replacement fertility, but most underdeveloped countries (UDCs) are very far from it. Their population growth is likely to end tragically.

The pressure of more and more people encourages such self-reinforcing trends as overfishing, overgrazing, and the irreversible loss of genetic variability of crops. Providing ever greater quantities of fuel for more and more people accelerates the depletion of energy reserves. Sucking the oil supplies dry helps push a lethal nuclear fission technology upon us. The collapse of one industry has ripple effects within national economies, and the collapse of one nation endangers other nations. Malnutrition and poverty breed disease and epidemics, which in turn cause economic disruptions that create more poverty and malnutrition. We could go on and on—the list is long. And whatever happens, Americans will be profoundly affected.

Given the interdependence of nations, especially over-developed countries (ODCs), and the approaching food and resource crunch, several broad-gauge predictions can be made about the course of the international system in the next few decades:

1. Escalating resource "needs" of ODCs will lead to both increased interdependence and increased competition among them. There is, of course, always the possibility that competition will upset the "balance of terror" and cause a thermonuclear war.

2. The increasing demand for resources by the ODCs, combined with efforts of various UDCs to limit supplies and raise prices of raw materials, will probably lead to increased "resource imperialism" and quite possibly to limited recolonization of UDCs. If recolonization is attempted, UDCs may defend themselves with nuclear or chemical-biological weapons and perhaps trigger World War III.

3. Rising prices of resources, especially oil, will greatly damage the economies of many UDCs, especially those not richly endowed with surplus commodities that can be marketed internationally.

4. Although awareness of the deepening plight of mankind will gradually dawn on the governments of the world, these governments will probably find it impossible to take effective joint action in most crisis situations. Acting *before* a crisis arrives will be beyond their capabilities.

5. Regional and national collapses, brought on by the collision between growing populations and diminishing resources to support them, are virtually certain, and these will have global repercussions.

Before discussing what influence such events might have on your personal plans, let's examine each of these predictions in greater detail.

## Interdependence and Competition Among ODCs

The trend toward interdependence is best exemplified by the "we give you wheat, you give us natural gas" agreements between the US and the USSR. It is an interesting spectacle to see such "bitter enemies," each having built thermonuclear strike forces capable of destroying the other many times over, purposely becoming dependent upon one another. Some of the many other manifestations of ODC interdependence include Soviet gas flowing to

western Europe, the existence of the European Common
Market, European dependence on American grains, and
Japan's heavy dependence on ODC markets for its manu-
factured goods.

As shortages increase, and more and more capital-in-
search-of-investment-opportunities accumulates, this interdependence will no doubt reduce the probability of thermonuclear war being triggered directly by the major powers.
The probability of direct triggering of Armageddon may
also be reduced by the growth of fission-power technology,
assuming that this potentially lethal trend does continue.
The existence of large numbers of fission reactors and fuel-
reprocessing facilities above ground makes any country
that has them vulnerable to radioactive releases from
ruptured nuclear facilities. This is an especially severe
hazard in the USSR, where fission reactors are being built
without containment buildings. The consequent vulnerability of these power plants to blast damage is presumably a powerful deterrent to the USSR against starting
World War III.

As ODC interdependence grows, the prospects of deadly
competition among these nations are, ironically, also growing rapidly. Major areas of competition will be for agricultural products, fisheries yields, minerals, and energy
(especially petroleum). Some portents of the future can
be seen in the fisheries situation, where competition is
already intense. The "Cod War" between Britain and Iceland showed how seriously a small country can take a
vital threat to its economy. Iceland was willing to enter
into a limited military confrontation with vastly stronger
England. Such conflicts over fisheries resources seem destined to grow steadily more severe, especially as Japan's
food situation grows more desperate.

More dangerous, however, may be the competition
among ODCs, especially the US, Japan, and the nations
of western Europe, for the petroleum and other mineral
resources of the Third World. The not-too-subtle message
in the early 1973 reports that American Marines were
training for desert warfare was surely understood by the
oil-producing nations of the Middle East. It also un-

doubtedly was clear to our European and Japanese competitors for Arab oil. The "everybody for himself" reactions of the petroleum-consuming ODCs to the Arab oil embargo—the groveling of the Japanese, the maneuvering of the French and British, the announcement of plans for American self-sufficiency—were far from reassuring.[4] Such behavior almost certainly foreshadows the response of ODCs to the more critical shortages of the future, as a nationalistic world faces problems that have no prayer of solution except through international cooperation.

Finally, we cannot ignore the possibility that Arab nations might threaten a total oil embargo against the US and other ODCs if certain transfers of food are not made to hungry nations. This would not be consistent with traditional Arab behavior, but in the Middle East traditions have been crumbling rapidly. Americans may eventually have to choose between filling their gas tanks and filling their stomachs.

## Resource Imperialism

International law specialist Richard Falk of Princeton University has written about the possibilities of partial recolonization of parts of the Third World during the closing decades of the twentieth century.[5] Anyone who wants to be forewarned of a trend in this direction should carefully watch ODC propaganda—especially that of the US. Loud declarations of Arab "holdups" as oil prices continue to rise, for instance, or public discussion of whether resources rightfully belong to those who discover or develop them, rather than to those who happen to live in their vicinity, are likely to precede any overt moves to secure critical resources by force of arms.

Such intervention might be a cooperative venture among two or more ODCs, like the joint attempt of England, France, and Israel to gain control of the Suez Canal in 1956. It is unlikely, for instance, that the Soviet Union would go to the mat to prevent a group of nations that includes the US from gaining access to more Arab oil by force. The USSR has abundant oil of its own and presumably would not want to jeopardize its access to North American grain. An attempt to take over Mideast oilfields may seem remote now, considering the almost certain demolition of the fields, the prospect of long-term guerilla warfare, and the uncertainty about a Soviet response. But the petroleum crunch may, by the 1980s, make a joint military venture seem attractive to those who are still wedded to the idea of perpetual material growth.

At present, however, competition rather than cooperation among ODCs seems more likely. There are barely enough available resources to meet soaring demand in the US alone for long, let alone enough for an equitable distribution among all the resource-hungry countries in the world. There is, then, considerable potential for armed conflict among the ODCs if they persist in an "expand the supply" rather than a "moderate the demand" approach to their resource problems. Thus, continuing to expand fossil-fuel consumption may spell disaster in still another way—by leading to war. How such conflicts might escalate is anybody's guess; one can only hope that the kind of restraint shown thus far by governments in the fisheries wars would prevail, and that a nuclear catastrophe could be avoided.

Therefore it is frightening to observe recently announced changes in American nuclear-strike policy that are supposed to make "limited" nuclear wars an option open to the President. "Limited" nuclear wars are a figment of the uninformed and unbalanced imaginations that float to the top of our military-industrial-government complex. Even a strike aimed *solely* at destroying American (or Soviet) nuclear missiles would, through blast, fire, fallout, and environmental destruction, be a far greater disaster than any yet recorded in human history.

A renewed period of colonialism would carry other hazards besides war among the colonial powers. Some UDCs, like India, already have the wherewithal to produce nuclear arms; others will certainly gain that capability if the present proliferation of fission technology continues. In addition, some capability in chemical and biological warfare is within the grasp of all but the poorest nations. Although no UDC could expect to "win" a war with a major power, the possibility of nuclear or chemical-biological "blackmail" remains. Would the US, for instance, dare to occupy Libyan oil fields if the Libyan government threatened in retaliation to destroy New York City with a smuggled A-bomb?

Quite apart from the potential hazards of a war over resources, we must all reckon with a changed international situation as a result of the "energy crisis." A fundamental power shift is underway which will totally change the pattern of ODC-UDC economic relationships that evolved in the decades after World War II. The era of abundant, cheap commodities and raw materials moving in enormous quantities from UDCs to ODCs is over. So is the time when countries like the Soviet Union and Japan could buy food from the US at bargain-basement prices. In early 1974, wheat reached a price of $5.93 a bushel in Chicago, as opposed to $2.40 at the beginning of 1973. During roughly the same period, raw cotton went up from 30 to 90 cents a pound, copper from 54 to 95 cents, and crude oil from $3 to as much as $20 a barrel.[6]

This shift in the economic situation has enormous consequences for all peoples, both in the ODCs and UDCs. In resource-poor countries like Japan and most of western Europe, prosperity has depended on the flow of cheap commodities, and the lower strata of many ODC societies are now clamoring for their share of the prosperity. In Great Britain, for instance, in the winter of 1973–74, coal miners showed a willingness to bring the British economy to its knees rather than remain near the bottom of the economic heap. As inflation continues (driven up by the rising cost of raw materials), pressures from the lower end of the economic scale seem bound to increase. The poor will feel even poorer, especially since inflation also amounts to a hidden rise in income taxes. Even if pay rises fast enough to keep pace with inflation, the increased number of dollars buys no more but moves the earner into higher tax brackets. This pressure from the poor of ODC societies thus may push those governments toward imperialistic foreign policy decisions. Some people claim that the era when strong nations could push the weak around is over,[7] but that hypothesis has yet to be tested in a world of genuine scarcity.

The outlook for the US is somewhat better than that for much of western Europe and Japan because we come much closer than they do to being self-sufficient (although not as close as the Soviet Union—at least as far as mineral wealth is concerned). But the economic costs of becoming self-sufficient would be colossal. Suppose, for instance, that the US proceeded to substitute its primitive nuclear burners for fossil fuels with the idea of supplying half the country's energy needs through fission by the year 2000. The cost of the plants alone would be something on the order of $425 billion—or some 40 percent of the 1972 US gross national product.[8]

This estimate does not include the amounts required for uranium enrichment plants (and the power plants required to run them), waste repositories, or the cost of converting much energy-using equipment from fossil fuels to electricity. The additional hundreds of billions of dollars in costs if there were a few catastrophic accidents along the way are not figured in, either. There is some question whether the nation could find the capital to finance such a huge undertaking, even if only $450 billion were necessary. But even if such an enormous amount of capital could be made available, the required reallocation of resources would cause great economic difficulties. But undoubtedly, numerous economists and politicians will nevertheless step forward to explain how it can all be done. We are all familiar with the standard spiel: "Our great nation, with its vast industrial plant and immense store of know-how—our human capital—can meet the challenge of the nuclear era . . . etc., etc."

Maybe those who make such speeches are right—in the narrow context that they are capable of perceiving. *If* the economic conditions of the 1950s and 1960s were to continue, and *if* there were no other pressing demands on our capital, perhaps such a nuclear "solution" to our energy problems could be fashioned. But, as we have noted, economic conditions have changed. Commodities are in short supply and going up in price, and it is unlikely that classic economic mechanisms will bring the prices down in the foreseeable future. Most of the easily accessible sources of fossil fuels and mineral resources are long gone, and the rising prices reflect the necessity to dig deeper, travel farther, and refine lower-grade ore in order to obtain them. Basic foodstuffs—especially grain for people and livestock—must be wrested in larger and larger amounts from roughly the same amount of land. This means increasing the energy subsidy, which itself is increasing in cost. Struggle as commodity suppliers might to increase production and take advantage of higher prices, in most cases demand should stay well ahead of supply, at least until a generalized economic collapse overtakes the ODCs.

There is considerable reason to believe that many UDCs, rather than trying to make more money by increasing supplies of commodities, may strictly limit flows in order to keep prices high. Why should the Arabs pump their oilfields dry in a few decades in order to supply cheap crude to the ODCs?

The success in jacking up oil prices of the first producer cartel, the Organization of Petroleum Exporting Countries (OPEC), did not go unnoticed by other suppliers of raw materials. The principal copper exporters outside North America—Chile, Peru, Zaire, and Zambia—have within the past five years wholly or partially "nationalized" their mining operations. They have formed a cartel called Conseil Intergouvernmental des Pays Exportateurs de Cuivre (CIPEC), which may soon follow OPEC's lead. And OPEC and CIPEC will almost certainly be followed by organizations of the small groups of countries that control bauxite (aluminum ore), tin, natural rubber, and timber.[9]

It looks as though many UDCs are now in a position to turn the tables on the ODCs, to use the industrialized nations' enormous greed for resources as a means of carving up the economic pie in a new pattern. Whether they will have the unity to do it, or will use the wealth they get more intelligently than the ODCs have, remain to be seen. The response of the ODCs also remains in doubt. In any case, reduced flows and higher prices of commodities, along with factors such as increasing market saturation, will make the last quarter of the twentieth century a very different political and economic ball game from the third quarter.

Unfortunately, the US is not making any serious effort to reduce its dependence on imports of many nonenergy materials. For instance, Table 1 shows that we import at least 25 percent of many of the minerals we consume. Some of these are imported simply because it is cheaper to do so than to use domestic supplies (iron and aluminum ore are examples), whereas others are never likely to be supplied from domestic sources.

## TABLE 1

### US Mineral Imports

Percentage of US mineral requirements imported during 1972, based on data from Mining and Minerals Policy 1973, a report by the Secretary of the Interior to the Congress.*

| Mineral | Percentage imported | Major sources |
|---------|---------------------|---------------|
| Platinum-group metals | 100 | UK, USSR, South Africa, Canada, Japan, Norway |
| Mica (sheet) | 100 | India, Brazil, Malagasy |
| Chromium | 100 | USSR, South Africa, Turkey |
| Strontium | 100 | Mexico, Spain |
| Cobalt | 98 | Zaire, Belgium, Luxembourg, Finland, Canada, Norway |
| Tantalum | 97 | Nigeria, Canada, Zaire |

| Aluminum (ores and metal) | 96 | Jamaica, Surinam, Canada, Australia |
|---|---|---|
| Manganese | 95 | Brazil, Gabon, South Africa, Zaire |
| Fluorine | 87 | Mexico, Spain, Italy, South Africa |
| Titanium (rutile) | 86 | Australia |
| Asbestos | 85 | Canada, South Africa |
| Tin | 77 | Malaysia, Thailand, Bolivia |
| Bismuth | 75 | Mexico, Japan, Peru, UK, Korea |
| Nickel | 74 | Canada, Norway |
| Columbium | 67 | Brazil, Nigeria, Malagasy, Thailand |
| Antimony | 65 | South Africa, Mexico, UK, Bolivia |
| Gold | 61 | Canada, Switzerland, USSR |
| Potassium | 60 | Canada |
| Mercury | 58 | Canada, Mexico |
| Zinc | 52 | Canada, Mexico, Peru |
| Silver | 44 | Canada, Peru, Mexico, Honduras, Australia |
| Barium | 43 | Peru, Ireland, Mexico, Greece |
| Gypsum | 39 | Canada, Mexico, Jamaica |
| Selenium | 37 | Canada, Japan, Mexico, UK |
| Tellurium | 36 | Peru, Canada |
| Vanadium | 32 | South Africa, Chile, USSR |
| Iron | 28 | Canada, Venezuela, Japan, Common Market (EEC) |
| Lead | 26 | Canada, Australia, Peru, Mexico |
| Cadmium | 25 | Mexico, Australia, Belgium, Luxembourg, Canada, Peru |

\* Source: Table modified from *Science*, vol. 183, p. 185, 18 January, 1974.

We should at present be doing comprehensive research to develop methods of conserving and recycling vital minerals, to find more economical and ecologically sound ways of exploiting those we have, and to devise substitutes for those we don't have. The battle that we and thousands of other conservationists and "ecology freaks" have been fighting for conservation, for reduced consumption of consumer products, and for reusable rather than disposable materials is much more than a battle for a garbage-free environment. It is a battle to preserve our children's resources. Its importance may be overlooked because it is fought on such familiar ground—in your kitchen and your local supermarket and recycling center.

Failure to establish a comprehensive national minerals policy has been one of the most elementary—and stupid—errors made by the US in the past few decades, perhaps exceeded only by our failure to establish population, food, and energy policies. All four mistakes are bound to have far-reaching effects; they could easily lead the US into "growing economic colonialism, international frictions, steadily deteriorating balance of trade, and a tarnished global image of the nation,"[10]

But perhaps the most idiotic error made by many politicians and economists in proposals for the future is "spending" our capital many times over. Much more must be done to see the US through to the year 2000 than building a lot of nuclear (or solar, or geothermal) power plants. Hundreds of billions of dollars in investments will be required for things like building mass transit systems, renovating the railroads, developing new water supplies, reducing air and water pollution, reorganizing the agricultural system, and making all of the conversions necessitated by revision of the energy system and by substitution for scarce resources. If the costs of urban renewal, prison reform, decent medical care for everyone, and so on are added in, the bill becomes astronomical.

We Americans ignore any or all of these projects at our peril; at the very least there would be dire consequences for the quality of our lives. With planning and cooperation, we might be able to meet our most critical needs without pursuing a neocolonial foreign policy. At the moment, however, all the signs are that government and big business will stick with blundering as their major tactic. You'd better plan as if the US will miss the boat (we'll give some more specific suggestions later), and then be pleasantly surprised if it doesn't.

## Resources and the Poor

For some countries—India, for example—the boat has already sailed. Although the Indian government has shown little sign of recognizing the country's plight, increased petroleum prices have produced a further deterioration in India's already precarious food situation. India does not use much petroleum—about 200 million barrels per year in the early 1970s, some 70 percent of which was imported. However, about 85 percent of that oil is used in "development" activities, including irrigation and the production and transport of fertilizer. With greatly increased oil-import costs, India will have to spend as much as 80 percent of her export earnings on petroleum in 1974. As recently as 1970, India's oil imports cost only $140 million. The bill for imported oil in 1974 was expected to exceed the $1 billion in foreign aid that had been pledged to India for that year by various nations.[11] And that mammoth bill would buy only 12 million tons of oil and oil products rather than the 17 million tons originally planned for.

Thus, price hikes for oil, which may mean dimes more per gallon of gasoline to American motorists, may literally mean the difference between life and death for millions of Indians.[12] Less foreign exchange will be available to buy grain or vitally needed fertilizers, of which India must import about half of what she uses. Moreover, the price of of each ton of fertilizer is also higher because of a worldwide shortage, caused in turn by the higher petroleum prices. Shortages of oil also depressed domestic production of fertilizer in India and hindered its distribution.

The Indian government responded to the oil crisis with a variety of measures, most of which will not yield immediate dividends, and some of which may ultimately prove to be disastrously bad decisions. Among the latter was a decision to slash the family-planning budget nearly in half in order to save the funds for food and oil. Some of the family-planning funds were later restored, however, after the international community protested.

To meet the oil crunch directly, India is planning to increase domestic oil production (in 1972, about one-third of India's oil was domestically produced and nearly all was refined there) and coal production. There are also plans for developing more hydroelectric power, and in rural areas making more use of wood where feasible (a disaster for what remains of India's forests). Wood and cow dung are now the principal sources of fuel in rural areas. But none of these projects can produce results overnight.

The fertilizer shortage is the most crucial short-term problem facing India. In 1973–74, domestic fertilizer production was about half what was planned, and India was having trouble buying it abroad. What was available for the spring crop in 1974 was about 45 percent short of what was needed. The ministry of agriculture frantically tried to mobilize urban and rural compost and sewage to help make up the deficit; but, again, erecting plants to process the waste takes time.[13]

By January 1974, it was already clear that the oil and fertilizer shortages were hurting Indian agriculture. Indian government production estimates of 115 million metric tons of wheat for the 1973–74 year were then revised downward to 110–112 million tons and later to about 103 million tons, only slightly better than the harvest of 1972–73—the year of the disastrous drought. Meanwhile, India's population continues to grow by 14 million hungry mouths per year. India was expected to require at least 7.5 million tons of imported grain in 1974. Together with an inadequate monsoon, the fertilizer-fuel shortage might just be the straw that breaks India's back, plunging the nation into a major famine.[14]

Bangladesh may be in an even more precarious position than India. Its population, already the world's densest (1300 per square mile), is growing even faster (3 percent per year)[15] than India's. The nation is also extremely poor, which makes importing food and fertilizers difficult. A monsoon failure, tidal wave, or large-scale flood could have just as catastrophic effects on Bangladesh's 75 million as on India's 580 million people.

Bangladesh is only one of several Asian nations (besides India) expected to need grain imports in 1974. The others are China, Sri Lanka (Ceylon), Indonesia, South Korea, South Vietnam, and Cambodia.[16] The latter two countries were once grain exporters, but the war in Southeast Asia has severely disrupted their agriculture. Cambodia's rice harvest in 1973 was only one-quarter the size of its 1970 harvest. If the monsoon fails completely, the grain deficit for all of Asia in 1974 could be as high as 50 million metric tons—a figure that dwarfs even the enormous 13 million tons bought by the USSR from the US in 1972. There is no way that the surplus-grain-producing countries (the US, Canada, Australia, and Argentina) can fill such a gap without causing severe shortages at home.

Nor is Asia alone in feeling repercussions from the energy shortage. Even if a massive food deficit doesn't develop, higher prices of commodities—especially fertilizers—and the resultant cost increases in manufactured goods are likely to shatter the development dreams of many UDCs. Some, like the oil-rich Arab nations, control so much capital that they may be expected to weather the storm (unless they are invaded). But most others, with their meager supplies of capital already eaten away by rapid population growth and recent worldwide inflation, will find that increased returns from selling their own commodities are insufficient to prevent a decay of their economic situations.

The People's Republic of China (PRC), the largest and most important UDC, may be an exception to this rule. Despite the frequent statements of American economists that inflation is "worldwide," the PRC, with about one-fifth of the world's population, has a slowly falling price level. The contrast between India and China is striking. While there is more political freedom in India, there is more freedom from hunger and poverty in China—and few would contend that the average Indian is better off than the average Chinese. India has been a colossal failure at population control; China shows every possibility of success. It is clear that many underdeveloped countries could learn a great deal from the Chinese example, and there are quite likely many valuable insights to be gained from that model even by the ODCs. Keep an eye on the relationships between China and other UDCs; the world's oldest civilization may well play a dominant role in helping to save some of the youngest nations.

## Governmental Cooperation

The present world system of nation-states seems to be in unstable equilibrium. Any major disturbance of the international system is unlikely to be resolved by a return to what was until recently thought of as normal. Once seriously disturbed, the system could drift toward a much more decentralized, neo-feudal structure, in which greatly reduced numbers of people lived at a near-subsistence level. Or, at the opposite extreme, a widespread realization of mankind's interdependence might miraculously lead to the rapid evolution of a true international government. Needless to say, the former seems more probable, with the disintegration starting in the weaker UDCs, Japan, and western Europe, then gradually encompassing the Soviet Union and the US.

Our pessimism about the potential for governments to cooperate and weld nations together into that often-sought One World is founded on the deep-seated tribalism of human beings. Even national identities seem to be thin veneers that, in most cases, cover a basic loyalty to a much more restricted group. That a feeling could develop in most people of belonging to a group as large as all of humanity may be a forlorn hope. You don't have to look to the overt tribalism of Africa to see examples of this. You need only consider the Catholics and Protestants in Northern Ireland, the Flemings and Walloons in Belgium, the Basques and Catalans in Spain, the Serbs and Croats in Yugoslavia, those of Greek and Turkish descent in

Cyprus, the French- and English-speaking Canadians, the Blacks and Whites in the US and Brazil, the Montagnards and Cambodians in Southeast Asia, the Hindus and Moslems of India, and the numerous minorities of the Soviet Union in order to see that many—perhaps most—individuals owe their primary allegiance to a sub-national ethnic or religious "in-group." And, as we have already noted, class strife within ODCs (at least) is likely to increase. Governments will therefore tend to focus their attentions inward, toward reducing civil strife and maintaining themselves in office. Foreign policy will be focused, not on the long-term good of the nations and the world, but, as always, on the short-term good of the nations (or, more accurately, of the governments). Governments will try to make special deals for commodities, will manipulate their currencies in attempts to "export" domestic financial problems, and will always focus on winning the next election (or suppressing the next revolution).

## Regional Collapses

The recent famines in the region of Africa just south of the Sahara, discussed earlier, are likely to foreshadow far more widespread tragedies. How far the disruptive effects of these events will extend remains to be seen, but the *relatively* small total population of the African areas affected (about 50 million people) and their comparative isolation from the world trade system indicate only a small global impact. This is especially true since the populations threatened are also among the poorest and least powerful in the world,[17] which, sadly, means that they can easily be ignored by the affluent and comfortable. Therefore, the likelihood that a collapse of sub-Saharan societies will cause severe disruption of other nations is quite small.

Where are other collapses likely to occur? Among the underdeveloped areas, the Indian subcontinent is a key area to watch. Pakistan, Bangladesh, and India are reeling from the aftereffects of a catastrophic war and disastrous climatic events. About 20 percent of the human population (750 million people in 1973) inhabit this region, which, though poor, commands substantially more wealth and power than the sub-Saharan region. The Indians, for example, have built their own twin-jet supersonic fighter[18] and have detonated their first atomic bomb. (The existence of nuclear reactors in India presaged her ability to become a nuclear power.) To date, India has not signed the nuclear nonproliferation treaty. (Neither has Israel.) If in the 1970s there is another failure of the Indian monsoon as serious as the 1972 failure, the utter disintegration of the Indian economy is possible, accompanied by tens (or even hundreds) of millions of deaths. Should there be two such monsoon failures consecutively, *such a disaster is certain.*

The extent and results of such a collapse are exceedingly difficult to predict, especially since systematic attempts to make projections have been largely suppressed by taboos against "thinking about the unthinkable." This trend now appears to be changing. At a recent UN conference,[19] physicist Amory Lovins openly broached the topic, discussing the need to find ways of "uncoupling" collapsing areas from the world system in order to limit the spread of misery. The audience was unreceptive, to put it mildly, but at least the idea was on the table.

With little systematic information to draw upon, what can be said about regional collapses and their potential to propagate? First of all, it is probable that, in the immediate future (say before 1985), food shortage will remain the most likely cause of collapse, and weather changes will be the major critical factor affecting agriculture. The characteristics of the south Asian monsoons will be especially critical. They occur between June and October and should be monitored closely by anyone interested in following the world situation. The progress of the monsoon rains is reported fairly thoroughly in British newspapers, and there is also adequate coverage in the *New York Times.*

However, the probabilities of collapse will not be predictable from information on the monsoon alone. The effects of partial agricultural failures can be relieved by shipments of grain into stricken areas. For instance, in October, 1973, the USSR agreed to "lend" 2 million metric tons of grain to India to help tide that nation over until November harvests. The following January, the USSR offered to sell more grain to the US to tide us over until the June harvest. The increasing food interdependence of the world is illustrated by the original source of all that grain—it had been purchased earlier from the US by the Soviets.

Some knowledge of the state of the world food stocks is obviously essential to any evaluation of the probability of collapse. Some information on food stocks can be found in the *New York Times* and in UN Food and Agriculture Organization and US Department of Agriculture publications.[20] But even knowing the state of stocks does not provide all of the necessary information. Something must be guessed or discovered about the intentions of overdeveloped nations to keep or export their reserves. It is clear, for instance, that the Soviet Union, with its traditionally shaky agriculture, has been buying and stockpiling food (hence its willingness to send grain to India in 1973 and to us—at a profit—in 1974). The US, on the other hand, accustomed to having vast food surpluses, in 1972 and 1973 permitted its food reserves to be heavily depleted.

What does all this mean to you? The immediate effect of bad harvests abroad and the consequent depletion of American grain reserves by foreign buyers was a sudden rise in food prices, especially of meat. Effects from the famines in Africa were minimal, except that tight US grain supplies made it difficult to send significant amounts of food to the starving. On the other hand, a severe famine in India, a country that buys in the international food market, could have profound effects on domestic US food supplies. Therefore, in order to anticipate high food prices and serious shortages, one must watch the monsoons as well as the agricultural situation in the overdeveloped countries.

Particularly critical to the latter will be the size of grain and soybean surpluses (if any) in the US and Canada. These two nations now are the breadbasket of the world,[21] and it seems likely that the Soviet Union will remain partly dependent on foodstuffs imported from North America for some time at least. The Japanese are also likely to continue depending on North America for wheat and soybeans.

Another factor, directly involved in the Japanese situation in particular, is the state of the world's fisheries. As the per capita yield declines faster, which appears inevitable, the Japanese will devote increasing capital to the purchase of protein-rich foods—especially soybeans—on world markets. Rising Japanese and Soviet demand for foodstuffs could, indeed, soak up whatever world surpluses might otherwise be diverted, say, to preventing an Indian collapse.

A scenario for collapse brought on by famine is easily constructed:

A year of spotty monsoon on the Indian subcontinent (some areas get adequate rain, some are flooded, and some receive too little) is followed in the next year by a complete failure with a resultant general drought. India, Pakistan, and Bangladesh, all perpetually short of foreign exchange, are unable to purchase enough grain even to begin to meet their needs. No foreign supplies are available free or even on concessional terms. Famine spreads rapidly, as do food riots and flows of refugees. Cholera, typhus, plague, and other diseases become epidemic; civil servants and technicians desert their posts; and transportation and distribution systems break down, exacerbating an already catastrophic food situation. Rioting develops along ethnic and class lines as governmental restraints disappear, massive destruction in cities and the countryside follows, and the subcontinent sinks into a new dark age. After more than 400 million people have perished, a quasi-stable situation develops, with perhaps another

350 million survivors living at a subsistence level in small feudal political units.

This grim but by no means impossible scenario does not, however, present the worst possible situation. What is the likelihood that the effects of such a collapse would spread? To use a description once popular with American militarists, could we expect a "domino effect"? The answer is "perhaps." The most humane result would occur if short-range compassion overrode long-range compassion. Suppose, for instance, the world responded too late (as it might well, if the record of international aid to the sub-Saharan region is any standard) by shipping the last of its food reserves to the subcontinent. If collapse were already underway, failure of transport systems (tottering before the collapse) could easily prevent food from reaching any but those in seaports, which is what happened during the Bihar famine of 1965–66. Thus reserves might be stripped without significant gain, and the future capability of the world to deal with subsequent shortage would be severely damaged.

Remember, *there is no guarantee that years of bad weather are necessarily followed by years of good weather*. If Professor Bryson and others are correct, mankind may be in for a long siege of rapid climatic change and an escalation of agricultural difficulties.

There are several other possible sources of a domino effect. Large-scale burning from civil disorders stretching over an entire subcontinent would add more particulates to the atmosphere and could contribute to further undesirable climatic change. But it is more likely that the collapsing area would serve as a focus of disease. Such events as the recent smallpox and European cholera scares,[22] and the even more frightening Marburgvirus incident (in which a fatal disease was transmitted from monkeys to human laboratory workers shortly after the infected monkeys had passed through London Airport),[23] remind us that mankind's ability to contain epidemic disease is marginal. Finally, of course, the political and ecological implications of the collapse of a country like India, which has both nuclear reactors and nuclear weapons, are ominous, to say the least. The chances that nuclear-reactor containment buildings might be breached or bombs detonated may be slight, but the consequences of such events would be catastrophic. And what are the chances that a desperate government, threatened with total chaos and mass starvation, might attempt to extract large shipments of free foreign grain by nuclear blackmail? India protests peaceful intentions loudly, but has been among the most warlike nations in the recent past.

But even such a colossal disaster as the complete collapse of southern Asia might not have the worldwide repercussions that a similar collapse in Japan would produce. It is very difficult to predict how the Japanese would react if they were unable to import the food they feel is a necessary minimum or if they were cut off from other vital resources. But one thing is clear: Japan, as a highly technological nation, at least potentially has the economic and military power to take what it needs from the less powerful. There is a substantial minority sentiment in Japan in favor of developing nuclear weapons, and it could be armed with them almost instantly. Any move toward remilitarization, as the nation's situation continues to deteriorate, would be an ominous portent. Even without a return of militarism, however, the economic "ripple effects" from the disappearance of industrial Japan could well trigger a worldwide depression. The global economic effects of an Indian disaster would be much less severe; Japan is involved about ten times as deeply in world trade as India.[24]

## What You Can Do

Unfortunately, there's very little that you can do about the international situation, except to keep informed about it. This will at least allow you to prepare for dire repercussions such as severe food shortages or—at absolute worst

—all-out war. We have warned you about some of the more probable dangerous trends, such as increased competition for resources and declining cooperation among governments. About all you can do against these is to encourage international cooperation on the part of our government and support a strong United Nations. Probably nothing can protect you if World War III erupts, although a fallout shelter might be better than nothing if you live a long way from a major population center. Short of major war, your best defense against repercussions from international events is to stay informed and particularly to watch some of the more sensitive trouble spots of the world, then make your financial and other plans accordingly.

Besides some of the specific places we have already discussed, there are several key areas to watch if you want to have some clue to international political trends. One is western Europe, where the advantages of international cooperation are most obvious. There the facade of growing unity was shattered by the relatively minor stresses of the Arab oil embargo, revealing the age-old hatreds and stupidities that have long made the continent a bleeding ground. Future major crises in Europe, such as one caused by severe food shortages, for example, will no doubt be met with more cries of "the hell with you, Jack, I've got mine." Keep an eye on France in particular—she can probably feed herself, something most other European nations cannot do. The precariousness of Europe's economies was clearly demonstrated by Italy's bankruptcy and the dissolution of its government in late spring 1974. England, too, came close to the brink in the wake of the oil embargo coupled with the coal miner's strike. Her investment in North Sea oil is what sustains her economy.

A second key area is tropical Africa, where international boundaries enclose neither economic nor ethnic units. Nigeria is calm again, due largely to the intelligence and humanity with which the Ibos, defeated in civil war, were treated by the victors. But if things get tight, there is nothing to guarantee that Ibos, Hausas, and Yorubas won't once again be at each other's throats. In East Africa, the test of nationhood will come soon in Kenya, where aging Jomo Kenyatta has kept the show going since 1963. The critical question is whether a strong government can hold the nation together after his departure, or whether a power struggle between the dominant Kikuyu and Luo tribes will tear it apart. The many smaller tribes are fearful of domination (except perhaps the Masai, who are frustrated warriors), and Kenya could easily disintegrate into civil war.

As important as Kenyatta's succession, or more so, is that of relatively young President Julius K. Nyerere (born in 1922) of Tanzania. Enormous progress has been made in that nation under Nyerere's charismatic and intelligent leadership, but he must eventually face the difficult challenge of preparing others to take over the reins of government. In addition, the futures of Tanzania and Kenya are tied to that of Uganda, the third member of the East African Community, and Tanzania also has very close links with Zambia. Uganda has more or less fallen by the wayside. Its government was taken over by an unbalanced military dictator, Major General Idi Amin, in January, 1971. Its economy has been badly damaged, and border strife has occurred between Uganda and Tanzania. Clearly, much can be learned about the long-term viability of nation-states in Africa by watching these nations over the next few years. If these recently formed states can rise above tribalism and maintain themselves as nations, it will be a very hopeful sign for the future of humanity.

By watching critical European and African areas, and by assessing the food situation in India and Bangladesh, you should be able to anticipate international trends and use the information to your own benefit. It can help even with relatively minor decisions. For instance, the obvious shakiness of the English economy might tend to stiffen your resistance to TV ads encouraging the purchase of English automobiles (where will parts come from if Great Britain's economy collapses?). Knowing that Kenyatta cannot last much longer might persuade you not to put off a long-anticipated visit to the game parks of Kenya.

But keeping informed can also help with major decisions, such as how much urgency should be felt about making preparations to ride out a severe depression in the US, or worse. Remember, our economy is closely interwoven with the world economy, and *the collapse of any other country can threaten us*. To understand further the influence other countries have on the health of the world environment and the global economy, let's look in greater detail at two nations in particular—one underdeveloped and struggling to become overdeveloped, and one overdeveloped and struggling to avoid collapse.

# 4

# Miners' Canaries

"Japan is an octopus eating its own legs."
—Japanese fisherman arrested for
protesting construction of a huge
petrochemical complex, 1973 [1]

"In Brazil, as in so many nations on earth,
reality emerges as very different from the
image which mankind's dreams and hopes
have constructed."
—Georg Borgstrom, 1967 [2]

WHETHER WE LIKE it or not, the fate of some countries—India, for example—is largely sealed. While an awakening within India coupled with imaginative and compassionate aid from other nations might help cushion its collapse, no human agency is likely to prevent the disaster. A run of miraculously good weather might delay it—perhaps for a decade, maybe even to the end of the century—but the train of events leading to the dissolution of India as a viable nation is already in motion.

Therefore, if we want to observe more sensitive indicators of the state of the world system, nations whose fates are not so clearly predetermined should serve us better. Our choices are Japan and Brazil, both now embarked on suicidal courses, but each still having a chance, however small, of changing direction.

## Japan: The Dying Giant That May Never Awaken

Even though we were intellectually prepared for our visit to Japan in the spring of 1973, the reality came as quite a shock. Japan is world-famous for the intensity of its agriculture, but the pressure of population on food supplies takes on a new reality when one discovers, for instance, that there are no "vacant lots" in Japan. Every available bit of flat land is under cultivation, with vegetable plots penetrating the margins of even the largest cities. In those cities themselves, the conversion of the Japanese to an American-style "my car, my home" value system is evident everywhere. After arriving at the Osaka airport in the early evening, we were treated to a two-hour crawl down the Osaka-Kyoto freeway at a snail's pace reminiscent of a Los Angeles rush hour. Only occasional signs in Japanese characters reminded us that we had left California.

The Japanese have managed to retain some small garden areas as tranquil refuges in and around their cities, but even these are often invaded by noise pollution from busy streets, and the plants themselves are damaged by air pollution. Traditional values are rapidly disappearing along with the tranquillity. Japan, with its tradition of quiet beauty, has been transformed into a transistor-and-plastic culture that in many ways surpasses the junk culture of the United States. In Japan, even the restaurant menus consist of plastic replicas of the food (produced, rumor has it, by simply adding a polymerizer to the real thing, which is already laced with 351 legal additives)! [8]

Those who would like some idea of what the future holds for the US may learn much from observing Japan, since much of what is now occurring there may soon be repeated in the US. But there is another reason for observing the behavior of the Japanese closely. Their actions as they slide rapidly downhill will inevitably affect much of the world.

Japan is, in many respects, a front-runner in the population-resource-environment crisis. The country is, of course, vastly overpopulated. The degree of overpopulation of a country is frequently (and often inaccurately) judged by its population density—and by that standard Japan certainly qualifies. There are about 105 million people crowded into an area the size of California. A century ago, Japan's population density was four times the present population density of the US. Today, with 750 people per square mile, Japan has a population density thirteen times that of the US. The grossly overpopulated Netherlands has well over 750 persons per square mile, but since only some 16 percent of Japan's land is arable and suitable for habitation, Japan is, in terms of habitable land, by far the most densely populated of the Earth's major nations.[4]

A much more reliable measure of overpopulation than people per square mile is the relationship between numbers of people and the availability of resources to sustain them. While all industrial nations depend to some degree on imports, those that cannot even come close to supporting their people with internal resources are in the most precarious position. They will suffer most if the world trade system breaks down or if ocean fisheries collapse. In terms of self-sufficiency, the true degree of Japanese overpopulation becomes clear. Although Japan is self-sufficient in rice, it imports massive amounts of other grains and legumes, about 14 million and 3 million metric tons respectively in 1969, roughly 50 percent of Japan's total grain supply (including rice), and 85 percent of its legumes.[5] Indeed, Japan completely dominates the Asian food-and-feed-import picture, importing 55 percent of all the cereal that flows to that continent, over 70 percent of the soybeans, almost 60 percent of the meat, over 60 percent of the meat meal, more than a quarter of the milk and more than half of the fishmeal.[6] Yet, Japan has only about 5 percent of the total Asian population.

Japanese fishing fleets in 1970 harvested more than 9 million metric tons, over 13 percent of the world fish catch. Japan has spread its fishing operations around the world—to the waters off Baja California, the Caribbean, the South Atlantic, and the Mediterranean—to keep the all-important flow of fish moving toward its overpopulated islands. According to agricultural expert Georg Borgstrom,[7] in 1964–66 fisheries provided Japan with an amount of animal protein that would require almost *four times* Japan's total tilled land to produce as milk. Indeed, in that same period Japan was able to produce only 17 percent of its own food, depending on fisheries and imports for the rest. And the picture is even worse today.

The Japanese are in a similar situation with regard to most other resources. In 1970 Japan produced less than 17 percent of the energy it consumed. Domestic sources of iron supply only 5 percent of Japanese industrial needs,[8] and all of the bauxite and most of the copper required must be imported. Japan imports ten times the value of the forest products that it exports,[9] which has helped to drive the price of lumber in the US to record highs.

A third standard by which Japan is vastly overpopulated is the way in which the Japanese exploit and overstress the natural ecological systems of their islands. The enormous damage they do in their environment is not surprising, considering the amount of industrial activity that is compressed into a small space. Energy consumption per unit of land area is eight times higher than that of the US, 2.5 times that of the United Kingdom, and 1.8 times that of West Germany.[10] Even within Japan's limited land area, activities are concentrated, with about 60 million people living and working in the Tokyo-Osaka megalopolis alone. Tokyo-Osaka produces roughly the same amount of steel as all of England. It is a miracle that the famous Tokyo smog is not even worse!

If Japan has been a leader in overpopulation, however, it has also shown the way in population control. Awareness of population problems among the Japanese people played a major role in the passage of the 1948 "Eugenic Protection Law," which legalized abortion and voluntary sterilization. This law also set up an office under the Ministry of Health and Welfare that established a network of 850 centers distributing family-planning information throughout Japan.[11] As a result of these heroic measures, the birthrate dropped quickly from over thirty-four per thousand in 1947 to less than eighteen in 1960, and fertility has fluctuated around the replacement level since about 1955. If that level is held, Japan may reach ZPG (Zero Population Growth, a stationary or nongrowing population) before 2025 with a population size of 130–150 million. Interestingly, however, knowledge among the Japanese of population problems outside of Japan until recently has been quite limited.[12]

The public-health problems associated with environmental deterioration in Japan have received worldwide attention: extreme air pollution, mercury poisoning, and cadmium poisoning[13] are outstanding examples. Some 40,000 Japanese people have already suffered severe injury or death diagnosed as related to major pollution incidents (air and water pollution, adulteration of food). And this is a conservative estimate—the actual numbers are certainly much higher. Thus, the Japanese are deeply aware of the *acute* health problems related to pollution, but they share with the American public a naive lack of concern about the long-term effects of chronic exposure to poisons.

For instance, the Japanese are serving as involuntary guinea pigs for "experiments" on the long-term effects of chlorinated hydrocarbon poisoning, just as are Americans. A survey made by the Sanitation Research Institute indicates that Japanese foods contain six to sixteen times as much DDT, benzene hexachloride, aldrin, and related pesticides as similar foods in Europe and America.[14] The Japanese have also suffered numerous cases of acute poisoning with PCBs, industrial relatives of DDT. PCB contamination of Japanese waters recently required the banning from market of some large fish catches. Interestingly, when we were in Japan, environmental protest over high PCB loads in fishes was directed mainly at forcing polluting companies to compensate fishermen whose catches had been confiscated. Hardly any alarm was expressed in the press over the dangers of chronic PCB exposure to the health of the individuals who eat the fish. The threat of pollutants to oceanic ecosystems (and thus to the supply of fishes itself) was not even mentioned. Indeed the Japanese are notoriously insensitive to the concept of conserving the world's oceans—a lack of sensitivity symbolized by their efforts to hunt the great whales to extinction as rapidly as possible (a colossally stupid game in which the only other remaining major player is the Soviet Union).

In all likelihood, the more subtle and perhaps more dangerous effects of human abuse of the environment will appear in Japan and in the adjacent oceans before they appear in most other areas of the world. It would be fitting for Japan and perhaps the UN to carry out intensive monitoring programs in the hope of providing other nations with some warning of expected patterns of breakdown.

## Japan as a Harbinger

Other citizens of overdeveloped nations can thus look to Japan for portents of their own futures. Japan provides an opportunity to study the behavior of a highly literate, technologically sophisticated people facing problems that will soon be universal in ODCs. For instance, the government in Japan is controlled by industry to an even greater degree than that of the US. Therefore the patterns of government-industry interaction in Japan, as the nation comes to grips with scarcity, environmental deterioration, and the demographic changes leading to ZPG, will be of great interest to Americans and Europeans. Will American politicians, for instance, prove to be as naive in population matters as the government of former Prime Minister Eisaku Sato? In 1969, urged by business interests, Sato called for an *increase* in the Japanese birthrate because of an impending "labor shortage." [15] This population policy could not stand up under economic analysis, which showed that Japan's overall economic condition (although not necessarily that of certain wealthy businessmen) would benefit from a lower birthrate. [16] Needless to say, the most elementary ecological analysis indicates that any attempt to increase the Japanese population would be utter insanity.

Japan in many ways is making the same mistakes that

the US has made. For example, the Japanese are installing nuclear power plants of the same potentially unsafe water-cooled design discussed in Chapter 2.[17] Japan has an installed electrical generating capacity of slightly over 68,000 megawatts, and slightly over 1000 megawatts are in this type of nuclear reactor.[18] When atomic power plants now under construction are completed, about 10 percent of Japan's power will be generated by using the heat of nuclear burners.

A second parallel to the US is the interest among Japanese politicians in "solving" population problems by population redistribution—a popular idea in American government circles also. Unfortunately, many of the most serious problems associated with overpopulation (such as environmental deterioration resulting from the use of pesticides in agriculture) are affected little by population distribution, and others (such as the loss of agricultural land to development projects and the destruction of fisheries in adjacent waters) would be made worse by it. In Japan, redistribution has meant relocation not only of people but of heavy industry—together with the pollution it generates—to remote areas. Redistribution may be beneficial in certain special circumstances (such as relieving congestion and concentrated air pollution around Tokyo), but by no stretch of the imagination can it "solve" the problems of overpopulation in either Japan or the US.

At a more personal level, other nations can learn much by studying Japanese attitudes toward childbearing, which might be of help in moving other nations toward ZPG. After all, the Japanese have achieved and maintained replacement reproduction for two decades[19]—and without the aid of any obvious social mechanisms to maintain that level. How, then, has this happened? How much has the relative homogeneity of the Japanese population, and the resulting freedom from fears of different birthrates among different racial or ethnic groups, contributed to this? How important have housing shortages and other economic conditions been? What roles have high literacy rates and population education played? The phenomenon richly deserves study.

The pronounced drop of the birthrate in 1966, the Year of Fire and Horse (thought to be unfavorable for childbearing),[20] indicates that the Japanese people have considerable control over their fertility. It seems unlikely, therefore, that propaganda from business or government is likely to produce a significant upturn in fertility unless the population as a whole sees benefit in it.

It remains to be seen whether the Japanese can attain similar control over their environmental destruction, especially since many changes that deal with ecological problems will probably be opposed by industry and an extraordinarily economy-oriented government. But ecological and consumer activism is on the upswing; employees in water works have refused to supply some polluting corporations, and women have organized to boycott certain products.[21] The courts have belatedly begun to compensate the most severely affected victims of environmental deterioration—although the amounts awarded have until recently been small by American standards. In March, 1973, victims of "Minamata disease" (methyl mercury poisoning) were awarded $3.6 million in damages from Chisso Corporation, the company responsible.[22] According to the final settlement, each victim was awarded between $51,000 and $59,000 and a lifetime pension. Of 659 known victims in the Minamata area, 81 had died and many of the remainder were horribly crippled. Perhaps as many as 10,000 latent victims may exist who will develop symptoms some time in the future.[23]

The most important question about Japan, however, involves her future international behavior. Japan is the ultimate example of a highly industrialized, resource-poor nation playing the role of an economic "middleman." From the narrow viewpoint of the classical economist, Japan is in a strong position. From the broad viewpoint of the ecologist, it teeters on the brink of disaster. What, for instance, will the Japanese do as the world fisheries move toward collapse from overfishing and pollution? Where will Japan turn for food if exporting nations like the US find they require more of their own supplies at home, or if they have to choose between exporting food either to Japan or to the Soviet Union?

In 1973, an Industrial Planning Roundtable made a far-reaching proposal to export Japanese heavy industry (along with its pollution problems) to underdeveloped areas where raw materials were available, mainly in Asia.[24] Japan itself would concentrate on less polluting and energy-intensive activities such as finance, advanced technology, communications, clothing manufacture, transport facilities, and a variety of social services for its people. Essential food imports would be ensured by exchanging modern agricultural techniques, fertilizers, and pesticides for them. Depending on how such a plan were implemented, it might be a way around Japan's vulnerability in the age of scarcity. But the Japanese have already run into opposition in Indonesia and Thailand to their aggressive capitalism and the pollution side-effects from exported industry. Such opposition is likely to escalate unless they control the environmental damage from their industrial projects much more carefully than they have in their own country.

The year 1973 gave the Japanese a foretaste of what the future holds for them. Shortly after our visit, President Nixon shocked the Japanese by restricting the export of American soybeans,[25] forcing Japan to search desperately for other supplies. But the soybean shock—which was only temporary—was nothing compared to the shock of the Arab oil embargo. Japan imports practically all of its oil, some 84 percent from the Middle East, about half of that from Arab nations and half from Iran.[26] In December, 1973, despite a humiliating change in its Middle Eastern foreign policy from neutral to pro-Arab, Japan was receiving 20 percent less oil than it had expected before the Middle East War.[27]

As a result, in late December 1973, Prime Minister Kakuei Tanaka declared an unprecedented national crisis, prices were fixed on a wide variety of goods, driving was banned on Sundays and holidays, and various other austerity measures were taken.[28] These were later relaxed as the Arabs partially restored the oil flow, but Japan's economic growth was at least temporarily slowed, and its national psyche had been dealt a substantial blow. Even with full oil flow restored, its greater cost will give continuing trouble to the Japanese. It will increase Japan's recent balance-of-payments deficit, created by a strong outflow of Japanese capital in search of investment opportunities all over the world.[29]

It will be most instructive to see whether Japan ignores the handwriting on the wall and plunges on in search of an ever greater gross national product, constantly increasing its dependence on imports and decreasing the quality of its citizens' lives. Will the already legendary economic aggressiveness of the Japanese continue to increase in spite of the growing protests in Southeast Asia over their "economic imperialism"? Will the Japanese return to military aggressiveness as suppliers become unwilling or unable to maintain flows? Or will they instead move toward an equilibrium, low-throughput economy, doing everything possible to reduce their dependence on imports? Will they completely change and de-industrialize along the lines of the Industrial Planning Roundtable's proposal? Will they become leaders in establishing international controls over the exploitation of fisheries and the pollution of atmosphere and oceans? Will they fall back on their enormous cultural resources and return to valuing beauty and tranquillity more than an expanding GNP? Knowledgeable people in other industrial countries will be watching Japan closely, much as old-time miners watched the canary in the cage.[30]

## Brazil: The Awakening Giant That Soon May Die

If Japan is the epitome of a nation suffering from a lethal dose of overdevelopment, Brazil is certainly the underdeveloped country most hell-bent on catching the disease. Among UDCs, Brazil is the homeland of that pernicious ecological fallacy—the idea that the degree of overpopulation (or underpopulation) of a nation can be judged accurately by population density. Brazil in 1971 had some 28 people per square mile, as contrasted to 57 in the United States, 435 in India, and 733 in Japan.[31] Most Brazilians, like most Americans, have not yet realized that the critical aspect of overpopulation is *not* people vs. brute space, but the pressure of numbers of people on resources, the environment, and values. And by those standards, Brazil is already an overpopulated nation— although not so obviously overpopulated as India or Japan.

To naive economists, Brazil (like Japan) appears to be a success story. Between 1959 and 1969 the annual rate of growth of the Brazilian GNP was almost 6 percent, and by 1970 it was pressing 10 percent.[32] Brazil is viewed as "A New Japan," [33] a country that in 1973 was roughly in the position occupied by Japan in 1960. Robert Campos, former Minister of Planning and "father of Brazil's economic miracle," predicted in 1973 that it would take not even a dozen years for Brazil to reach Japan's 1973 level of industrialization. That investors are "bullish" on Brazil is clear. In 1972 international businessmen invested at least 3 billion dollars in Brazil, a larger sum than they invested in all of the rest of Latin America. The Brazilians themselves invested 9 billion dollars, helping to fuel the economic boom.

The boom mentality is exemplified by ads in the *New York Times* placed by Brazilian banks and business groups, shouting such slogans as "Brazil is open for business" and "Come to a booming state in a booming country, if you have a booming industry." [34] This mentality is based on the rapid turnaround of the Brazilian economy following the establishment of a military dictatorship in March, 1964. The regime ruthlessly tackled problems of corruption, disorganization, and inflation, all with substantial success. Confidence in government and currency were restored, and an inflation rate of 100 percent per annum in 1964 was reduced to some 18 percent by 1973.[35] This led to phenomenal economic growth, based in no small part on comparatively low costs of labor. By the early 1970s, Brazil was producing well over half a million motor vehicles annually. Its automobile production was about one-tenth that of Japan and seven times that of India, the only other UDC with substantial production.[36] Brazilian assembly-line workers were paid about $100 per month,[37] giving Brazilian manufacturers the advantage of a labor cost only 25 percent that of their Japanese and West German competitors. Brazil is now exporting, in addition to automobiles, such sophisticated products as "jumbo" oil tankers and ore carriers, jet planes, and electronic equipment.

Given this boom, why shouldn't we be "bullish" on Brazil? After all, Brazil has a huge area, rich natural resources, and a talented population less bound by tradition than those of most Latin American countries. But in spite of this we must be bearish. The reasons are a combination of rapid population growth, social injustice, distorted priorities, and ecological insanity.

Brazil in 1973 had a population of 101 million people, a birthrate of 38 per thousand, a death rate of 10 per thousand, and a population growth rate of 2.8 percent a year.[38] Should these rates persist, Brazil's population will reach 143 million by 1985, and will be over 200 million at the turn of the century. Thus in the year 2000 Brazil may have a population density higher than that of the United States in 1970. If so, it is likely that by sometime in the last quarter of the twentieth century, Brazil will have lost any opportunity to provide the majority of its people with a reasonable standard of living because, rich in natural resources as Brazil is, it is nowhere nearly as well-endowed as the US.

Most of the reasons for this gloomy conclusion are related to Brazil's unfortunate agricultural situation. It may seem strange to use the term "unfortunate" at a time when Brazilian agriculture seems to be booming and past dependency on cash crops (coffee, cotton, cocoa) for foreign exchange appears to be ended. In the first five months of 1973, agricultural exports rose to $4.5 billion, an increase of 42 percent over the equivalent period in 1972;[39] Brazil is investing a major portion of this bonanza in food crops —especially soybeans, of which 6 million tons were expected to be harvested in 1973. A lucrative market for these legumes, a prime source of high-quality protein, has opened up in Japan. Soybeans are a crucial item in the Japanese diet, and demand for them has traditionally been met by imports from the US. When that source of supply was threatened in 1973, the Japanese turned to Brazil, among other places.

Is Brazil, then, to become a larder for the world? Hardly. An important thing to remember, first of all, is that the *ability to export food does not necessarily mean that a country is well fed*. Unhappily, while Brazil is "booming" and exporting soybeans, many of its citizens are slowly starving.

One of the principal clues to Brazil's future, and that of other development "successes" among the UDCs, can be found in the income disparity between the rich and the poor—a gap that has been widening within Brazil in the last few decades. In the 1950s and 1960s, the ratio of the average income of the richest 20 percent of the population to that of the poorest 20 percent increased from 15-to-1 to 25-to-1.[40] Similar increases in the inequity of income distribution have taken place in other developing countries, including Mexico, Pakistan, the Philippines, and Ghana.[41] In these and many other UDCs, "development" is leading to a two-tiered economy, with one segment of the population reaping handsome rewards and the other remaining in abject poverty.

In Brazil, the city of São Paulo is, indeed, "developing," while the vast northeastern part of the country remains a disaster area. Southern farmers with large holdings in soybeans prosper, while *flagelados* (flagellated ones) in the Northeast migrate in search of work and food.[42] While automobile factories churn out vehicles for the privileged, Indians are systematically being exterminated in an ill-fated attempt to develop the Amazon Basin. In short, while one segment of Brazilian society seems to be following Japan into the morass of overdevelopment, another seems to be going nowhere—doomed to perpetual privation.

The Brazilians are an independent, cultured, and sensitive people. Many well-off Brazilians are concerned about the fate of the less fortunate, and they, like their government, look to the "immense riches" of the Amazon Basin to provide the wealth necessary to raise the masses from the depths of poverty. Brazil is once again attempting to expand its feeding base by opening the Basin to agriculture. This huge area (some 2.7 million square miles, almost the size of the continental US)[43] is covered in large part by tropical forests, and their lush growth has long misled laymen into believing that Amazonia could be converted into a rich farming area.

The truth is quite different. The Amazon Basin is not a rich, untapped agricultural resource like the great American prairie of 150 years ago. Amazonia, like many other tropical rain forest regions, tends to have thin, poor soils. Most of the nutrients necessary for plant life are contained in the lush vegetation itself. When plants or animals die, the nutrients released by their decay are rapidly absorbed back into the living forest plants through their extensive root networks, which lie just below the surface. Clearing land for farming disrupts this nutrient-recycling system. In the absence of vegetative cover, torrential rains wash the nutrients away, and soils, alternately leached by downpours and exposed to the tropical sun, undergo a process called "laterization" and turn into bricklike "laterite."[44]

Much of the Amazon Basin consists of such lateritic soils and consequently presents a severe challenge to agriculture. With great effort and care, successful agricultural programs could be developed to farm the so-called *terra firme*—land above the flood plains that are periodically inundated (and thus fertilized) by the Amazon. Such programs would involve the interlocking of farming with animal husbandry to make manure available for fertilizer (it tends to be much more satisfactory under tropical conditions than inorganic fertilizers). As biologist Harold Sioli pointed out, "no 'permanent recipe' for lucrative agriculture in Amazonia can be offered"[45] because continual adjustments to meet changing local and international market conditions will be required.

Brazil is now in the middle of a crash program of highway construction in the Amazon Basin. The central project is the construction of the Transamazonian Highway, begun in 1970.[46] When completed, the highway will connect such Atlantic Coast ports as Belém and Recife with Peru and Bolivia, through which they may someday be linked by road to the Pacific. The route of the Transamazonian runs roughly parallel to the river itself, about two hundred miles to the south. The highway is planned to tie in with an extensive additional network of roads crisscrossing the Basin.

The crash program was initiated by President Medici after he visited the drought-devastated Northeast in 1969, "to carry the landless population of the Northeast to the unpopulated lands of the Amazon."[47] The highway has been pushed forward rapidly, with plans calling for an *agritown* of forty-eight to sixty families planned every 6 miles along its 3000-mile length.[48] The government has expropriated all land within 50 miles of the road network (an area of almost 900,000 square miles—much larger than Mexico), on which it plans to establish colonists on 250-acre parcels.[49]

Some eight thousand Amazonian Indians are to be pushed out of the development area and onto reservations in a move reminiscent of United States policy of the last century. Although a group of eighty-four Brazilian social scientists signed a protest against the planned treatment of the Indians,[50] it is clear that the development project will be permitted to push them aside. The great Amazonian rain forest, complete with its rich array of animals and peoples, appears doomed to follow the tall grass prairies of North America to destruction. But the tragedy of the Amazon will be even greater. The European successors of the North American Indians were at least able to extract great wealth on a continuing basis from the lands they appropriated. But the current efforts of the Brazilians will merely net them a few harvests at the cost of irreversible destruction of the region. Amazonia will be turned into the world's largest parking lot.

The tragedy is the greater because there has been ample warning for Brazilians—warnings from home, not just from foreign ecologists. The failure of the agricultural colony set up by the Brazilian government in the Amazon Basin at Iata was one portent.[51] But the Brazilian government, like other governments, seems to find it impossible to learn from experience. It also turns a deaf ear to expertise when politics and special interests are involved. Scientific reports published by a government agency, Instituto Brasileiro de Geografia, pointed out the stupidity of the development program, warning that "a disaster of enormous proportions" would occur.[52]

Perhaps the essence of the problem is that Brazilians do not want to know the truth about Amazonia, for to do so would force them to confront the true dimensions of their country. Gone would be myths of untold abundance, of limitless resources, of future world power. Brazilians would have to face the biological and physical limits within which their nation must operate in order to survive—much as citizens of the US now are facing the limitations to their own power. But the Brazilians have a tougher job since they must confront reality *before* they have had their fling at being overdeveloped.

The apparent blindness of Brazilians to their plight shows most strongly at the international level. At the 1972 Stockholm Conference on the Human Environment, the essence of the Brazilian message to the overdeveloped countries seemed to be, "You've had the opportunity to foul up your environments for fun and profit . . . now it's our turn." In 1973 at a congress of the World Wildlife Fund, we were confronted by a Brazilian who was enraged at our criticism of his government's policies in Amazonia. He refused to believe that disaster could strike, his strongest argument being, "Of course, we must cut down the forest; we are not animals that can live in trees."

There are a few cheering signs that Brazilians are becoming concerned over "pollution,"[53] as is the rest of the world. But there seems to be little appreciation of the more subtle (and, in the long run, more lethal) aspects of environmental damage. Within months, or at most a few years, after injection of pollutants into the atmosphere is halted, the atmosphere will cleanse itself. Similarly, given time and effort, many forms of water pollution can be abated. But once the Amazon Basin is turned into a wasteland, it may never be converted into an area useful to man, and the many vital free "services" provided by the natural ecosystem of the rain forest will be lost forever.[54]

What can we expect to occur in Brazil in the rest of this century? What are the chances that, for instance, the Brazilian government will halt its massive "chop down and farm" assault on the Amazon Basin in favor of a more gradual development within the framework of the tropical forest ecosystem? The *terra firme* is suitable for silviculture (forestry, timber, and orchards) and the exploitation of some fish and wildlife. Will the Brazilians institute a crash program of population control in an attempt to reduce the strain on the resource capacity of their country? At the moment there is little sign of such a development, although the government is beginning to cooperate with private family-planning groups.[55] Will they turn from the course of industrialization at any price?

It would be diplomatic to say we are hopeful, but the time for diplomacy is long past. We believe that Brazil will continue on its current path, even though it clearly leads to disaster. Just as the US made no move to put brakes on its profligate use of energy until it was in the midst of a crisis—and then only tapped the brakes lightly —Brazil is unlikely to pay heed to anything but immediate political and economic expediency. As long as those in control are profiting, the tragedy will be played out— perhaps before 1985.

Any deflection of Brazil from its suicidal course will probably come from a grassroots revolution. As noted above, the disparity between rich and poor is growing, and poverty is not confined to the Northeast. For instance, while the city of São Paulo grew from 3.7 million in 1960 to 6.3 million in 1970, the infant mortality rate in that city *increased* from 62.9 to 83.8 per thousand births.[56] Such statistics indicate that the condition of a major portion of the population is worsening even in the center of the area that is most rapidly "moving into the twentieth century." How long the military dictatorship will be able to retain control is an open question, especially after the Brazilian economic bubble bursts.


## Lessons from Brazil


Brazil is one of the most advanced UDCs. If its position is shaky, that of most of the others is worse—*as long as population growth continues and development plans consist of efforts to repeat the errors of the overdeveloped countries.* Under these conditions, those countries are not "underdeveloped," they are "never-to-be-developed." [57] One has only to consider the great difficulties that the overdeveloped nations are having maintaining their prosperity to see the impossibility of today's UDCs attaining a similar level of industrialization. This does not mean that several centuries hence a world with a much reduced population might not provide a pleasant, energy-rich life for all—but the following statement can be made with certainty: *The environmental systems of the earth would collapse if the attempt were made to supply all human beings alive today with a European style of living.* To suggest that such an increase in living standards is possible for a world population *twice* the present size by the early part of the next century is preposterous. Of course, we do not think that this doubling of the population will occur, for reasons given in earlier chapters.

How will underdeveloped countries react as they realize that their rising expectations are accompanied by plummeting prospects? And what will the ODCs do, if anything, to help deal with the crisis? We doubt that sensible planning with realistic development goals will prevail in the UDCs any more than it has in the ODCs. Why should it? Plunging ahead into crisis seems to be the human way. Consequently, we anticipate an era of prevailing scarcity that could lead to regional collapses. The kind of self-interested, nationalistic squabbling that characterized

European reaction to the oil crisis may thus become a pronounced feature of behavior in the international arena. Both Brazil and Japan should be observed very closely by anyone who wants advance warning of whether or not these trends will materialize.

# 5

# Gentlemen
# Now Abed

---

"Sure there are dishonest men in local government. But there are dishonest men in national government, too."

—Richard M. Nixon [1]

THE WORLD'S IN trouble, and we're in trouble with it. One thing is certain—we can't count on our leaders to steer us through the times of crisis. We can only count on them to fumble the ball (if they can ever get their hands on it), and then try to tell us the fumble was a touchdown. Americans have grown accustomed to having their intelligence insulted in this way and have gradually come to expect lies from politicians.[2] Kindly old Dwight Eisenhower lied about the U-2, folksy Lyndon Johnson fibbed for years about Vietnam, clever Dick Nixon won the 1968 election by having a fictitious "secret plan" to end the war.[2a]

After Nixon became President, there were concealments of a series of military actions, followed by the Watergate cover-up and Agnew's oath that he would never resign. Public awareness of lying by politicians reached a zenith as the Nixon administration was revealed to be shot through with felons and frauds. Among them, apparently only Agnew was criminally using his office to enrich himself in the great tradition of Credit Mobilier and Teapot

Dome. Much more frightening, Nixon and his friends, by contrast, were trying to steal our freedom. Often overlooked in commentaries on the Watergate mess was the systematic campaign waged by John Mitchell when he was Nixon's Attorney General to destroy the American system of justice.[3]

But the most serious offense was the attempt to use the power of the executive branch through extortion of funds and political sabotage to guarantee Nixon's reelection. Although elements of such behavior may have existed in previous administrations, the Nixon administration was the first to be exposed making a large-scale attempt to subvert the electoral system. Needless to say, democracy cannot survive if the President is allowed to use the full power of his office to assure his own reelection.

It is not surprising, then, that public trust in politicians as indicated by the polls was at an all-time low in early 1974. But there still were substantial numbers of people who had a childlike faith in politicians and who seemed unable to face the facts about the President and his cronies. It is an unhappy commentary on our educational system that so many people could not understand either the basic threat to our democracy posed by President Nixon or the Constitutional remedy for the problem—impeachment.

But the behavior of the Nixon administration did more than expose the extent to which the executive branch of the government could be corrupted. It also highlighted the fumbling inadequacy of the legislative branch. It became inescapably clear to the public that secrecy, deception, and outright lies had practically become a way of life in Washington—even to the point where different branches and agencies deceived and spied on one another.

Unfortunately, however, many Americans believed that Congress had played a major role in getting rid of Nixon. Actually, the gutty performance of Judge John Sirica and Nixon's incredible stupidity in first making and then preserving most of the incriminating Watergate tapes were far greater factors. The House of Representatives was pushed only very reluctantly into favoring impeachment.

The performance of the Judiciary Committee was better than might be expected, considering the overall record of Congress. But the committee's by then inevitable articles of impeachment were produced after debate marked not only by due deliberation and respect for the law of the land, but considerable anguish. Why, we wonder, should there have been so much agony in constitutionally removing a leader who so richly deserved it?

No, it wasn't our perennially paralysed Congress that banished America's chief crook to exile in his palatial mansion at San Clemente. It was an alert night watchman, a tough judge, a few dedicated public servants like Elliot Richardson, Archibald Cox, and Leon Jaworsky, a handful of investigative reporters, and the fumbling of Nixon himself and his arrogant but often not too bright gang members.

Yet some lessons from Watergate have apparently remained unlearned by many, as was demonstrated by the immediate near-deification of President Ford as soon as he was inaugurated. Nixon might have been removed from office much sooner and more painlessly if Americans had been less determined to regard him as a sort of irreplaceable demigod. Indeed, many of the abuses of office carried out by the Nixon White House crew might even have been prevented if others hadn't held them in awe.

The ultimate Watergate disaster was Ford's pardoning of Nixon, perhaps covering up once and for all the truth about the affair, and certainly establishing once and for all that there is a dual system of justice in the United States, one for the rich and powerful and one for the poor and powerless. The most charitable interpretation of the pardon is that it was a stupid act by an honest man. The least charitable is that Ford became Vice-President by agreeing to pardon Nixon if it became necessary. In the latter case the act would involve bribery and might be an impeachable offense in itself. We hope that it was the former, but considering the depths of corruption in Washington the latter cannot be discounted.

What has remained largely unrecognized, even in the

wake of Watergate, is the even more common indirect
deception indulged in by politicians, lies that even they
do not always recognize for what they are. Among these
lies are that you can give to everyone and take from no
one, that minor adjustments can keep the economy rolling, that the government is solving the problems of population growth, resource depletion, and environmental
decay, that more is always better, and that the entire
system is fundamentally sound and only needs a little
superficial repair. Perhaps the most misleading of all is
the idea that everything will always come out all right.

Many politicians believe these lies themselves, which
only indicates their inability to analyze even simple situations. We have had thousands of letters from high school
students who, upon reading *The Population Bomb,* immediately grasped the consequences of the world population doubling every thirty-five years and wanted to know
what they could do about it. Only a handful of congressmen have shown a similar concern. Relaxed as they are
about the straightforward threat of rapidly growing populations, it is not surprising that they are unexcited by the
even more rapid growth in the use of energy and many
materials—since the consequences, although at least as
serious, are less straightforward. Apparently most politicians believe that what they don't know can't hurt them.

Politicians are now held in low esteem by the public
for the direct lies they have told; it is high time they were
held to account as well for the indirect lies they tell. Ignorance of the laws of nature is no excuse. American citizens
must also stop believing the indirect lies, which are usually
even more obvious than the direct ones.

In the future, Americans *must* plan on being lied to by
their government, regardless of who is in power. The
crooks and deceivers of the Nixon-Agnew era may have
represented a new low in the caliber of public officials,
but they (and their fates) are inconsequential against the
backdrop of the real governmental problem that confronts
our society. That problem is best expressed by the first
and second laws of post-industrial government:

1. Governments, as now organized, are incapable of solving either the national or international problems ahead.
2. No form of governmental reorganization will permit these problems to be solved until the attitudes and expectations of the citizenry have been profoundly modified.

These laws make liars out of all governments. They apply especially strongly to the US, but are also applicable in large degree to all other governments. The fundamental dilemma faced by governments is that the average person expects his or her "standard of living," as measured on a material scale, to go on increasing. In our world of growing scarcity (and growing demand for redistribution of wealth from rich to poor), this is an impossibility, and no amount of governmental reorganization will make it possible.

Faced with trying to do the impossible and being unable to admit that it *is* impossible, politicians have no choice: they lie.

## Establishing Faith in Ourselves

A phrase now often heard from the lips of politicians is that we must "restore faith in our leaders." We disagree. Rather than "restore faith," we must *utterly destroy the last remnants of it*. We can't afford to put faith in people who *must* present a false impression to the public. Americans must learn to have faith in themselves and to monitor the behavior of politicians continuously and with great skepticism. Independent thought and eternal vigilance must always be the price for preserving democracy. A political leader may earn a degree of trust from his or her constituents on the basis of performance—but total unquestioning *faith* in political leaders must always lead in the end to fascism. Indeed, such faith in *any* leaders—

military, business, religious, scientific—will only make the
next decades more perilous.

Fortunately, the process of eroding such misplaced faith
is already underway. The bungling and systematic deceit
of the Kennedy and Johnson administrations in their
handling of the Vietnam war started the trend of public
distrust in the military [4] that paralleled the decline of trust
in politicians. In addition, the prestige of big business has
also fallen to new lows, as corporate executives have
proven themselves fully as out of touch with reality as
their friends in government and the Pentagon.

Religious leadership needs little comment—just tune in
to a televised Billy Graham revival for an hour. Listening
to him exhort his followers to "render unto Caesar," one
sees quickly how he became chaplain of the Nixon gang.
And in 1974, when millions were dying of famine and
hundreds of millions more were threatened with hunger
in an overpopulated world, Pope Paul was still stating
that nations that practiced contraception or abortion were
doomed,[5] and the Chief Rabbi of New York was urging
Jews to have large families. Small wonder people are flee-
ing western organized religion in droves, either to think
for themselves, to take up an eastern religion, or join one
of a rash of modern cults.

Scientific leadership has, if anything, been worse than
religious leadership. In theory at least, scientists ought to
know better, but they sent men to the moon when cities
on Earth were dissolving, and transplanted hearts in
preference to tackling the problems of overpopulation and
mass starvation. It is no surprise that people have become
disenchanted with scientists and technologists who promised them the good life and gave them smog, pesticide
pollution, sonic booms, nuclear missiles, biological weapons, poison gas, brainwashing, electronic surveillance, and
a computer-ridden dehumanized society. Only the naive
still have faith that science can pull some kind of technological rabbit out of the hat at the last minute to save
us. The more sophisticated are beginning to realize that
such rabbits tend to have big appetites and superabundant
noxious droppings. Faith in science can be just as danger-

ous as the religious faith that it has largely superseded.

The way truth has been abused in the US is extreme, but not atypical of the rest of the world—and the blame for it lies not just with venal politicians, stupid corporation executives, outdated religious leaders, and mad scientists, but with *all of us* for putting up with them. We have let hypocrisy become a way of life in America. The time is now ripe for politicians, generals, businessmen, ministers, scientists—in fact *everyone*—to face the true state of our nation and the world, and to start a trend toward real candor in the name of survival. Such candor, however, first requires facing honestly what the future holds. This would permit us at least to begin planning for the multitude of poorly defined crises ahead.

We are not, as you may have guessed, optimistic about the political future of the US. In spite of Watergate and consequent efforts at governmental reform, we expect the medium-range trend to be one of increased concentration of power in the executive branch and further erosion of power of Congress and the courts. Crises will sweep over the nation and the world with increasing frequency as the end of the century approaches, and Congress will probably continue to flounder, bicker, and maunder in its traditional manner. There will be cries for strong leadership and an increasing tendency for presidents and governors to "call out the guard" to stop violence in labor disputes, protests against runaway inflation, food riots, and the like. It is quite possible that the ultimate strong man could gain the presidency and, during a crisis, solve his problems with Congress by declaring martial law and sending the senators and representatives home "for the duration." The problems of America would thus be solved by destroying its greatest asset—the relative liberty of its citizens.

Should no strong president appear, the results might be even worse for freedom because the alternative may well be anarchy. Unless dramatic reforms are forced on Congress and the average caliber of legislators is vastly improved,[6] it will never be able to guide the nation through the time of crises. It will continue to be a patsy to industry and the military, a promoter of the pork barrel, and a roadblock to most reforms a democratic-minded president might wish to institute. It might well remain paralyzed while the nation tears itself apart.

In short, you'd better expect a further deterioration in the performance of politicians—difficult as this is to believe—since a downward trend in political performance is self-reinforcing. The lingering stink of Watergate will not do much to encourage honest, intelligent, and compassionate people to seek the highest office in the land. Neither will the rock-bottom rating in the public mind that Congress achieved in the early 1970s. Cynicism among the voters will increase, and the lower politicians sink in the eyes of the public, the more difficult it will be to recruit better ones.[7]

Suppose that, in spite of this depressing prognosis, you (like us) would like to try to effect a change. As we have told many people, the only chance of success is through concerted political action. If you want to help, you must be willing to work long and hard for and against political candidates and (even more important) to recruit more people into the effort. A dramatic change in the political cast of characters is badly needed, but a simple house-cleaning will not do—the cast can be changed back too easily. Some progress along this line was made between 1968 and 1972, especially in the Democratic Party. But unless public concern is maintained, the party may revert to old forms and again become the exclusive property of self-serving party hacks.

There must be a return to an old idea in our republic—that we send people to Washington who we think have brains and integrity and who we hope will make wise decisions, attempting to balance our local interests with a concern for the good of the nation and the world. This means that we must acquaint ourselves with the overall performance of our representatives. If we are employed by a university, we must not automatically oppose Senator X, who voted against more funds for higher education, but rather must ask the reason for the opposition. Perhaps Senator X honestly thought other things should have priority, and, stepping back mentally, we may see that in the broad view he was correct. Especially where we are emotionally or financially involved, it is incumbent upon us to examine a politician's performance carefully.

"Okay," you say, "political action is the way. But specifically who should we be for and who should we be against?" That's really one for *you* to answer. Groups like the League of Women Voters, the League of Conservation Voters, and Common Cause can supply you with the voting records of your senators and representatives, and you can analyze them for yourself. A helpful source is the *Almanac of American Politics—1974*,[8] which among other things gives the ratings of congressmen by a variety of organizations spanning the political spectrum. Just to stick our necks out, in Table 2 we list some of the "good guys" and "bad guys" in the 93rd Congress from our perspective, with some indication of how they earned our blessings or brickbats.

## TABLE 2

### The Good and the Bad in Congress

#### Senate—Good Guys

| | | |
|---|---|---|
| J. William Fulbright | Ark. (D) | His opposition to the Vietnam War overrides a relatively weak civil-rights record (Arkansas should be ashamed of encouraging his segregationalist votes). Unhappily, he was defeated in the 1974 primary election. |
| Alan Cranston | Calif. (D) | His support of welfare payments for Lockheed is the only major blot on an otherwise excellent record. |
| John V. Tunney | Calif. (D) | Very much concerned about the approaching age of scarcity. He and Cranston make a matched set—California is relatively fortunate in its senators. |
| Abraham Ribicoff | Conn. (D) | A gutsy and independent liberal. |
| Lowell P. Weicker, Jr. | Conn. (R) | A gutsy and independent conservative. |

| | | |
|---|---|---|
| Herman E. Talmadge | Ga. (D) | A smart conservative who performed well on the Watergate Committee, powerful chairman of the Senate Agriculture Committee. |
| A. E. Stevenson, III | Ill. (D) | Good voting record. |
| Birch Bayh | Ind. (D) | Active, effective leader in Senate against Nixonism, pushed through Equal Rights Amendment. |
| Edmund S. Muskie | Maine (D) | Strong environmentalist. |
| Charles M. Mathias, Jr. | Md. (R) | Supporter of reform of political system. |
| Edward M. Kennedy | Mass. (D) | Activist, good record. |
| Edward M. Brooke | Mass. (R) | Frequent critic of Nixon Administration. Outstanding voting record. |
| Philip A. Hart | Mich. (D) | Quiet, effective liberal and champion for the consumer. |
| Walter F. Mondale | Minn. (D) | Idealistic, effective. A leader in promoting good social legislation. |
| Clifford P. Case | N. J. (R) | Independent, enemy of political corruption. |
| Jacob K. Javits | N. Y. (R) | An outstanding exception to the need to retire older senators, a steadfast opponent of Richard Nixon. A prime mover for pension reform. |
| Robert W. Packwood | Ore. (R) | A rather liberal Republican who has championed the cause of population limitation. He's a good example of an honest politician, whom we support despite some major disagreements with him—especially on military legislation. |
| Ernest F. Hollings | S. C. (D) | A moderate who has waged a courageous campaign to feed the hungry in the United States. He was also a prime mover behind legislation to save what remains of our coastal lands. |
| George McGovern | S. D. (D) | Good at almost everything but running for President. Especially a leader in the battle against hunger and opposition to Vietnam War. |

| James G. Abourezk | S. D. (D) | Second of a pair of senators South Dakota can be proud of. Liberal, strong supporter of the rights of Indians—not necessarily a popular position in South Dakota. |
| Frank E. Moss | Utah (D) | A liberal in a conservative state, opponent of the Vietnam War. |
| William Proxmire | Wisc. (D) | One of the best—he beat the SST and fights to trim the fat off the military. "Conservative" on some of the more dubious liberal domestic programs. |
| Gaylord Nelson | Wisc. (D) | Fine record on war, environment, and consumer protection. |

## Senate—Bad Guys

| James B. Allen | Ala. (D) | Threatened filibuster to halt the bill to reform campaign spending; filibustered against a bill to make voter registration easier for the poor. Generally bad voting record. |
| Edward J. Gurney | Fla. (R) | He tried to get Carswell on the Supreme Court, was Nixon's man on the Watergate Committee. Got into legal trouble in Florida. Voting record better than many conservative southerners, but not good enough to balance his other shortcomings. |
| James O. Eastland | Miss. (D) | A political dinosaur, staunchly opposed to twentieth century, superannuated. |
| John C. Stennis | Miss. (D) | He and Eastland would make a good pair of bookends of some historical interest. |
| Roman L. Hruska | Neb. (R) | Famous for wanting mediocrity to be represented on the Supreme Court. |
| Carl T. Curtis | Neb. (R) | A man fully as brilliant as Hruska. |
| James L. Buckley | N. Y. (Cons.) | Attempted to enshrine Catholic religious doctrine in an anti-abortion amendment to the Constitution. Showed lack of faith in the Constitution by his early call for Nixon to resign, *not* because of Nixon's despicable behavior, but because he felt impeachment and trial would be divisive. |

| | | |
|---|---|---|
| Hugh Scott | Penn. (R) | Very powerful nineteenth-century legislator, soon hopefully to retire. He opposed bringing criminal charges against Nixon because he felt forcing him to retire to his palatial mansions on $150,000 per year in pay and expenses (and numerous other perquisites) was equivalent to "hanging" the ex-President. |
| Strom Thurmond | S. C. (R) | A bigoted old man—hopefully we'll be rid of him in 1978. |
| William E. Brock, III | Tenn. (R) | A dreadful senator, enemy of both nonwhite people and the environment. |
| John G. Tower | Texas (R) | A "young fogey" who supports a big military force and environmental destruction. |

## House—Good Guys

| | | |
|---|---|---|
| Morris K. Udall | Ariz. (D-2nd) | A bright maverick in a House suffering under the leadership of the senile. |
| John E. Moss | Calif. (D-3rd) | An independent champion of open government. |
| Ronald V. Dellums | Calif. (D-7th) | Black, radical, smart—a breath of fresh air. |
| Fortney H. Stark | Calif. (D-8th) | Can you believe, a radical banker? Another bright new face. |
| Don Edwards | Calif. (D-9th) | A classic liberal, opposed Vietnam war early, major backer of Equal Rights Amendment. |
| Paul N. McCloskey, Jr. | Calif. (R-17th) | A true conservative whose stands against the Vietnam war and opposition to Nixon have brought him national fame and the eternal enmity of the spoilers and troglodytes of the Republican Party. Good conservation record. |
| Yvonne B. Burke | Calif. (D-37th) | A progressive black woman with broad support among white voters. |
| George E. Brown, Jr. | Calif. (D-38th) | At least as good a man as John Tunney, who beat him in the 1970 senatorial primary. |
| Patsy T. Mink | Hawaii (D-2nd) | Early opponent of Vietnam war, good voting record, independent. |
| John N. Erlenborn | Ill. (R-14th) | An independent-minded conservative. |

| Robert F. Drinan | Mass. (D-4th) | Liberal, activist, Jesuit priest. |
| John Conyers, Jr. | Mich. (D-1st) | Outstanding member of Judiciary Committee, opponent of Nixon, good voting record. |
| Donald W. Riegle, Jr. | Mich. (D-7th) | Outstanding conservationist. |
| Peter W. Rodino, Jr. | N. J. (D-10th) | Good civil rights record; performed well as Chairman of Judiciary Committee in impeachment proceedings against Nixon. |
| Shirley A. Chisholm | N. Y. (D-12th) | A smart black woman who has become a national political figure —better 1976 "presidential material" than most, if not all, male candidates usually mentioned. She has announced plans to retire, but hopefully will change her mind. |
| Bella S. Abzug | N. Y. (D-20th) | Another outstanding woman legislator from the Empire State; strong environmental record. |
| Charles W. Whalen, Jr. | Ohio (R-3rd) | Liberal antiwar Republican. |
| Barbara C. Jordan | Texas (D-18th) | Her eloquence provided a high point in Judiciary Committee debate on impeachment. The first black woman representative from the South is also a new bright light in the Congress. |
| Les Aspin | Wisc. (D-1st) | The people of his district should be proud of this fine congressman. Deadly enemy of the soft, bloated, military hierarchy, friend of the environment and the consumer. He exposed oil industry payments to Nixon's campaign. |
| Henry S. Reuss | Wisc. (D-5th) | Another good congressman from Wisconsin; senior, strong environmental record, enemy of corruption. |

## House—Bad Guys

| Robert R. Mathias | Calif. (R-18th) | A seemingly not-too-bright "young fogey." |
| Chet Holifield | Calif. (D-19th) | His behavior on the Joint Committee on Atomic Energy (JCAE) has made him one of the most dangerous men in the House. Fortunately retiring in 1974. |

| | | |
|---|---|---|
| Carlos J. Moorhead | Calif. (R-20th) | One of the "irresponsible four" congressmen voting against authorizing the Judiciary Committee to investigate whether there were grounds for impeaching Nixon. |
| Delwin M. Clawson | Calif. (R-23rd) | A powerful, but little-noticed, ultraconservative. |
| John H. Rousselot | Calif. (R-24th) | Fanatically in favor of turning back the clock—a John Bircher. |
| Craig Hosmer | Calif. (R-32nd) | His JCAE activities make us delighted that he has chosen to retire. |
| B. B. Blackburn | Ga. (R-4th) | Another of the "irresponsible four." |
| Earl F. Landgrebe | Ind. (R-2nd) | Another of the "irresponsible four." He has an unbelievably bad voting record and favored retaining Nixon as President even after Nixon was shown unequivocally to be a crook. |
| David C. Treen | La. (R-3rd) | The last of the "irresponsible four." |
| Edward Hutchinson | Mich. (R-4th) | Conservative with a terrible voting record, ranking Republican on House Judiciary Committee. |
| Jamie L. Whitten | Miss. (D-1st) | Representative Richard Bolling wrote in 1969, "Study the unpardonable problem of malnutrition and even starvation in this country and you'll encounter Representative Jamie Whitten of Mississippi, Chairman of the Appropriations Subcommittee on Agriculture and lord of certain operations of the Agriculture Department." Whitten also has been an active supporter of ecocide as practiced by the pesticide industry. |
| Wayne L. Hays | Ohio (D-18th) | One of the most powerful men in the House, often uses that power to oppose reform (as in opposing campaign spending restrictions with real teeth). |
| William R. Poage | Texas (D-11th) | The epitome of a bad congressman, Chairman of the Agriculture Committee who has opposed programs to feed the poor and supported welfare for the rich. Retiring would be the greatest service he could do for the US. |

In both the Senate and House we list more "good guys" than "bad guys." This is because the lists contain only the names of people we personally know something about—and such people naturally tend to be prominent. But large numbers of mediocre and incompetent legislators never become prominent—they do their damage by representing their own interests rather than the public interest, or by representing the interests of their constituency to the virtual exclusion of the nation's interests. They are men like William Dickinson, representative of the 2nd District of Alabama, whose sole claim to fame according to the *Almanac* was his charge in 1965 "that the Selma marchers —who passed through his district—engaged in obscenities; though he promised to document the accusation, he never did."

Dickinson votes for bombing Cambodian children, but he has compassion in his heart for the highway lobby. He likes consumers to stand on their own two feet in confrontations with giant corporations—they should certainly not have "communistic" help from the government. He wants kids to be able to pray in school (presumably to protect themselves from the governmental corruption and environmental destruction that his other votes promote). But Dickinson did not make our "bad guys" list—his kind of rotten apple is a dime a dozen in the 536-apple congressional barrel, as an evening spent perusing the *Almanac* will convince you. Dickinson is merely an example of many legislators who, usually with good and generous intent, have risen far beyond their levels of competence.

Congress is truly the "sapless branch" of the US government—slow, stupid, floundering, and ruled by old men, many of whose minds have not been sullied by a new idea in decades. Its hypocrisy is legendary. While zealously searching out signs of wrongdoing in the executive branch, and while subjecting Cabinet and Supreme Court nominees to relentless scrutiny for such things as conflicts of interest, it has no code of ethics of its own worth mentioning. Conflicts of interest abound in Congress, as do many other means of undercover financial aggrandizement. Nepotism and junketing are ways of life.

One of the saddest things about our list of "good guys" is the relative absence of "conservatives" who consistently support the individual against the government, the military, and big business, and who stand for the protection of America, including her environment. One of America's outstanding nominal conservatives is John Ashbrook, Republican of Ohio (19th District), who ran against Nixon in the 1972 primary because he disapproved of the rapprochement with China. Although we disagree with his stand on China, it is a logical one for a man to whom freedom of individual choice is perhaps the most cherished political goal. He also opposed the bombing of Cambodia and supported cuts in military expenditures. His opposition to forced busing was also understandable. (We are at best lukewarm about this particular liberal "solution" to problems of racial injustice, as are many people of all races. There clearly are better ways to solve the problem if we can generate the political will.)

But Ashbrook supports strip-mining, which destroys rather than conserves the US, and favors big corporations over the individuals who must live with the mess the corporations have made. Similarly, he supported the highway lobby against the people and has voted consistently to give corporations the biggest possible advantage over individuals in the political process. So he didn't make our "good guys" list. The US needs more thoughtful conservatives to balance its relative abundance of thoughtful liberals.

You will note that we list, proportionately, many more "good guys" in the Senate than in the House. This is partly a matter of prominence, but we also think it reflects a genuine difference in overall quality. The six-year term may permit senators more time to vote their consciences before turning their attention back to the parochial demands of their constituents. Moreover, they represent a broader constituency.

Above all, remember that the lists represent our own prejudices and judgments. There is abundant information available for you to make your own list. The *Almanac* is a good place to start—we recommend it most highly.

After that, consult the annual ratings issued by the League of Conservation Voters and Common Cause.[9]

Our local newspaper has recently begun a regular accounting of the votes of local representatives and senators in Congress. Such information is highly valuable in determining how your congressman is performing and where he may stand on issues not mentioned during campaigns. If your paper doesn't carry such a feature, it might be worthwhile to request that it do so. Better yet, encourage your friends to make a similar request—and make use of the feature if it appears.

Don't hesitate to let your representatives at any level in government from city council to President, know how you feel about their actions. This includes not only votes or positions you don't like, but also—and this is important—the ones you *do* like. Everyone likes to hear if he's doing a good job, and politicians are decidedly no exception. Perhaps if Senator Hughes and Representative Chisholm had received more encouragement and recognition of their achievements from their constituents, they wouldn't have decided to retire.

## Economists and the Failing Economic System

The gross failure of the political system in recent years is matched by the gross failure of the economic system. And this failure is of even greater concern to most Americans than the political failure, to which it is closely related. Rather than moving toward reasonable prosperity for all the people in America or the world, the economic system has produced enormous affluence for a few and pseudo-affluence for the middle class, which is now losing ground in maintaining its standard of living. For the world, the system has perpetuated poverty and misery for the vast majority and mortgaged the future of all.

The reasons for the failure of the economic system are many, but to some degree responsibility must rest with professional economists. For twenty years following World War II, economists deluded themselves and many leaders whom they advised into thinking the system was working. Then, when failure was evident, some of the finest minds of the profession—men like Galbraith, Samuelson, Spengler, Boulding, Heilbroner, Georgescu-Rogen, and Daly—attempted to discover what was wrong with the system. They recognized that the gap between the rich and the poor wasn't closing, that society was strangling in its own wastes, and they tried to figure out what to do about it. So far their successes have been very limited. Perhaps the most seminal contribution was Boulding's contrasting of "cowboy" and "spaceman" economies; the most innovative proposal was probably Daly's suggestion (discussed below) of placing quotas on resource depletion.[10]

But these men are a few among the multitude. The vast mass of mediocre economists are entrapped in their own unnatural love for a growing gross national product. Growthmania is surely the most pervasive social disease in America, but sadly it cannot be cured with a simple dose of penicillin. Rather, it is exacerbated by economists who believe in miracles (how else can infinite growth be achieved on a finite planet?) and by presidential economic advisors whose often irrelevant charts, graphs, and statistics attract politicians looking for simple answers to complex problems.

One economist who believes in miracles is Richard Zeckhauser, an otherwise obscure Harvard professor who gained temporary fame by publishing the notion that the only reason we don't reburn the same oil many times over in our power plants is that nuclear power is cheaper! [11] Of course, to produce power by reconstituting oil from its combustion products and then reburning it ("recycling oil," as Zeckhauser put it), would take very many times more useful energy than could be produced—unless Congress could be persuaded to repeal the Second Law of Thermodynamics.

The Second Law of Thermodynamics is a fundamental law of nature which underlies all economic processes.[12] It specifies the *direction* in which spontaneous physical processes proceed: heat moves from hot to cold, concentrations of anything disperse, order becomes disorder. This law tells us the universe is inexorably "running down." At the Stockholm conference described earlier, several economists refused to accept the consequences of the Second Law, and one even said, "After all, who knows what that law will be like in a hundred years?"

The answer given by the physicist present was, "I do, and so does every other scientist." He could make the statement with such conviction because the Second Law is not based on high-flown theory, but on trillions of observations made every day by all human beings. If the Second Law doesn't exist in a hundred years, oil will indeed be recyclable, squashed cats will reassemble themselves on the highway and trot off, salt and pepper can be kept mixed in the same container since sorting them out will be as easy as mixing them is today, and toilets will become obsolete because it won't be necessary for you to produce waste products. These tongue-in-cheek examples only hint at how preposterous is the notion of a world without the Second Law. Such a world is literally unimaginable.

Considering the failure of most economists to understand the physical, biological, and social constraints operating on the economic system, it should hardly come as a surprise that most economists cannot give sensible advice on how to deal with the kinds of change that the world now faces. To explain to one of them the inevitability of no growth in the material sector, or the ideas that commodities *must* become expensive, that worldwide markets for many manufactured goods may soon be saturated, that special drawing rights are unlikely to replace gold as money until there are vast changes in the human psyche, that the next "recession" might well turn out to be the *final* depression, would be like attempting to explain odd-day–even-day gas distribution to a cranberry.

The situation in economics is not entirely bleak, however. There are many ways that economists, once they become oriented to physical and biological realities, could help humanity in the coming crises. Economist Herman Daly, for instance, has suggested that the government impose quotas on the depletion of key resources. This would slow the rate of human attack on the nonrenewable resources of the planet and raise the prices of some raw materials. Price rises would encourage recycling, the development of substitutes, and the reclaiming of pollutants. Perhaps most important, controls could be imposed at a point that would not require the creation of a huge regulatory bureaucracy. Although many details remain to be worked out, Daly's ideas are examples of the kind of innovation that may be expected from economists once they realize that the system requires a complete overhaul.[13]

## Sorting Sense From Nonsense

Regardless of their potential capabilities, however, we have little faith that politicians and economists will be able to guide the US or the world through the trying times ahead. They have too much to learn in too little time.

As we have said, "faith" in any authority or group of authorities should be avoided; people must instead put their trust in *themselves* and learn to live without depending on authorities for everything. We believe that the rewards of so doing would be enormous, not just for the individual, but for society as well.

This, naturally, raises the question of why you should take our word on these or other matters. The answer, of course, is that you shouldn't. Whenever you are doubtful, check it out. The Ehrlichs say that most economists are hooked on growth the way junkies are hooked on heroin. Don't take their word for it; read what economists are writing. If you doubt us when we say that the market for airbuses is near saturation, read Professor K. E. F. Watt's analysis of the situation.[14] You don't trust Watt? Go to the original industry sources.

There are many habits that can be developed for helping to sort sense from nonsense. The basic tools of the trade are simplicity itself—a pencil and pad when you watch TV to jot down numbers and preposterous statements, and access to basic reference books and good newspapers and news magazines as mentioned at the end of Chapter 1. If you want to be well informed about the state of the world so you can make an impact on society and/or plan your own future, *there is no substitute for zealous reading and note-taking, followed, where necessary, by some thinking and calculations.*

What sort of calculations? Suppose you hear an executive of some big oil company claim that our petroleum problems can be "solved" by drilling in a certain offshore area where wells can be expected to contribute 100,000 barrels per day to our supply. You whip out your most recent copy of the *Statistical Abstract of the United States* and discover (Table 820, p. 506 of the 1972 issue) that in 1971 we consumed 28,049 trillion British Thermal Units (Btu) worth of petroleum. Now comes the arithmetic. In the fine print at the head of the table, you discover that each barrel of oil contains 5,623,000 Btu. Dividing the total Btu by Btu-per-barrel tells you that some 5 billion barrels were consumed by the US in the year 1971. Dividing the yearly total by 365 shows that some 13.7 million barrels a day were used up. The oilman's "panacea" turns out, if his numbers prove accurate, to be a supplement of much less than one percent of the 1971 level of demand—a level that has long since been exceeded.

You note also that there is no statement of *how long* this flow can be expected to last—probably just long enough for the oil company to realize a huge profit. When the field is exhausted and the beaches thoroughly tarred, the oil barons will use those profits as capital to fund some other rape of the environment for short-term gain. You are now in a much better position to decide whether the aesthetic and environmental costs of the drilling project are justified by the potential benefits—especially if you remember our slogan for evaluating oil-company public-relations efforts: "Exxon doesn't want you to know."

With your simple tools, you are also in a position to play the Watt Game, named after its inventor, Professor K. E. F. Watt. When economists make predictions (usually carried in newspapers and newsmagazines), clip them and later check how accurate they were. Watt reports some of his results in his splendid book, *The Titanic Effect*.[15] Needless to say, the inaccuracy of their predictions don't build confidence in economists. In his State of the Union address in early 1974, President Nixon, presumably for political reasons and without serious objection from his economic advisors, guaranteed "no recession" in 1974. Considering the record of "Nixonomics," that statement could be considered a signal to buy gold-mine shares and be prepared to do a lot of short-selling in other stocks. The big bear market must have been just over the horizon. (Nixon's confidence could, of course, have been just a cover-up for an intention to avoid a depression temporarily by stimulating more inflation.)

In the medium term, what's coming economically seems fairly certain—a long-lasting production-depression which, at best, will phase into a steady-state economy very different from anything in the past. Whether or not it will be accompanied by a runaway monetary inflation, like that which hit Germany shortly after World War I,[16] is an open question. The possibility can't be ignored, especially as long as governments can delay the onset of a depression by printing money. Of course, the longer they postpone the inevitable consequences of decades of government spending more money than it made, the bigger the bust will be when it comes.

Although, as we enter the age of scarcity, the broad economic trends seem clear, the likelihood of short-term fluctuations makes personal economic planning difficult. For instance, it is possible that a temporary "solution" to the petroleum shortage may trigger a boomlet that lasts several years or more—possible, but not likely.

Your personal financial plans must, of course, vary with your personal circumstances, but a few general suggestions are in order. Economic conservatism seems prudent from here on out. By the end of 1973, smart investors around the world had moved much of their money into gold (the classic haven for capital when currency becomes superinflated), as evidenced by a market price of over $170 per ounce. Should there be another boom, the price of gold will almost certainly drop; and if it goes below $100, gold stocks may become a very attractive investment. Indeed, they may well still have been bargains at their early 1974 prices. It depends on those hard-to-judge short-term fluctuations that are always superimposed on the long-range trends.

Many, if not most, Americans consider how to protect themselves from financial disaster the most important problem in their lives. They are faced with a steady erosion of their buying power due to inflation, while depression seems to threaten just over the horizon. Unfortunately, the optimal personal strategy for dealing with the situation will depend on how badly world society bungles its financial affairs. For example, if the transition to a steady-state economy is managed without a financial collapse, a program of financial conservatism may suffice for people with secure jobs and adequate incomes.

Financial conservatism would include such things as never buying a new car until the old one is uneconomical to repair, minimizing the purchase and use of energy-consuming devices like air conditioners, owning the smallest house in which one can be comfortable, keeping one's money in such things as gold stocks, Swiss banks, or US Treasury bills, rather than US banks or savings and loans, which are less than adequately insured.[17] If investments are made in stocks or property, they should be made with an eye toward steady increase in value at a rate of perhaps 10 to 15 percent a year rather than attempting to double one's money annually by speculating.

Needless to say, for the many Americans who have been dealt out of the affluent society, these options are unreal. They would be happy just to get out of debt or to find work to feed their families. To them the concept of sending money to a Swiss bank or buying a Treasury bill (requiring an investment of almost $10,000) is simply absurd. Perhaps the best they can do personally is not

nurture unrealistic hopes about aid from the rest of society—the middle class will itself be on the road to
poverty, and the rich won't give a damn. In theory, our
society could be reorganized to abolish poverty, but the
gap between theory and reality is huge. But everyone will
be better off if society doesn't completely drop the ball.
As long as the system manages to stagger along, some
efforts, probably increasingly inadequate, will be made to
help the poor—both out of compassion and because the
nonpoor fear them. But programs to help them will probably remain bungled and degrading. Some, like the giant
Social Security fraud, a regressive tax program that benefits the middle class at the expense of the poor, are
positively harmful.[18]

Collectively, the poor might be able to improve their
condition vastly if they were able to organize. But thus
far, attempts to organize them have been feeble and
largely unsuccessful because the interests they oppose are
too powerful. If a *majority* of the poor came to realize
how they are being ripped off, and if they banded together to do something about it, something might be
accomplished. But until that day comes, we're sorry to
say, the poor will have to depend on themselves and
their neighbors to solve their problems at very local
levels, not on some nationwide movement, and certainly
not on politicians or economists.

## Some Economic Facts of Life

Whatever your financial status, it would be wise to keep
some basic economic facts, often ignored by "professional"
economic commentators, firmly in mind. At the most basic
level, money can be thought of as a commodity that
people value as a medium of exchange. For practical
purposes in today's world, this means silver or, especially,
gold, although in the past such diverse commodities as
cattle and sea shells have served. Without such a uni-

versally valued commodity, all economic transactions would be by direct barter—for instance, we might personally trade you the valuable contents of this book for, say, a can of tuna. Obviously, if there were no money, only barter, large complex societies could not function (consider, for instance, the problems you would have simply filling your daily needs by trading things with people). Gold is the closest thing there is to an ideal all-purpose medium of exchange. It is rare, virtually indestructible, easily divided, and has high intrinsic value because of its beauty and its numerous applications in industry.

"But wait a minute," you say, "I use money all the time, but I've never handled any golden money. How come?" The answer is that gold as a medium of exchange is still far from perfect. For instance, the amount of gold necessary for small purchases, such as, say, buying a newspaper, is too small for gold coins to be convenient—they would have to be microscopic. And for large transactions, gold is too heavy. So people long ago put their gold in warehouses, now called "banks," and the banks issued receipts for the gold.

The receipts were much more convenient to carry around and trade with than the gold itself was, and thus currency was born. So was inflation. If the bank issued more receipts than it had gold, the value of each receipt decreased, and more receipts would be required to obtain a desired product from a knowledgeable merchant. Although a receipt might say "receipt for twenty ounces of gold," if the merchant knew that a thousand such receipts had been issued by the warehouse and that the warehouse had only ten thousand ounces of gold, he would also know that the receipt was really only good for ten ounces. For, if there were a run on the warehouse, it would either have to limit each receipt-holder to ten ounces, or give full value for the first five hundred receipts presented and nothing for the remainder.

For the past hundred or so years, governments have been empowered (either through coercion, or the devotion of their citizens, or, most commonly, a combination of the two) to determine what should be used as a medium of exchange. The commodity that was most acceptable to the citizenry when governments took over this role was gold, and it still is gold to this day. Monetary theorists notwithstanding, gold is still the medium of exchange that more people in the world would accept, given the opportunity, than any other. Although they cannot eat it, live in it, or drive it, they do have confidence that they will be able to exchange it for food, a house, or a vehicle.

Governments and most economists, however, like to pretend that gold has no special value. In economics texts, money is, quite logically, described as what you use to buy things—currency and checking accounts (demand deposits) in commercial banks. Indeed, money is normally created by central banks, such as the Federal Reserve System—the "Fed"—of the US, in the form of new demand deposits. Money can also be destroyed by the Fed, and if the system is functioning "properly" (we cannot deal with its complexities here), the supply of money can be kept appropriate to the wealth of the nation. This ability to adjust the supply of money so that it coincides with the needs of the economy is why economists prefer that people not think of gold as money, because the supply of gold is subject to the vagaries of discovery and mining, rather than the functioning of central banks. But even the governments that pretend gold is unimportant strive mightily to amass it. During the Stalinist period, the Soviet Union expended hundreds of thousands of human lives to drag gold out of the ground, and in the early 1970s the US desperately sought more of it. In spite of its many imperfections (e.g., strict adherence to a gold standard has stood in the way of prosperity on occasion), gold continues to play a key role in the international monetary system and in people's ideas of money and value.

Considering the psychological importance of gold, a significant measure of the confidence that people have in their government and their society is their willingness to accept something other than gold (like paper certificates) in its place. If people *believe* that paper currency has value, it *will* have value. But governmental behavior can easily erode that confidence, as it has in the US in the early 1970s. And one of the easiest ways for a government to erode confidence in itself is to inflate its currency continually.

Banks, of course, played the game of inflating their currencies before governments established central banks and currencies became national. But banks were pikers compared to governments when it came to inflation. When governments decide they want to do costly things, such as send men to the moon, or support hundreds of generals or rich farmers with welfare schemes, or give research grants to university professors, and they are afraid to raise taxes to get the required money, they can turn to inflation. In the old days they would print more receipts for nonexistent gold and use those receipts to finance their projects.

More recently in the US, governmental fiscal (taxation and expenditure) and monetary policies were adjusted to increase the money supply more rapidly than the material wealth of the nation expanded. In "printing" money that wasn't backed by increased holdings of gold (or by increased productivity of the economy), governments weren't creating wealth, they were simply redistributing what already existed. Supernumerary generals, weapons manufacturers, subsidized rich farmers, grant-getting university professors, people who worked for or sold material and equipment to NASA, and other recipients of government largesse were better off, at least temporarily. They got more receipts, enough to balance the decline in value of each receipt. So did some clever enterpreneurs who saw inflation coming and took appropriate steps. Everyone else, of course, lost, since they got only reduced buying power.

In the early 1970s, most governments, including that of the US, had only enough gold on hand to return a few pennies on the dollar on their "receipts" (demand deposits and currency) if they were willing to redeem them all simultaneously. Even the Swiss franc, although much stronger than most currencies, had only about 25 percent gold backing. Thus even "strong" currencies demand an act of faith on the part of citizens that their governments will not simply create so much money that it would decline precipitously in value. For many people, the ability and willingness of a government to back its currency in gold enhances that faith because they realize that gold is likely to retain some value regardless of what economic or social problems arise. Government printing presses have a tendency to roll faster and faster, since politicians do not want to threaten *their* jobs by liquidating the untenable programs they have created (e.g., those that taxpayers would be unwilling to support if they could see the real costs). There are just too many people who are (or think they are) getting something for nothing who would raise hell. Look at the fuss that people at Lockheed raised when the market was about to liquidate that uneconomical enterprise!

"Well," you might say, "why can't the government go on redistributing wealth forever by using inflation?" The answer is that sooner or later people wise up. At first it is only the people on fixed incomes—pensioners, for instance—who really suffer, and they can be ignored. But soon the waste of the government-supported boondoggles begins to pinch almost everyone. Then the people who realize what is happening begin trying to redeem their receipts before they lose any more value. In a country like the US, where the government won't redeem currency with either gold or silver, smart people with enough money to make it worthwhile may convert dollars into Swiss francs or buy silver, gold bullion, old gold coins, or stocks in goldmines. (Owning gold other than in coins or jewelry has been illegal in the US—part of the government's scheme to convince people that ten-dollar bills have intrinsic value—but shortly after the publication of this book it is scheduled to become legal again.) People will also try to spend their money as rapidly as possible, purchasing things of intrinsic value before their paper "money" becomes valueless.

Since the only thing that keeps unbacked currency (or gold, for that matter) valuable is the value people *think* it has, inflation feeds on itself. The more people doubt the paper, the more the prices of gold, food, automobiles, or whatever people think has intrinsic value is bid up. In a country where many people are *paid* to make things like C-5A transports, nuclear missiles, and atomic submarines *that no one can purchase* on the open market, there is a lot of money around with which to do the bidding. Prices rise ever more rapidly, the paper currency plunges in value, and inflation starts to run away. Eventually, people are being paid millions of dollars (paper) an hour and bread costs $750,000 (paper) a loaf. The rate of inflation may become so rapid that employees demand to be paid first daily and then twice a day so they can spend their wheelbarrows full of currency before it loses more value. Sound fantastic? That is what happened in Germany shortly after World War I, and that wasn't the first time.

When inflation reaches that point, if total collapse is to be avoided, the government must step in and reestablish faith in the currency by, for instance, issuing a much smaller amount of a new currency backed by whatever gold (or other commodity that people value) it has or can lay its hands on. To end the German runaway inflation, a new currency was issued, "backed" by claims on German agriculture and industry. The "backing" was largely phoney, but it restored people's *faith* in the currency—which is the key to the situation when such an inflation is to be stopped. Deficit spending also must come to an end, and uneconomic enterprises must be liquidated. The economy then undergoes a convulsive readjustment called a depression. People in many sectors that previously received government handouts find themselves unemployed, as do many who supplied them with goods and services (a ripple effect). Until the economy is reorganized to meet the needs of the population more closely, rather than doing what the government thinks is best, there is a great deal of hardship.

There are two important lessons to be gleaned from this oversimplified discussion of the classic aspects of inflation.[19] First, when the government tells you funny stories about how paper is valuable money and gold isn't, ignore it—it's just one more lie. Value is something that people give to things and few people in early 1974 would trade an ounce of gold for 43 one-dollar bills—the "official" US government rate. Indeed, many people were busily trading 150 or more dollar bills for an ounce of gold. Whenever people lose their confidence in governments and currencies, they always try to get gold; and if they can't get gold, silver. That tells you what people value.

The second lesson is that as long as the government spends more than it collects in taxes, the inflationary trend will continue, ending in an inevitable deflation and depression. The longer the government waits before permitting the readjustment, the worse the ultimate crunch will be. If a runaway inflation is allowed to proceed, then a total collapse of the economy will occur, leading to chaos. It would be decidedly better to have a relatively brief and orderly depression early. *"Recessions" do not provide the necessary readjustment;* they are merely small downturns in an inflationary trend.

Such a long inflationary trend was three decades old by the early 1970s. When government economists talk about "fine-tuning" the economy, maintaining "acceptable rates of inflation," and the like, don't be fooled into thinking that anything is being done to correct a basic cause of inflation: *Its use as a political device for the covert redistribution of wealth in ways that would be unacceptable to most people if they realized what was going on.*

On top of these problems created by government bungling, there are even more fundamental difficulties. Inflation is often defined as too much money chasing too few goods. In the classic "demand-pull" kind of inflation outlined above, the government prints too much money, which it then uses to bid up prices on goods. If it buys steel to waste in building aircraft carriers, there is less steel available for appliance manufacturers. The price of steel is bid up, and the additional cost is passed on to you when you buy a refrigerator. But if you are a worker, you will expect your wages to be increased to compensate for the loss of buying power of your dollars. Thus both prices and wages are "pulled" upward by increases in the money supply (that is, in demand).

In so-called "modern-mixed" economies, prices also rise *before* goods become scarce, basically because of the rising expectations of both business and labor. Labor asks for wage increases unjustified by increases in productivity, and business grants them because it plans to pass on the higher costs as higher prices. Both "expect" the government to create enough demand (money) to pay for this increased GNP. This kind of "cost-push" inflation occurs because the Fed must increase the money supply to meet these expectations; otherwise the lack of money to buy the more expensive output of society will cause the quantity of goods purchased to decrease. Output will then decrease, and unemployment will increase. Thus, money is created faster than productivity can increase the real wealth of society, and "cost-push" inflation ends up where "demand-pull" does—with goods scarce relative to the amount of money available to buy them.

*But scarcity can also originate from sources other than government printing presses or the expectations of labor, most notably from the finite nature of many resources.* As the human population has grown and per capita demand has increased, those resources have become proportionally scarcer. There is, for instance, much less first-class farmland per capita today than there was in 1900. Not only does the same land provide food for more than twice as many people, but much of the land—more than a million acres per year in recent years—has been "developed." This should have meant a great increase in the price of food, but to a large degree the reduction of farmland per capita has been compensated by technological advances. Thanks mainly to advances in plant genetics and a large fossil-fuel subsidy, much more food can be grown on an acre today than could be seventy-five years ago.

In many areas of the economy, enormous reserves, technological change, and substitutions have prevented the prices of resources from skyrocketing as demand has increased. But now that era is ending, even though most economists remain blissfully unaware of it. Many of the reserves are approaching depletion—the world's supply of liquid petroleum is an outstanding example. There are limits to how much technological change can make up for depletion. For instance, in many areas of the world, it is unlikely that agricultural productivity can be increased much further by technological advances. And for some substances, such as silver, substitutes are likely to be difficult to find and expensive to put into use if found—for example, the use of silver in photographic processes.

Thus, at a time when government policies and rising expectations are creating a rapidly escalating inflation, genuine scarcity will also add its push. Furthermore, other resources that in theory might be made available may remain scarce because society is unwilling to accept the high costs or environmental risks of mobilizing them. For instance, the US might (wisely, in our opinion) make do with less energy rather than deploy the nuclear-burner technology, or choose to continue farming in Iowa and Illinois and grazing in Montana rather than strip-mining.

The fundamental solution to these economic problems is simple: people in general, and Americans in particular, must change their expectations and learn to live within their means. Once the limits to the Earth's resources are recognized, the *basic* value question—*how those finite resources are to be distributed and used both within and between generations*—can be faced squarely. Once everyone realizes that economic growth will not close the gap between the rich and the poor *and* that such growth will soon end anyway,[20] then economists can descend from dreamland, and we can get on with the job of designing an economic system based on equilibrium.

## Economics in the Future

With many uncertainties clouding our view of the next few decades, it is impossible to forecast economic trends with any hope of detailed accuracy. General comments seem appropriate, however, to provide some guidance in personal planning.

First it is important to recognize that in the future the value of labor is likely to decline relative to capital. People are in abundant supply and, barring disaster, will be in even greater supply each year for some time to come. In contrast, resources are finite and will be dwindling annually. Unemployment, overt and disguised, is likely to increase, although the trend may be dampened somewhat by a return to a more labor-intensive agriculture and a greater substitution of men for machines in other areas as energy becomes short.

The trend toward concentration of industrial power seems bound to continue as scarcity of resources increases and technologies designed to deal with scarcity become more complex. Big corporations, able to generate capital internally, will have the capacity to control what resources are available and will be able to pay for expensive substitutes when supplies are simply unavailable. Small manufacturers will increasingly find that suppliers are reserving limited stocks of raw materials for their larger customers. In many cases, multinational corporations should be in an especially strong position because of their ability to manipulate their tax situations and control diverse sources of raw materials.

Among consumers, too, it will be the big and steady customer who gets the goods in time of shortage. Now is clearly the time to become a faithful customer to a variety of local merchants—remember that at many gas stations, regulars were favored at gasoline pumps during the "energy crisis." In general, the safety and quality of products will deteriorate as the government presses to have demand met at any cost. Americans are used to being superconsumers, and American politicians will be loathe to tell their constituents that their expectations cannot be fulfilled—even if the politicians themselves realize that the end of the "disposable society" is at hand.

The Nixonian response to the economic problems connected with scarcity showed the way. In his economic message in late July, 1974, the message was clear: remove environmental restraints and increase production. To growthmaniacs, poisoning the consumer and mortgaging the future of society are a small price to pay for one last fling at affluence. The major question now is whether that fling will materialize. Will the US (and perhaps certain other overdeveloped nations) manage one more boom, perhaps covering several decades, before the final bust? We think probably not. The food crunch is likely to undermine the world economy and result in political instability that will affect every corner of the globe. But a temporary boom is *possible*—accompanied by short-term gluts of commodities like meat, wheat, and gasoline— although the long-term trend is clearly downhill. The Dow-Jones average might even hit 2000!

We hope a last fling does not occur. Such a boom would all but destroy any remaining chance to make a smooth transition to an equilibrium society. Irreplaceable resources would be squandered and irreversible destruction visited upon the ecosystems of the planet. The long-term carrying capacity of the Earth for *Homo sapiens* might be so reduced as to make it impossible for any industrialized society to persist after the collapse. The final growth spurt of the cowboy economy would be like the sudden brightening of a light bulb just before it goes out.

With or without a terminal boom, what will the long-term trends look like from the viewpoint of most Americans? The big feature of future economics will probably be a reversion to conditions similar to those that prevailed during most of human history, conditions still experienced by the majority of human beings. Instead of being concerned with "keeping up with the Joneses" in terms of newness of car and number of household gadgets, people will increasingly worry about how to keep nutritious food in their children's stomachs and roofs over their heads. The purchase of food will take a bigger and bigger portion of the household budget, and, unless the grow-it-yourself movement really catches on, the quality of the average American diet will deteriorate. Just as energy czars have argued successfully that they should be permitted to relax pollution controls in order to produce more energy, food barons may argue and win the case for more fillers and preservatives to "stretch" short food supplies.

Rising costs of land, lumber, aluminum, roofing materials, plastics, and the like will make the single-family home an unattainable dream for most people. Many who already have homes will find themselves hard pressed to pay for gas or electricity for cooking and heating, or for water to keep their gardens growing.

Once basic needs are met, the big problem for future Americans will be to provide themselves and their families with security for the future—an even bigger order for them than it is for us today. A combination of inflation, the growing bankruptcy of the Social Security system, and the unwillingness of a country that is getting poorer to provide welfare payments in any form will make it more and more difficult for people to assure themselves even a minimum income in their retirement years. This problem is compounded by the manifest inadequacy of private pension funds, which are necessary to make up part of the gap between what a worker was earning before retirement and Social Security, which is normally about a third of that amount. Problems with pensions have included inadequate reserves to supply promised benefits (sometimes as the result of embezzlement of the funds), poor or no provisions for transfer when a worker moves, and trick or hidden clauses in the contract which may deprive a person of retirement income that he or she had been led to expect.

These abuses and others are so severe that they have come to the attention of Congress. The Senate Labor Subcommittee discovered in 1970 that one-third of the pension funds were only large enough to pay *one-half or less of the promised benefits*.[21] Recently passed legislation should make a significant improvement in this situation in the future.

There are, indeed, "hard times a-coming." Even if there is no final boom and bust, the economic world of the near future will be a very different place from that of today. We suspect that it will be much less complex. On one hand, there will be a relatively few gigantic corporate entities, private or nationalized, attempting to fill basic needs: food, housing, clothing, transportation, and medicine. On the other hand, there will be a resurgence of small family-based enterprises—farms, shops, maintenance businesses—through which people attempt to provide for themselves the security that is otherwise unattainable. The vast diversity of businesses that manufacture and distribute the goods of our "cowboy" economy will have largely disappeared. Most of the Japanese firms that today shower us with electronic gadgets will have gone defunct as Japan's situation deteriorates, and the higher costs of necessities will have so reduced demand for television sets, radios, tape decks, and the like that few new firms will have entered the market. Similarly, a wide array of non-essentials, from convenience foods to recreational vehicles, will have largely vanished along with the companies that produce them.

Probably before 1985, a general recognition of the changed economic status of the nation will lead to a stock-market collapse even more severe than the one that preceded the onset of the depression of the 1930s. This time, however, the public will be aware of the depth of our economic difficulties, and confidence in the market as a place to make money may be more or less permanently eroded. It is very likely that before the end of the century the stock market, as we know it, will disappear as a factor in the lives of individuals. The approach to a steady-state, survival-oriented economy and the decrease in the number of competing big businesses will destroy the rationale of private market investment, even for those so fortunate as to have accumulated spare capital.

In short, we are saying what politicians are reluctant to say. In material terms, we will in the near future be poorer, not richer. As the famous economist Schumpeter predicted in 1942, the day of the pioneering capitalist will pass, not because of the dullness of big business, as he envisioned, but from a lack of the unlimited resources and infinitely resilient environment that the ignorant capitalists (to say nothing of the equally ignorant socialists) have always assumed existed.

If we decide to plan our economic future, rather than simply let it overrun us, the practical questions to be answered will be tough indeed. Are we obliged to preserve a certain quantity of resources for future generations, and if so, how much? Are the thrifty obliged to help the spendthrifts out of trouble (the ant-and-grasshopper dilemma)? Should everyone in the US (or the world) be provided a minimum standard of living, whether they work or not? How should family sizes or the population growth rate to be considered in any plan to allocate scarce resources?

There are technical questions to answer also. Since the days of Adam Smith, it has been recognized that the wealth of a nation was *not* the amount of a yellow metal it stored, but the skills, tools, and productivity of its citizens. But no one has figured out how to make a paper receipt redeemable in gold by, say, one-trillionth of America's productivity on January 1, 1974. Economists have for good reasons tried to find a way to eliminate people's psychological dependence on gold, but as the gold market shows, they have failed. We suspect that, despite all the drawbacks, increased backing of currencies with precious metals may be required before the coming economic crises can be dealt with—not for "sound economic reasons," but for "sound psychological reasons."

As for your own financial planning, perhaps the most important thing to keep in mind is that gold and silver are commodities that people desire for their intrinsic beauty and industrial usefulness *and* because of strong traditions (especially in the case of gold) that give them psychological value. Currency of course is desired for what it will buy, but unlike gold it is not useful in itself, and also unlike gold it has a reputation for occasionally becoming valueless. Loss of faith can and has in the past reduced paper money to just so much paper. So far in human history, this has never happened to gold.

Some people, such as writer Harry Browne,[22] claim

that the greatest good for a given number of people would be achieved if there were no governments at all, if currency were backed 100 percent by gold, and each person sought to maximize his or her own personal happiness. In a perfect world where resources (except gold!) were infinite, price mechanisms were never sticky, expectations were not on the rise, monopolies were banned by God, and sadism was banished by eugenics and behavior control, the ultimate in laissez-faire might be fine.

But in this less-than-perfect world, people, in their attempts to find personal happiness, will band together to do as a group what they cannot accomplish as easily (or at all) singly. That's how partnerships, corporations, governments, social contracts, and paper money come into being. But governments grow, become ends in themselves, employ economists who think the GNP can grow forever, print too much money, and create inflation.

Perhaps then, in the simplest terms, humanity's great economic task is to find a way to have global and national governance that is strictly limited to doing things considered to be in the common interest *at a known cost to society*. To accomplish this, most members of society will have to become aware of how the economic system works. They must remain constantly on the alert against the kind of hocus-pocus that governments use to conceal the true state of the economic system from the majority of people. Much of the needless complexity must be removed from government economic operations, since it tends to obscure what is actually going on. Especially in the area of taxes, reduction of complexity will also tend to remove gross inequities.

This is a tall order, one that we frankly doubt will ever be filled. But if you inform yourself and attempt to inform others, you will not only be moving society in the right direction, you will also become aware of ways to protect yourself if continued government bungling shoves society over the economic brink. Among the things you should "stockpile" to assure yourself of a reasonable future are skills. If you know how to grow food, build and maintain simple machinery, make your own clothes, care for the sick, and so on, you will be in a relatively strong position if the worst materializes.

If there should be an economic collapse, most of us, middle class or poor, will be in much the same boat. Then perhaps only farmers, physicians, and others with valuable skills will be relatively secure, since the outstanding needs of people will be for basics such as food and medical care. If our highly interdependent society breaks down, food-distribution systems will break down and lawlessness will prevail until new, small, survival-oriented political units evolve. The chance that a collapse will go that far seems to us rather remote, but not impossible. It is quite conceivable, however, that the Western world will decline to the state of Germany after the runaway inflation of the 1920s. In those days, people commonly had to travel on foot out of urban areas to barter their possessions with farmers in exchange for food.

## Catch 22

It would obviously be to everyone's advantage to work cooperatively in an attempt to ease the transition to a steady-state economy—especially advantageous for the middle class and wealthy since they have much more to lose than the poor. Ironically, the only way out of the coming dilemma may be for the "haves" to reorganize America (and eventually the world) to give the "have-nots" a chance. The cooperative efforts required will never be made, however, in a society shot through with gross economic and racial inequities. We are in a Catch 22 situation. To solve the problems of maldistribution, we need cooperation, but such cooperation is blocked by class and racial tensions largely created by the maldistribution.

It is simple to perceive the need for cooperation in solving the problems faced by humanity; it is another thing entirely to devise ways of getting around the xenophobia and greed that stand in the way of such cooperation. How many of us are Nixonian philanthropists, talking a good line of charity while giving nothing? Can we blame the poor for rebelling if the "richest nation in the world" can't manage to supply adequate food to some 15 percent of its citizens, forcing many to go hungry or to suffer the degradation of eating pet food? We have created a society where even the wealthy can feel economically insecure, where accumulating a fortune today seems essential to assure a minimal existence if misfortune overtakes one in the future. We think ourselves "advanced," but there have been few "primitive" societies where some people had empty stomachs when the group as a whole had abundant food.

The inability of American and global society to come to grips with problems of equality and the distribution of wealth has led to a shocking rise in terrorism, which cannot be condoned, although it is easy to understand. We are reaping what we and our predecessors have sown. As long as our society permits some individuals to have hundreds of millions of dollars while others starve, violent attempts at redistribution seem likely to continue. Such events may be met, nationally and internationally, by increased attempts at repression—in the long run probably doomed to failure—or by attempts to reorganize society so that poverty diminishes greatly while equity increases. We hope the latter course will be taken; we fear the former will be.

What has all this to do with your future? Simply that the government, which has failed to meet even the minimal standard of ensuring that all Americans are well fed at least in times of affluence, is unlikely to perform better when the real crunch comes. Complete polarization of the rich and the poor can only lead to social chaos if there should be an economic breakdown. You could be reduced to the elemental position of defending yourself and your means of survival alone.

The only real hope of lessening the horrors that may follow the inevitable end of growth is the possibility of a miraculous political awakening in the US and throughout the rest of the world. Just perhaps, if much larger numbers of people become informed and involved, the governmental and economic structure could be reformed, the hack politicians and robber barons thrown out of power, and a nation forged that would have a reasonable chance of developing appropriate responses to the coming flood of crises. Twenty million informed activists could do it; ten million might. Social change is virtually never pushed by a majority; but the majority may go along with a knowledgeable and persuasive minority.

The public concern over population growth and destruction of ecosystems generated by environmentalists in the US in the late 1960s and early 1970s is a good example of how a relatively small group can change the awareness and behavior of the majority of people. Birth rates dropped, "ecology" became a word in everyone's vocabulary, and battles were won (or successful delaying actions fought) on many fronts—over clean air and water, the SST, nuclear reactors, the Alaska pipeline, the Highway Trust Fund, offshore drilling, abortion-law reform, bans on importing furs of endangered species and whale meat, and so on.

One area in which your personal efforts to change society are most likely to enhance the quality of your life in the future is your local community. If our predictions are correct, there will be an accelerating trend toward decentralization in the next few decades, and gradually your relationships with your neighbors and your local community will increase in importance while those with federal and (probably) state governments will tend to fade. Indeed, the strength and cohesiveness of your community may be *the* dominant factor in determining whether or not you can successfully ride out a time of troubles.

Of course, you can always wait until troubles arrive before taking action. In New York City during the great power failure, individuals banded together to get food and water to elderly people marooned high in buildings; but such altruistic emergency behavior is unlikely to persist or be very effective in a widespread and lasting crisis. The time for planning for such events with your friends and neighbors is *now,* not at the eleventh hour. If the people in your immediate community (block, apartment house, subdivision, township, or county) are aware of the difficulties they may soon be facing and are making cooperative preparations to meet them, the chances for everyone in the community will be increased. If everyone has stored some food and water against times of shortage, there will be less likelihood of conflict when the shortages materialize. And, perhaps more importantly, if local government is of the highest quality, formal contingency plans and emergency preparations for the community can be devised in advance and implemented promptly when the need arises.

Therefore, we would like to encourage increased citizen attention to and participation in local politics (up to and including the county level). A concerned citizen tends to feel, with some justification, that he or she can have little impact on our national "leaders," who are busy playing golf with their millionaire buddies and zooming around the world negotiating cosmic bungles with dignitaries from other nations. But that same citizen can have dramatic impact at the local level—as has been amply demonstrated by the capture of the Berkeley city government by "radicals" from the community and by the recent winning of various city and county posts around the country by members of minority groups or people normally thought of as "too young" to hold office. Much of the key political action of the future is likely to take place at the local level. If you have never thought of running for local political office, you might start thinking about it now.

Only determined political action at the grassroots level seems to have a real chance of averting social polarization between the rich and the poor. And it seems likely, at least at first, that the ranks of those willing to put in the time and energy will remain thin. Most politicians, economists, scientists, and just-plain-citizens will remain on the sidelines. Others will be summer soldiers, putting in some effort and then fading away—as many did after the ecology fad peaked in 1970. Nevertheless, we cannot give up, if only because the problems will not go away. If the long struggle gets you down, perhaps the vision of glorious (if improbable) victory can sustain you. It may be difficult when you read a statement by someone attacking "doomsayers" and urging complacency because "everything is under control," or when you can't get some friend to help fight the good fight. At such times, we find it soothing to recall the words Shakespeare put in the mouth of Henry V, as the king addressed his men before the decisive battle of Agincourt:

> And gentlemen in England now abed
> Will think themselves accursed they were not here
> And hold their manhoods cheap whiles any speaks
> Who fought with us upon St. Crispin's day.

# 6

# The Most Basic Need

"... industrial man no longer eats potatoes made from solar energy; now he eats potatoes partly made of oil."
—Howard T. Odum, 1971 [1]

In the winter of 1973–74, Americans seemed most worried about the state of their future fuel supply. But we should have been more concerned about the quality, quantity, and price of our future food supplies. People in other parts of the world may face food problems that are more immediate and severe than those we will confront, but Americans will soon be forced to make drastic changes in their eating habits. With some understanding both of the international food situation and of the agricultural system, you can tell what is coming in a general way and put yourself in a position to anticipate more specific trends.

Two essential points should always be kept in mind when considering the system that supplies us with food. First, food is obtained at an inevitable cost to the environment, a cost that is dependent both on the number of people supported by a given area of farmland and on the quality of the diet being consumed. A sparse population subsisting on a mainly vegetarian diet generally makes less of a demand on the environment than either a sparse meat-eating population or a dense vegetarian population.

Second, a huge amount of energy is consumed in order to maintain high levels of agricultural productivity. In general, the more intensive the agriculture, the greater is the energy subsidy and, of course, the greater is the accompanying deterioration of the environment.[2]

Affluent Americans, 80 percent of whom have probably never had to worry about where their next meal was coming from, have largely forgotten the importance and value of food. Even among developed countries, Americans spend the smallest percentage of their incomes for food—an average of 16 percent in 1973. By contrast, people in Japan were spending an average of 31 percent of their incomes on food in 1973, and in Calcutta food took more than 50 percent of a family's income.[3]

Because Americans have long taken food for granted, when food prices began rising rapidly in the US in 1972, the reaction was widespread consternation and then rebellion in the form of abortive meat boycotts. Public concern was reflected in ill-advised attempts by the Nixon administration to control rising food prices—actions that did little to ease the blow to consumers. By inducing shortages, price controls only served to complicate and aggravate the situation.

In 1973, food prices rose nearly 20 percent, while the average disposable income in the US rose only a little over 10 percent. In the first half of 1974, some prices declined at the wholesale level, but consumers found most price changes at the retail level were upward.

## The American Cornucopia

Two myths have long dominated American beliefs about food: (1) that the US is completely self-sufficient in food, and (2) that the US feeds the world. These, like many other myths, contain elements of truth, but much is left out. The US does export more food than it imports, but it still imports a good deal. Consumers are at least vaguely aware of such imported foods as tropical fruits and nuts, vegetables from Mexico, coffee from Colombia and Brazil, Dutch chocolate, French cheese, and Danish ham. These add variety to our diets, but are by no means essential to our health and well-being. Most Americans are unaware, however, that we also import large quantities of fishmeal and oilseed presscakes which are fed to livestock and pets. One factor in the 1973 meat price rise was a severe shortage of fishmeal, due to the near disappearance in 1972 of the anchoveta fishery in Peru, a major source of this important livestock feed.

The US undoubtedly *could become* self-sufficient in food, unless its population grew substantially larger. There would, of course, be a high energy cost and some sacrifice in the variety of foods available, but the nutritional quality of the average diet would remain high. The same cannot be said for very many other nations.

In exports, the US falls far short of "feeding the world," even though it is the world's largest exporter of food. Our food exports are mainly grains and soybeans. In most commodities, our contribution is a very small fraction of world production; for example, in 1971 we exported about 5 percent of the world's total production of wheat.[4] Our shares of the soybean harvest and export market are larger—we exported about 25 percent of world production in 1971—but most of the exported soybeans go to other ODCs.[5] And most of this valuable protein food is fed to livestock, both here and abroad.

Moreover, the vast bulk of our exports are *sold*, not given away. In 1972, the Food for Peace program exported 5 million metric tons of grain, most of which was merely sold at below-market prices, not given away. In 1973, squeezed by grain shortages, the program was severely curtailed—at a time when it was desperately needed. Twelve percent less grain was made available for sale at lower prices than in the previous year, and no allowance was made in the budget for higher grain prices in purchasing for the program. The budget for Title II, the part of the Food for Peace program that does give grain free to the needy, was slashed by 30 percent for fiscal

1974. Growth of the export market for grain is mainly responsible for this change in policy. A decade ago we produced far more grain than we could consume or sell, and Food for Peace absorbed more than ten times as much of our surplus production as was sold abroad. By 1973 the situation had reversed. With a booming world grain market helping our balance-of-payments deficit, the attitude of the US Department of Agriculture was, if wheat can be sold for a high price, why subsidize giveaways? [6]

By 1973, nearly all of the free Food for Peace was being sent to South Vietnam and Cambodia to help fill a food gap the US was largely instrumental in creating. Moreover, those governments sold the food and used the proceeds to finance the continuing war. The starving people of Africa depended mainly on UN and private agencies for relief food; the US participated in that emergency only belatedly and inadequately.

Alarmed by the drops in food production in 1972, the subsequent disappearance of grain reserves, and the apparent drying up of the few programs that distribute free food to the world's hungry, a few world leaders began in 1973 to call for the establishment of a global grain reserve as a hedge against famine.[7] The time was ripe for this idea twenty-five years ago; but better now than never —if it isn't already too late.


## What's Next?


One general prediction can be made with confidence: the cost of feeding yourself and your family will continue to increase. There may be minor fluctuations in food prices, but the overall trend will be up. How much costs will rise depends on many unpredictable events: the weather in many parts of the world, how the international community reacts to food shortages, and whether societies and governments devise humane ways of meeting such shortages. If the international distribution of food continues to be governed purely by short-term economic considerations—if, for example, wheat goes to the highest bidder regardless of need—the poor in the US will be very hungry, and even the middle class will be in for some bad times.

Even if the subtropical monsoons regain the dependability of the last few decades—none too great at that, with an average of two failures in each decade in the Indian subcontinent—and if the 1974 midwestern drought isn't repeated, the inexorable 2 percent annual growth of the world population will continue to strain mankind's food-producing abilities. Even if food production manages to keep pace with population growth for a while, the energy subsidy and environmental costs of agriculture will continue to rise, and food will become more costly for the rich as well as the poor.

On the other hand, if as seems likely, the weather situation deteriorates, chronic shortages of various foodstuffs will become commonplace in ODCs, while famines will spread in UDCs. If the international community organized itself intelligently, fairly, and promptly, the famines in UDCs could be relieved with relatively minor sacrifices by people in ODCs. And if governments of nations planned and regulated their agricultural policies, sudden domestic shortages could be avoided. But these positive statements refer *only to the short term,* perhaps the next decade. Without both planning and organization on the food front *and* a rapid decline in world fertility to below replacement level, the prognosis for 1990 and beyond is completely negative. A massive die-off from starvation will be unavoidable.[8]

If the botching of the US agricultural policy goes on, however, Americans can expect more unpleasant surprises like the one of winter 1974, when they discovered that nearly all of the wheat crop was disappearing on the foreign market, and bread prices were rising accordingly. Fortunately, one of the major buyers on this occasion (the USSR) was willing to delay delivery of some wheat purchases until the new crop was harvested, but such cooperation can hardly be counted on.

The USSR, in engineering its massive grain purchases in

1972, had dealt directly and secretly with several US grain dealers.[9] None of them knew what the others sold, and the government—with the exception of one Assistant Secretary of the Department of Agriculture—did not know how much was sold until the deals had been signed. Moreover, it was all sold at low prices subsidized by the US government. The total cost to taxpayers of subsidized foreign grain sales in 1972 was some $300 million. Curiously enough, history repeated itself the following year, with both the USSR and the People's Republic of China making very large grain purchases (but this time not subsidized by the US government). Altogether, between 70 and 80 percent of the 1973 wheat crop was sold abroad. Some way to monitor foreign sales of essential foodstuffs and to limit such sales if they unduly threaten domestic supplies is a badly needed element of any new agricultural policy.

Recent food and agricultural policies have been mainly a hodgepodge of regulations supposedly aimed at protecting the health of consumers, keeping farmers from bankruptcy, and inhibiting overproduction. Even with these limited goals, success has been mixed. The safety, quality, variety, and abundance of food available to most Americans are undeniable. But the increases in productivity and efficiency (measured in terms of manpower and yield per acre) in our agriculture have been achieved at the cost of huge energy subsidies and the rapid disappearance of the small family farm. The costly subsidies have generally benefited agribusiness tycoons far more than small farmers— one more example of the American system of socialism for the rich and capitalism for the poor. "Overproductivity" appears to be a problem of the past, partly because of an increased population of American consumers (including a higher-than-usual proportion of young adults— the biggest eaters) with expensive tastes and the money to indulge them, and partly because of the increased demand from overseas.

The US Department of Agriculture is gleefully anticipating a continued tight seller's market for the next several years. But even those eternal optimists admit that a brisk international trade in grains is likely to hinder the establishment of a large reserve grain supply, whether a domestic one or an international storehouse, in the near future.

Thus, American consumers can look forward to higher prices both for staples like bread and for meat, poultry, and dairy products, which are indirectly produced by using feedgrains. Continued foreign demand for wheat and feedgrains will force prices still higher (wheat prices at the farm level tripled in less than two years—from 1972 to 1974), and the costs of producing animal foods will rise with them. Even more disturbing, some relatively inexpensive protein substitutes for meat—peas and beans —quadrupled in price within a year. Very good luck with weather, producing record yields over much of the world, could lead to temporary reversals in this pattern of price escalation, but they will certainly be only temporary.

Taking the longer view, how well Americans eat in the future will depend not only on how well the rest of the world manages to meet its food needs, but how intelligently we manage our own food-production system. The trends followed in past years, if continued, could lead us straight to disaster. How well you will eat depends on how well you can adjust to and compensate for scarcities of some foods—whether you can maximize your nutrition as the variety of available food becomes severely restricted.

## Feeding the Affluent American

Although it spends much less of its budget on food, the average American family eats much more sumptuously than a comparable family in almost any other nation, as measured by the amount of high-protein animal food (meat, poultry, fish, eggs, and dairy products) consumed. Indians on the average consume about seven pounds of meat per person per year, the Japanese about twenty-five

FIGURE 3.     **WORLD MEAT CONSUMPTION**

Related to Income and Population*

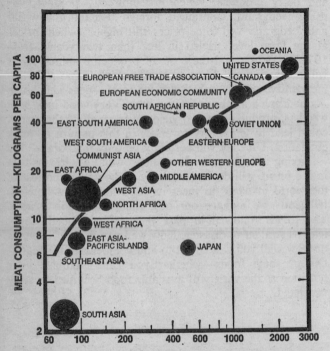

Real Per Capita Gross Domestic Product—U.S. Dollar Equivalent

*The areas of circles are proportional to population*

REDRAWN FROM U.S. DEPARTMENT OF AGRICULTURE

pounds per person (Japanese consumption of meat has risen rapidly in recent years), and Americans nearly two hundred pounds each. Figure 3 shows the level of meat consumption in various parts of the world and its relationship to income.

American grain consumption reflects our rich diet—it is over four times as high per person as the grain consumption of people in UDCs. However, more than 80 percent of our grain is first fed to the animals from which we get our meat, poultry, eggs, and dairy products. Most of this grain is thus lost to human nutrition. Figure 4 shows the disparity in grain consumption among nations. The difference between total grain consumption (circles) and direct grain consumption (squares) for each country is what is fed to livestock.

With American livestock-feeding methods, it takes about three pounds of grain to produce one pound of poultry, five pounds of grain for one of pork, and ten for one of beef.[10] The ratio of *protein loss* is even more startling. As much as twenty-one pounds of protein in animal feed are needed to produce one pound of beef or veal protein, eight pounds for a pound of pork protein, and a range of three to six for poultry, milk, and eggs.

Looked at another way, the grains and high-protein supplements (soybeans, oilseed presscakes, and fishmeal) now fed to American cattle, pigs, and poultry would go a long way to alleviate hunger among people around the world. It has been estimated that the protein alone would make up 90 percent of the world's protein deficit.[11]

The shame of all this is that so much of it is unnecessary. American agriculture, while being gloriously productive, is also incredibly wasteful. Among livestock, only swine are necessarily competitive with people for the same food. Cattle and sheep can be raised on forage unsuitable for human consumption grown on land unsuitable for human crops. These animals have been shown to be capable of manufacturing protein for themselves from a diet of urea, starch, ammonium salts, sucrose, and cellulose.[12] Very adequate meat can be produced with very small supplements of grain.

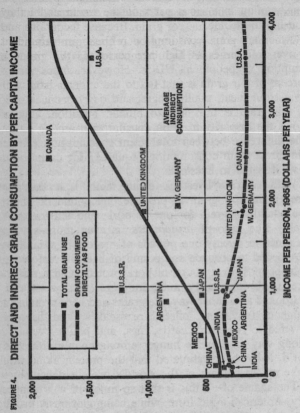

FIGURE 4.    DIRECT AND INDIRECT GRAIN CONSUMPTION BY PER CAPITA INCOME

POUNDS OF GAIN PER PERSON PER YEAR

Source: "Population and Affluence: Growing Pressures on Food Resources" by Lester Brown, *Population Bulletin*, 1973. Based on data from Food and Agricultural Organization, *Food Balance Sheets, 1964-66 Average.*

Like other economic activities, however, agricultural ventures are run to make profits. The meat, dairy, and poultry businesses have developed to maximize profits, not to maximize the efficient use of valuable resources, be they soil, water, fertilizer, fuel, or grain. Because feedgrains and protein supplements have long been cheap and abundant in the US, our steers are fed the mixture that will produce the heaviest animals in the shortest time. The result is an excessively fat, but tender and tasty, meat. The carcass of an American grain-fed steer is one-fifth fat, a pig is one-fourth fat, and a lamb one-third fat. Small wonder so many Americans die of cardiovascular disease!

Livestock production could clearly be conducted far more efficiently, in the sense of competing much less with human beings for food, and the current increases in grain prices may help to bring that about. If grain finishing (fattening of cattle before market on feedgrain) becomes more expensive than keeping cattle in pasture for longer periods, stockmen will change their methods. The trend could be encouraged if rents for grazing land were kept relatively low (perhaps through subsidies or tax discounts) and if the marketing system encouraged leaner meat, which is also preferable from the standpoint of human health. While many Americans would prefer leaner beef, present grading standards are based directly on proportions of fat.

If the grading system were changed so that it was based on tenderness rather than fat proportions, cattlemen might thereby be encouraged to raise leaner, more tender breeds of cattle—like those preferred in Europe. European breeds require far less grain finishing. Another alternative is the "beefalo"—a recent successful cross between cattle and buffalo that reputedly is a far more efficient animal to raise and has flavorful, tender meat. You as a consumer can encourage such changes by expressing an interest in these new meats to your butcher (European beef is being marketed in Denver and beefalo in Los Angeles) and by writing to the Federal Food and Drug Agency in support of changing meat-grading standards.

Some moves in this direction were initiated in late summer 1972, when it was announced that beef grading standards were being slightly lowered. A little earlier a plan for marketing "baby beef," i.e., young animals that had been only grass fed, not grain finished, was put forward. The motive was to relieve stockmen caught by the grain shortage, but if the product finds a market, the American public could benefit by having cheaper meat and the world would benefit by having access to more grain.

Since well over one-third of the continental US land area is already used for grazing (now you know one thing "all that empty space" is doing for you),[18] there is clearly a limit to how far we can reverse present livestock-feeding practices without a risk of overgrazing. *The ultimate answer must be a reduction in American consumption of meat*—especially beef, which with present rearing methods represents by far the least efficient conversion of plant food to meat.

If grain finishing of beef and pork were significantly reduced, what would we do with all that corn? Assuming that midwestern droughts don't drastically reduce production, there could be an increase in the use of corn domestically for human consumption. Also, foreign demand for corn is likely to rise. In dryer parts of the corn belt, wheat could replace corn. We could also increase our crop of soybeans, a high-protein crop that could be invaluable for improving the diets of hungry people everywhere, and one for which the foreign market is growing. Even in the US, as meat prices rise, soy protein is becoming increasingly popular as a nutritious supplement to stretch ground beef.

## The Energy Subsidy

American agriculture not only wastes food resources, it is a gluttonous consumer of fossil fuels and is becoming increasingly dependent on them. Furthermore, most other agricultural systems in the world are eagerly striving to imitate ours—hardly the most prudent course as fuel reserves are being depleted. Of the gigantic amount of energy that the US consumes, some 12 to 13 percent is devoted to putting food on our tables. This sounds modest enough, until one learns that *six to nine times* more calories are used to cultivate and fertilize the land, grow the food, transport it, process it, retail it, and cook it than your body derives from it.[14] Table 3 shows a simplified

## TABLE 3

### US Food Energy Budget, 1963

| Activity | Percent of Energy Consumed |
|---|---|
| Agriculture | 18.3 |
| Food Processing | 32.9 |
| Transportation | 2.4 |
| Wholesale and Retail Trade | 15.9 |
| Home (storage, cooking) | 30.5 |
| | 100.0 |

Source: Eric Hirst, *Natural History*

breakdown of where the energy is used between the farm and the dinner table.

A detailed study has been made of the energy used in corn production.[15] Corn was chosen because it occupies the middle range of energy consumption for crops—it requires less energy to produce than fruits and some vegetables, and more than some other grains such as wheat. It should be pointed out that nearly all corn in this country is used as livestock feed, which is one reason the energy subsidy of American meat production is so high. Since 1945, corn yields per acre have risen 240 percent, while labor inputs declined over 60 percent. But while the energy subsidy (in fertilizer, tractor fuel, etc.) more than tripled, the caloric return (calories derived/calories put in) declined from 3.70-to-1 to 2.82-to-1. Much of the increase in yield is undoubtedy due to the energy

subsidy, but much could be done to reduce the subsidy
without loss in productivity, as we shall see later.

Taking a longer view, it is quite evident that we cannot
continue to play this game indefinitely, and we certainly
cannot extend it throughout the world. The energy inten-
siveness of various agricultural systems has been analyzed
relative to the density and size of populations they feed
and the amount of land available.[16] The results were extrap-
olated to determine how much energy would be required
to feed 13 billion people (the projected size of the world
population by 2040 if present growth rates continue) at the
western European standard. This standard offers somewhat less meat than Americans are accustomed to, but it is
still a more than adequate diet, and also uses much less
energy. Nevertheless, in both respects it is far above prevailing levels in the underdeveloped world.

Given 13 billion people to be supported by the world's
available land (assuming productivity can be maintained),
producing the equivalent of a western European diet would
require each year *as much energy as the entire world now
uses for all purposes*. This estimate, moreover, includes
only the energy for food *production;* it does not include
the amounts required to make farm equipment, or to transport, distribute, store, or cook the food. Also, the probable
horrendous ecological impact of such an enterprise was not
assessed, although it would obviously be horrendous. Indeed, the collective environmental repercussions would
no doubt bring the project to a halt long before the number of hungry mouths reached 13 billion.


## Streamlining the System


During the energy mini-crisis, the Nixon administration guaranteed American farmers all the fuel and electricity they needed—and rightly so, since shortages would
result in large-scale waste of food. Nevertheless, there is
room in our agricultural system for considerable energy

savings without loss of productivity.[17] Interestingly enough, many of the shifts would have beneficial consequences for the environment beyond reducing the direct impact of energy use.

One agricultural practice that requires large amounts of energy is the use of synthetic fertilizers. For instance, in corn production, nitrogen fertilizer is the greatest single item of energy input. Not only does fertilizer require energy in its manufacture, but nitrogen fertilizer is made with natural gas, which, like petroleum, is in short supply. It is thus not surprising that the energy shortage has been accompanied by a shortage of fertilizer, although the shortage was also partly caused by economic factors.

Yet a superior natural fertilizer exists in abundance—the sewage from livestock feedlots, most of which is simply dumped into our rivers, causing enormous water pollution problems. In addition, there is human sewage, which has long been used as fertilizer in Europe, China, and elsewhere.[18] Until now, it has been considered cheaper to manufacture and distribute synthetic fertilizer than to collect, treat, and distribute feedlot sewage; while human sewage has generally been considered by Americans as too unsanitary and requiring too much expensive treatment. (Of course, the cost of cleaning up our rivers, lakes, and bays was never included in the calculations.) As energy becomes even scarcer and more costly, so will fertilizers. The fertilizer shortage is already a calamity for UDCs (and they have no feedlot resources), but it might push Americans into more ecologically sound practices.[19]

Other substitutes for synthetic fertilizers are to rotate crops, or to plant legumes such as clover or winter vetch alternately (i.e., in fall) with a grain crop. Legumes enrich the soil, especially with nitrogen, and as cover crops they help protect the soil against erosion. They would also reduce plant-disease problems in the grain crop and the needs for herbicides, which are also manufactured from petroleum. And finally, legumes are excellent forage crops for livestock.

Much farmwork now done by machine—planting, cultivating, harvesting, pest-control operations—could be done by hand. This would increase the need for farm labor, which might not be a bad idea when unemployment is high and rising. (It is unlikely, however, that competent workers will be attracted to farms unless social justice and decent wages for farm labor can be provided.)

Further energy savings could be made by adopting such ecologically sound strategies as substituting biological and integrated pest control for chemical pesticides, and breeding for crop strains with greater resistance to pests and disease (though this will always be a running battle as the pests evolve means to penetrate the plant's defenses).[20] Breeding strains with lower moisture content could reduce the energy demand for drying.

A form of "free" energy especially suitable for use on the farm is wind power. In recent years, the efficiency of windmill designs has been greatly improved. Some are now in use in Australia; smaller-scale versions are being tried out in a few UDCs. Windmills could conveniently supply power for irrigation and to meet the electrical needs of the farmer. If electric vehicles were used, windmills could also be used to recharge the batteries.

So far we have discussed only how to reduce energy consumption on the farm, but actual production of food accounts for less than 20 percent of the US food energy budget (Table 3). The largest single chunk of the budget —nearly a third—is devoted to food processing. On the average, processed foods use three times as much energy as fresh foods (they are also often more expensive). The food-processing industry is the fourth largest energy-consuming industry in the nation, following primary metals, chemicals, and petroleum refining.[21] There are many degrees of processing, ranging from pasteurization of milk, which is essential for health reasons, to elaborate frozen TV dinners, in which nutritive value and flavor are sacrificed for convenience.

Like other high-energy industries, the huge food processors will soon be feeling the squeeze from the growing scarcity and costs of energy. Their increased costs, of course, will be passed along to consumers. If the captains of this industry are wise, they will begin to phase out the most energy-consuming items in their lines. But even if they don't, consumers are not required to buy them. We can expect that either processed food prices will become outlandish or quality will decline as processors try to reduce their costs. Either way, they'll lose customers.

Another big slice of the food-energy budget is consumed at the wholesale–retail level. Here also a lot of energy is wasted—one of the most obvious being the acres of open freezer and refrigerator cases found in every supermarket, and also the heat needed in the store to counteract all that refrigeration. You as a consumer could try to persuade your supermarket manager to keep his freezer and refrigerator cases closed. It's not that much trouble to open a case for milk or ice cream. At the very least, the cases could be closed when the market is closed. Eventually, rising power costs may force him to do it.

The last big opportunity for saving energy comes between the store and your table—and a big part of that is each householder's weekly or biweekly trip to the supermarket. A way to cut back here is for neighbors who shop in the same stores to form car pools. If you live close enough to your market, you might consider walking with a shopping cart. Also, it's good exercise. Or you might try a three-wheeled bicycle, which can carry quite a lot of groceries.

Perhaps the best solution would be to revive grocery-store delivery services. You could suggest it to your supermarket manager, perhaps with a petition signed by those of your neighbors willing to join you. Finding neighbors who would appreciate such a service might be easier than you think.

There are numerous ways, which have been well publicized elsewhere, to reduce food-related energy use at home. Here are some of them:

Don't buy an electric stove or oven if you can avoid it; get gas appliances.
If you buy a freezer, get one that opens at the top.
Keep your refrigerator and freezer reasonably full.

Open the refrigerator door as briefly and infrequently as possible.

Don't preheat your oven, especially for long-cooking roasts, and don't peek in.

Defrost before cooking.

Don't boil a gallon of water for one cup of coffee.

Use a pressure cooker if you have one.

Fit the pan to the burner.

Don't use the self-clean device if your oven has one.

Use a charcoal broiler (if the air isn't polluted).

Minimize your use of overprocessed foods.

Eat cold meals when feasible.

Don't run the dishwasher unless it is full.

Turn off the dishwasher during dry cycle; open it and let the dishes air-dry.

Voluntarily doing such things will save you money and will conserve some energy for society. But much more energy could be saved if, for instance, the extremely wasteful practice of installing electric stoves, ovens, and heaters in new homes could be made illegal—at least until the end of the fossil-fuel era. Similarly, open freezers in grocery stores could be legislated out of existence. Here, as in other areas, however, it is often difficult or impossible for individuals to behave in an environmentally sound manner because the necessary political leadership and legislative actions have not been taken, and the economic system operates against it.

## Maximizing Your Nutrition

As food costs escalate and shortages become commonplace, maintaining a well-balanced, nutritious diet will become increasingly difficult. At the same time, as life in general becomes more difficult and stressful, you will need more than ever to be well nourished in order to stay healthy and able to cope.

Many Americans are surprisingly poorly nourished, considering the variety of food available and their ability to afford it. This is a nation of snackers and soft-drink guzzlers—and frantic dieters. It's amazing how many people can be seen at lunch counters eating a piece of apple pie and a cup of coffee, thinking that this is a "lunch," or breakfasting on coffee and danish pastry. What's worse, many of them think they're dieting because they're eating only four hundred calories. Indeed they are, and very little else!

A few years ago, a Public Health Service survey revealed a shocking level of malnutrition among Americans, largely among the very poor, but also to a surprising extent among middle-class people who could easily afford plenty of good food.[22] Protein deficiencies were found to be very common, especially among children of very poor families; iron-deficiency anemia was found in one-third of the young children examined in a low-income area; vitamin A deficiency was found in one-third of people of all ages; and even widespread goiter—easily preventable by using iodized salt—was found in many areas. The nutritional deficiencies in the nonpoor families could have occurred only because the people either were ignorant of basic nutritional needs or didn't care.

The teaching of nutrition in schools is usually sketchy at best, limited to telling children they should eat food from each of the "four basic food groups" every day. (Unfortunately, nutritional training in most medical schools is not much better.) How these food groups are related to the children's nutritional needs is poorly explained at best. Small wonder they grow up thinking soft drinks and potato chips are good for them!

Everyone should become familiar with the various kinds of essential nutrients and in which foods they can be found. Essential nutrients fall into five categories: proteins, carbohydrates, fats, vitamins, and minerals.[23]

**Protein.** Protein is essential for life and health. Your body is largely made of protein and water; to keep it healthy, you must have a substantial amount of protein every day—about one gram for every kilogram of body weight for adults. Growing children and pregnant or nursing mothers need even more. Translated into everyday terms, this means that an average-sized man (160 lbs.) should have about as much protein as there is in eleven ounces of steak each day, and an average woman (125 lbs.) needs the equivalent of about eight ounces of steak (unless she is pregnant or nursing, in which case she needs the equivalent of another three to six ounces of steak). However, a 30-pound child needs more than half as much total protein as its mother does. For maximum benefit, a portion should be consumed with each meal. These estimates, of course, are averages. The quality of the protein affects how much an individual needs; much more low-quality protein must be consumed in order to ensure that protein needs are fully met. Moreover, there are wide differences among individuals in their needs for various nutrients. Some people just seem to utilize any given nutrient more efficiently than others do.[24]

Protein is found in virtually all foods (except heavily refined ones like sugar and cornstarch), but both the quality and quantity vary from very high to very low. Most people know that rich sources of protein are animal foods: meat, poultry, fish, eggs, and dairy products. But they may not know that many plant foods also contain quite a lot—although of lower quality. Among these are pulses (peas, beans, lentils), nuts, and grains. By judiciously combining plant foods so that they compensate for each other's protein deficiencies, one can still enjoy a high-protein diet while eating much less meat and spending much less money too.

Protein is made of building blocks called amino acids. Human beings can manufacture many amino acids, but eight amino acids cannot be synthesized by the body and hence must be obtained from food. High-quality or complete protein is protein containing all eight essential amino acids *in approximately the right balance* for meeting human needs. The highest-quality protein—that having the closest to ideal balance for human beings—is found in eggs, which have a net protein utilization (NPU) of 94. This means that 94 percent of the egg protein can be digested and used as protein in the human body. Left-over amino acids—those not matched by other essential amino acids in the right proportions, or simply not needed as protein—are broken down and used as fuel, as are carbohydrates (see below). Table 4 shows the NPUs of various common foods.

## TABLE 4

### Net Protein Utilization of Common Foods

| Food | NPU |
|------|-----|
| Eggs | 94 |
| Milk | 82 |
| Fish | 80 |
| Cottage cheese | 75 |
| Cheese | 70 |
| Rice | 70 |
| Meat and poultry | 67 |
| Soybeans | 61 |
| Wheat | 60 |
| Cashews | 58 |
| Lima beans | 52 |
| Corn | 51 |
| Walnuts | 50 |
| Peas | 47 |
| Peanuts | 43 |
| Kidney beans | 38 |
| Lentils | 30 |

Source: Lappé, *Diet for a Small Planet*

As you can see, the real protein value—NPU—of meat is not especially high, and those of many plant foods are not far below. Compensating amino acids, however, is less complicated than it might seem, once the basic patterns are understood.[25] Many societies have practiced some form of protein complementation in their traditional dishes. One of the best patterns is to combine a pulse (pea or bean) with a grain—thus long-popular and familiar American meals include Boston baked beans with brown bread, or hominy grits and black-eyed peas. Another example is succotash (corn and lima beans), originally an Indian dish and now usually considered only a side-dish. Tortillas and beans are the universal staple among the poor in Latin America. Many other combinations are commonly used by other cultures: the Chinese and Japanese supplement rice with soy products, beansprouts, and snowpeas; in India and the Middle East, wheat bread is combined with chickpeas or lentils; and so on. Of course, the people in those societies also add small amounts of fish, poultry, eggs, or yogurt to these staples, but their consumption of animal protein is very low by American or European standards.

High-quality animal protein or fully complemented plant protein is also known as "complete protein." To equal the complete protein of a nine-ounce steak, you need to eat ten ounces of fish, or six cups of milk, or seven eggs, or fifteen and a third ounces of dry beans, or fourteen and a third ounces of nuts. In calories, of course, these foods are very different. The fish and skim milk would give fewer calories per unit of protein than a lean steak, while eggs would be about the same, and whole milk, beans (except soy), and nuts would provide more, in that order.

## TABLE 5

Food Combinations to Improve Protein Quality

| Food | Complements |
|---|---|
| Pulses (dried peas, beans, lentils) | Rice Wheat Corn meal Soybeans Milk or cheese Nuts and seeds |
| Nuts and seeds | Soybeans Pulses Milk or cheese Seafood Poultry Meat |

| Grains and Cereals | Milk or cheese |
| | Yeast |
| | Pulses |
| | Wheat germ |
| | Eggs |
| | Poultry and meat |
| Lima beans, green peas, green vegetables | Sesame seed |
| | Brazil nuts |
| | Converted rice |

Source: Lappé

Table 5 shows how the protein of different types of plant food can be raised to high-quality standards by combining with other foods in the same meal. Table 6 shows

# TABLE 6

Protein Equivalent of Combinations to Steak

| Combination in best proportions | Steak protein equivalent |
|---|---|
| 2 cups rice + ¾ cup peas or beans | = 9.50 oz. |
| 2½ cups rice + ¼ cup soybeans | = 9.25 oz. |
| 1½ cups rice + 2 cups skim milk | = 7.75 oz. |
| 1½ cups rice + 2½ oz. cheese | = 7.75 oz. |
| 4 slices whole wheat bread + 1 oz. cheese | = 2.50 oz. |
| 1 cup whole wheat flour + 1 tbsp. nonfat dry milk | = 3.00 oz. |
| 1½ cups whole wheat flour + ¼ cup beans | = 4.60 oz. |
| 1 cup whole wheat flour + ¼ cup soy flour | = 4.10 oz. |
| 6–7 cornmeal tortillas + ¼ cup beans | = 2.60 oz. |
| ½ cup nonfat dry milk + 1 cup beans | = 8.33 oz. |
| ⅓ cup peanut butter + ½ cup skim milk + 6 slices whole wheat bread | = 10.10 oz. |

Source: Lappé

the protein equivalence in terms of steak that can be achieved by various combinations of plant foods with each other or with milk. With a little ingenuity, a family's protein consumption can be maintained or improved, even as grocery costs are reduced. Many of the foods involved, such as pulses, nuts, seeds, flour, rice, and dry milk, have the added advantage of being easy to store for fairly long periods of time. Frances Lappé's superb book, *Diet for a Small Planet* [26] is invaluable for those who wish to be prepared to maintain a healthy pattern of protein consumption as the food situation grows tighter. Her recipes can help you maintain a high protein diet at a minimum cost.

**Carbohydrates.** Along with fats, carbohydrates (sugars and starches) principally provide fuel for your body. They are found in abundance in most plant foods, but among animal foods they occur in large quantities only in milk. Carbohydrates are unlikely to be lacking in anyone's diet, except in cases of outright starvation. On the other hand, Americans often consume too many carbohydrates through foods loaded with refined sugars and flours at the expense of other nutrients such as protein, vitamins, and minerals. Money spent on soft drinks, doughnuts, potato chips, candy, most cookies and cakes, and the like is, nutritionally speaking, largely money down the drain. If your food budget is limited, you should avoid such junk foods like the plague.

Sugar and starch are both carbohydrates. Sugar is, of course, available in more or less pure form in sugar and syrups. It is also found in fruits, berries, milk, and foods made from them. Starch is most abundant in such vegetables as potatoes and yams and in grains and bakery products. There is also quite a bit of starch in pulses, nuts, and seeds.

**Fats.** Besides being a major source of energy, used directly or stored, some of the constituents of fat—fatty acids—are essential for metabolic processes. Three fatty acids cannot be manufactured in the human body and must be provided in the diet. These fatty acids are present in vegetable oils—safflower, soy, corn, cottonseed, etc.— but are poorly provided by animal fats. Americans consume a high proportion of their calories as fats. Yet so much of this is animal fat that they may still be deficient in the essential fatty acids.

An even more serious consequence of a diet high in animal fat appears to be the association with cardiovascular diseases—heart disease, stroke, thromboembolism, high blood pressure, etc. Although the relationship is not a simple one, and a variety of nutritional and other factors are involved, it seems that eating the high proportions of cholestrol and the saturated fats found in red meat, milk, eggs, coconut oil, and hydrogenated vegetable oils may encourage the development of cardiovascular disease. The fats in fish, poultry, some nuts, and olive oil are less saturated and apparently have no effect on levels of fat or cholesterol in the blood (high levels are associated with cardiovascular disease). The unsaturated fats—vegetable oils—appear to be positively beneficial if vitamin and mineral intake is also adequate.[27]

Here is yet another argument in favor of reducing your consumption of beef, lamb, and pork—especially of the fattier cuts. At the same time, obtaining polyunsaturated vegetable oil daily is essential, preferably in salad dressings. Oils can and should also be used in cooking, but some of their value may be lost if they are heated for long. For that reason, cooking oil or fat should never be reused. Unsaturated vegetable oils and their valuable constituents are also available in whole grains, nuts, and seeds. Hydrogenated oils (margarine, hydrogenated peanut butter) should be avoided because the hydrogenation process raises their saturation level and reduces their value as weapons against cardiovascular disease.

**Vitamins.** There are two basic kinds of vitamins: water-soluble and fat-soluble. The water-soluble vitamins include vitamin C and the B-complex of some fifteen vitamins, which are relatively fragile and may be lost or destroyed through exposure to heat, evaporation, or soaking in water. These vitamins also cannot be stored in the body for more than a few days. To preserve these fragile vitamins, fruits and vegetables should be cooked—if at all —only briefly and in minimal amounts of water. The cooking method for vegetables that best preserves vitamins is the quick stir-fry technique of oriental cooks, a method that also conserves energy.

Vitamin C is found mostly in fruits, especially citrus fruits, berries, and melons, and in tomatoes and green vegetables, particularly peppers. The entire B-complex is found in liver, yeast, and whole grains. Some of the B vitamins are also found in other organ meats, green leafy vegetables, eggs, milk, molasses, and nuts. Because these vitamins act in concert with one another, it is important to obtain all of them every day in the correct proportions. If one is lacking, the others may not be usable, even though provided.

Early in this century, when wheat, corn, and rice were first refined, deficiency diseases such as pellagra and beri-beri appeared. Even today, Americans eat a great deal of "enriched" bread, to which small amounts of a few vitamins and minerals have been added to replace the twenty-five or so nutrients milled out. Such "enrichment" is like "enriching" a bank by stealing $10,000 from it and returning $100! Although "enrichment" makes these extreme deficiency diseases rare in the US, many Americans may still fall far short of obtaining optimal quantities of all the B vitamins.

The fat-soluble vitamins—vitamins A, D, E, and K—are less likely to be destroyed or lost in cooking or storage than are water-soluble ones. They are also stored well in the body. Because they are stored even in excess amounts, not excreted as are the water-soluble vitamins, vitamins A and D have been shown to be toxic in very high dosages. No toxicity has been demonstrated for vitamins E and K, however. All these vitamins must be consumed with fat or oil to ensure their absorption.

Vitamin A is found in eggs, milk and milkfat products such as butter, cheeses, sour cream and ice cream, and in green and yellow vegetables and fruits. Vitamin D is the sunshine vitamin. If you live in a cold climate where your skin is not exposed to direct sunlight during long periods, you and your children should be sure to eat foods fortified with vitamin D or to take cod-liver oil. Vitamin E is found in vegetable oils, but it can be destroyed by over-refining or overheating. Vitamin K is normally manufactured by intestinal bacteria and is also widely available in foods; deficiencies therefore are very rare.

In general, the more refined and/or processed a food is, the more vitamins have been lost along the way. Thus, to be sure that you and your family have all the vitamins you need, try to use fresh foods as much as possible and minimize your use of refined and processed foods. When processed foods must be resorted to, remember that fresh-frozen, uncooked, or freeze-dried foods have probably suffered the least abuse. Pre-cooked combination frozen foods and canned combinations have probably lost the most food value.

Avoid packages with large amounts of preservatives. Not only do preservatives sometimes destroy nutrients, their safety is in many cases far from well established. This is particularly true for nitrates and nitrites, which are commonly used in bacon, sausages, ham, and hot dogs. Moreover, any food that needs a lot of preservatives to maintain a semblance of freshness has probably already lost much of its nutritional value. Similar warnings apply to foods loaded with colorings, emulsifiers, artificial flavorings, and the like. Recent research indicates that food additives may be a major cause of hyperactivity in children. If your children seem overactive, it might be wise to eliminate all foods with additives from their diets. The "tests" that are alleged to protect you from long-term consequences of consuming these materials are hopelessly inadequate, even when carried out honestly—and they sometimes haven't been.[28]

**Minerals.** Some seventeen minerals are essential nutrients. Even in the varied diets of Americans, some of these are often enough lacking to warrant discussion.

Calcium is abundantly found only in milk and milk products, less so in green leafy vegetables and in hard water. Since it is needed in large amounts by mothers and growing children and in smaller amounts by all adults, the consequences of not consuming milk (or an adequate substitute like yogurt or cheese) are serious.

Iron deficiency is distressingly common among Americans, especially teenage girls, whose needs for iron are high. Iron is readily available, however, in liver and other variety meats, meat, beans, molasses, oysters, apricots, and green leafy vegetables.

Iodine is often lacking in the diets of people who live far inland, leading to goiter. It can be easily obtained in iodized salt and is also available in seafood of all kinds.

Most other minerals are unlikely to be lacking in the diet of anyone eating reasonably well-balanced meals. Just as with vitamins, it is wise to avoid overprocessed and overrefined foods as a general principle. Unlike vitamins, minerals are not lost or destroyed by cooking or storage, although they may (along with vitamins) be poured down the drain with cooking water.

The field of nutrition has been fraught with controversy in recent years, owing to the incompleteness of nutritional knowledge and the prevailing ignorance of both the public at large and the medical profession of what *is* known about nutrition. Thus large segments of the public, rightly believing that what they eat has a direct influence on their health, are ripe to accept fraudulent, misleading, or unsubstantiated information on nutrition. The tragedy is that such misinformation comes to them both from the conservative food industry and the trained nutritionists it employs, and from far-out, untrained health-food nuts.[29]

When supposedly respectable professionals defend the commercial cereal industry by saying that cornflakes with milk is a very nutritious dish (virtually *anything* with milk is a nutritious dish), it is no wonder the public is misled. Those who have long functioned as paid consultants to the food industry tend to have a vested interest in it—"experts" who represent the food industry tend to be of the same breed as "experts" who testify to the great safety of nuclear reactors for power companies.

A few years ago, Dr. Roger J. Williams[30] presented his findings that young rats quickly died on a diet of commercially "enriched" white bread, while they remained healthy indefinitely eating bread enriched with all known vitamins and minerals. Far from expressing interest in similarly enriching their own products, the food industry attacked Williams on the grounds that rat nutrition is different from human nutrition and that people don't subsist entirely on bread, anyway. With some exceptions, food processors are much more interested in the health of their balance-sheets than that of their customers.

The other extreme of the controversy is equally appalling. Here one finds similar exploitation of consumers and sometimes semi-religious zeal in promoting "health" diets that are downright dangerous. Perhaps the most extreme case of the latter is the Zen macrobiotic diet favored in recent years by some hippies.[31] The advanced level of the diet is hopelessly inadequate for adults; for infants and children it is a disaster. By late 1972, as least one death was attributed to the diet, and a great many cases of advanced malnutrition had been reported, and many of them were infants and children. The parents of the malnourished children were not even feeding them milk! Even with dietary improvement, these children may never completely recover from their early deprivation. The tragedy is that it is preventable. No one with even a rudimentary understanding of nutrition would accept the diet in the first place, let alone inflict it on a baby.

Less obviously harmful are the many food faddists who mislead the public into thinking certain foods or vitamins can cure diseases or restore their youthful vigor. Many of these people profit from the gullibility of the public. Thousands of people, many of whom can ill afford it, waste money needlessly on special vitamin preparations, or overpriced health foods. Worse, others try to cure medical problems this way instead of consulting a physician. Nevertheless, there are many honest and reasonably well-informed health-food store operators who are concerned about health and are trying to provide a useful service. Where else can a consumer find noninstant powdered milk, soy flour, whole unmilled grains, or cold-pressed vegetable oils without preservatives? Not in your local supermarket!

The problem is to sort out the honest health-food dealers from the unscrupulous exploiters. For this, the only defense is knowledge, plus a healthy skepticism for anything that sounds like a far-fetched claim. Nutrition can do a lot of good for you, but the benefit lies more in prevention than cure (except, of course, for deficiency diseases). All the protein, vitamins, and minerals in the world won't cure cancer—or bunions. But improving your diet might very well make you feel more energetic and give you extra stamina and resistance to disease.

Above all, some basic knowledge of nutrition will aid you greatly in optimizing your diet during the coming times of food shortage. If there is an economic collapse, the food system, which is an integral part of the economic system, will collapse with it. In the next chapter we will discuss some other ways to ensure that you can continue to eat reasonably well—including storage of emergency supplies—even if our society breaks down completely.

# 7

# A Brighter Future:
# It's Up to You

"The cog in the big machine can look forward to nothing but spinning in place and wearing out."

—Ludwig von Spengenberg, 1926 [1]

"He who reforms himself has done more towards reforming the public than a crowd of noisy, impotent patriots."

—J. Lavater [2]

So AMERICA'S ECONOMIC joyride is coming to an end: there will be no more cheap, abundant energy, no more cheap, abundant food, and soon the flow of cheap consumer goods will suffer increasing disruption and rising prices. Thus far, spoiled Americans have met each new piece of bad news with disbelief and sometimes outrage. There has been a lot of talk about "who is to blame," and some groups have taken the position that they have been singled out for unfair treatment (for example, independent truckers during the 1973–74 energy mini-crisis, who were caught in a squeeze between price controls and rising fuel costs). The charges and countercharges have filled the air, clogged the media, and done nothing at all to hasten an adjustment of Americans (or Europeans, or Japanese, or citizens of UDCs, most of whom are worse off than we are) to new ways of life. The overall assumption has been that each scarcity is temporary—witness the rapid move back toward large automobiles, the pressure to raise speed limits from an energy- (and life-) saving 55 mph, and the desertion of mass transit that characterized the return of abundant gasoline supplies in Spring, 1974.[3]

There is bound to be a period of transition as Americans come to realize that the changes are permanent and alter their expectations and goals to fit new limitations. This must happen at all levels, from the family to the business corporation to the federal government. If we fail to make the transition in a spirit of cooperation and enterprise— meeting the challenges together—the result will be a spiral of ever-deepening economic and social chaos.

Given the rather dismal future that we have depicted, what can you do to help make things better for yourself and your fellow citizens? And what can you do to protect yourself and your family against hard times that cannot be avoided? Fortunately, most of the things you can do to help push American society toward making the right changes will also benefit you directly. What you do to protect yourself will benefit society only indirectly in the sense that it will foster feelings of independence. If you have confidence in your ability to look after yourself, you will be less inclined to run to the nearest government agency for help whenever things go wrong. When everyone depends on some authority to solve every problem, the problems don't get solved; usually they just get worse.

Energy consumption is a major key to the profligate American life, pervading nearly every aspect of it. Some of the most profound changes must therefore occur in the area of energy use and conservation. Citizens like you and ourselves can either help or hinder the process. But if you have a coherent view of where society can and should go, it will be much easier for you to cope with what's coming and to enlist the cooperation of others.

### Energy and the Future

The future would be much rosier if all Americans understood that energy limitations and costs must henceforth be taken into account in all decision-making, public and private. For example, about 18 percent of the nation's energy budget goes for space heating, while transportation of people and goods uses some 25 percent of it.[4] Significant amounts of energy could be conserved by making changes in the way our homes and offices are heated and cooled, in our modes of transportation, and in industrial processes. In the latter case, not only could the efficiency of the processes themselves (such as the production of steel) be improved, but they could be integrated with recycling programs, which would result in still further energy savings.

There is, however, little sign of such a happy trend so far. The conservation measures taken to meet the energy mini-crisis were generally regarded as temporary emergency steps, and some of them probably will be abandoned if petroleum supplies remain adequate at post-mini-crisis prices. But abandonment of conservation measures would be a serious mistake. If we persist in wasting energy in the same old way, we will sooner or later be faced with frequent unpredictable blackouts and brownouts, the continual need to devise more "emergency" measures, and the return of closed gas stations and long gas lines. Eventually the nation would go bankrupt.

But if we made *permanent changes* in the system, perhaps we could have a reasonable level of energy consumption in perpetuity. Over the next decade or two, Americans should try to cut their per capita energy consumption *in half*. This effort lies at the heart of any solution to national and world scarcity problems. Such a reduction, however, would require far more than such half-hearted measures as lower speed limits and reduced commercial lighting, although these help. Nothing less than a reorganization of the American way of life is required.

One of the arguments raised against making basic changes is that they would cause unemployment. This is true, but they also can lead to the creation of new jobs and even new businesses. The level of unemployment will be far higher if changes are forced on society by events, rather than planned in anticipation of the need for them. Detroit, for example, had at least four or five years' warning that energy supplies were getting short and a decade's warning that air pollution was getting serious. A partial answer to both problems would have been vigorous promotion of smaller, more efficient cars. Yet no serious attempt was made either to make more small cars and fewer big gas-guzzlers, or to promote the switch. Instead, the car manufacturers waited until the public got the message and switched on its own when the mini-crisis set in. The result was that over 150,000 auto workers were laid off in Spring, 1974. Meanwhile the industry was frantically—and fruitlessly—promoting Cadillacs and Continentals on television, something they had never done before.

It would be nice to think the leaders of the auto industry will now recover the foresight and initiative of their pioneering days and try experimenting seriously with alternative forms of transportation, but there is little likelihood of that. The industry is too monolithic. At best it will respond belatedly to consumer demand for small, economical cars, blind to everything else. But you as a consumer have at least some power to push the industry in the right direction. When you *must* buy a car, buy the smallest, most energy-efficient one that you feel safe in driving.

Much of what should be done is obvious. The entire pattern of transportation for the US should be changed, and this means that our settlement patterns must also change.[5] No one enjoys commuting to work, and yet we seem to be locked into a system that requires it of millions. Urban areas must be reorganized to allow people to work near their homes. The surface-transportation system, both locally and for long distance, should change from one dominated by private automobiles and trucks to one dominated by public transportation, especially railroads. Admittedly, these are very profound changes that would take several decades to bring about once the required political actions had been taken. But there are many smaller changes that can be initiated now to encourage such a trend and conserve energy in the meantime.

The government could immediately reverse the policies of discontinuing passenger-train service and tearing up railroad tracks, and effort should be put into improving and upgrading what service remains. Then money should be invested in building new lines, improved roadbeds, and modern, comfortable passenger cars (including pullmans). It would be costly at first, but should ultimately be profitable, since the days of the energy-inefficient auto are numbered. Each city could explore and plan for expanded commuter rail service where needed. It would also be practical to replace truck transport with rail where possible; as fuel costs rise, rail will automatically become more economically attractive. One of the cheapest forms of transport (in terms of energy consumption) is by water —barge and riverboat. This mode has also been in decline, but could usefully be revived. Such programs could help take up the employment slack created by reduced demand for cars, truck transport, and other economic changes related to energy conservation.

Needless to say, the multi-billion-dollar federal highway-building program—a form of welfare for the trucking, construction, and auto industries—should be ended, except for the completion of projects already under construction. This could provide a source of funds to invest in railroads and other public transport. Detroit could increase its production of buses, while reducing that of medium-sized cars. The large automobile should disappear entirely, except for some taxis, and these could be designed to run economically.

City councils can reverse the tax policies that have encouraged the construction of giant office buildings in large cities, destroying without replacing existing housing in the process. The possibility of converting some office buildings to housing should be explored. In this connection the appallingly inefficient thermal qualities of the majority of large buildings—especially offices, but also some apartments, stores and factories—should be corrected. Unopenable windows should be made openable; office layouts arranged to take maximum advantage of daylight and use minimum amounts of electric lighting; lighting adjusted to adequate, not excessive, levels; insulation added to walls and roofs; double-glass windows installed in cold climates; and adjustable outside shading devices put over south and west windows for summer. South walls can be painted dark colors, east and west walls and roofs painted light colors. In this way, buildings can be partially heated by the sun in winter, but will mostly reflect sunlight in summer. In many large, air-conditioned buildings, savings can be made simply by reducing the rate of air-flow and turning it off entirely at night when the building is empty. In most large buildings, the air-flow is set far higher than is necessary to replenish oxygen and keep the air fresh. The potential usefulness of solar power for heating and cooling each building should be explored, and solar units should be installed wherever feasible.

Some of these changes require only simple adjustments, while others would be expensive. But the savings in energy costs would eventually compensate even for the costs of making the structural changes. Incentives could be provided by tax breaks (at least for as long as the government continues to use taxes as instruments of policy). The slumping construction business would become very healthy doing all that remodeling. While the changeover took place, a moratorium on major building projects could help ensure the availability of materials. This interruption would also give cities and urban regions a breathing space for revising and reformulating their goals.

Changes in settlement patterns could be started immediately by planning the location of all new housing. The age of leapfrogging suburbs would come to an end—it has lasted altogether too long. Cities, towns, and emerging regional governments are discovering that they can control the location of housing developments through zoning regulations. In many areas, fed-up citizens are demanding an end to all such growth. Obviously, as long as the population keeps growing, new housing will be needed. But the location of the growth can be planned, providing an integrated mix of industry, commerce, and homes in each new development. Such integrated communities can provide additional opportunities for more efficient energy use.

Living conditions in city centers must be improved. One imaginative idea is the project in Baltimore where a low-income family is sold an abandoned, derelict house for one dollar with the understanding that the family will restore it to livable condition within two years. The city provides low-interest loans to finance the restoration. If cities can be made attractive places to live, while some businesses are moved to the suburbs (where many people already live), the dividends in reduced commuting would be enormous.

There are other opportunities for energy saving in industry beyond those related to building design. Wherever possible, industries should strive for maximum flexibility in the types of power they use. At the very least, they should be capable of switching from oil to coal or have pollution-abatement equipment ready if they must use high-sulfur coal. Some small operations may be able to supplement their conventional power sources with windmills and/or solar units, if only to heat or cool their buildings. Most industrial processes themselves can be made more energy-efficient; as fuel costs rise, more industries are likely to find such conversions economically attractive.

Much energy that is now wasted could be put to use. Heat that once went up the smoke stack could warm the factory and other nearby buildings. Some industries could also make use of low-temperature steam and heat now wasted by power plants. Waste heat from industrial plants could heat nearby homes, stores, and offices in integrated communities.[6]

The packaging industry, which is wasteful and destructive by its very nature, accounts for about 4 percent of the US energy budget in the production of materials alone (wood, glass, metals, plastics, paper, etc.). Additional large amounts of energy are required to dispose of them afterwards. Much packaging is unquestionably unnecessary, often adding cost to the product, and should be eliminated. Wherever possible, reuse of bottles and jars should be encouraged. Recycling of the glass is not enough—that still consumes far too much energy. It has been suggested that soft-drink bottles be standardized so that they can be returned to any company. A similar system could be used for foods that come in bottles or jars: baby foods, pickles,

and salad dressings, for example. Metals should be re-
cycled as efficiently as possible; changing some production
methods and urban waste collecting procedures could
facilitate this. Even more important, large consumer
products, such as automobiles and major appliances,
should be designed to permit easy recycling of their component materials.

Utility commissions could immediately help to reduce
energy consumption by reversing power rate structures.
Now the biggest energy users pay the lowest rate per unit
of energy. If the rates were changed so that the biggest
power users—all large industrial corporations—paid the
most, there would be a sudden scramble to streamline industrial processes. Recycling of materials, which uses far
less energy than mining and refining, might become a
more fruitful economic activity, thus opening more jobs.
The rate change could also be an economic spur to the
remodeling of factories, stores, and office buildings already discussed.

There are many relatively minor changes that, if made
across the nation, could add up to significant energy savings. Electrical-resistance heating (conventional electric
heating), which is the most inefficient of all, should be
banned in new homes and offices. Only where there is no
other alternative might exceptions be made. Electric heat
pumps (new and not yet in general use), on the other
hand, are relatively efficient. If the maintenance problems
they have been prone to can be eliminated, it would be
helpful to encourage their use, especially in areas where
natural gas is scarce.

Unnecessary lighting in offices and factories should also
be banned. Some 10 percent of the national energy budget
goes for commercial lighting alone. There should certainly
be a ban on lighting for business advertising when the business is closed. Security lighting can be reduced and in
some cases replaced with electronic alarm devices, which
use far less power.

Appliance manufacturers can be encouraged to make
their products much more efficient in energy use, especially big energy-eaters like air-conditioners, hot-water

heaters, clothes dryers, refrigerators, ovens and ranges. At the very least, electricity (or gas) consumption information should be posted on all appliances so consumers can take that factor into consideration when buying. Completely frivolous uses of power, such as gas yard lamps that are permanently lit, should be outlawed altogether.

As a longer-term change, vacationing by automobile could be discouraged, which would help reduce gasoline consumption. Vacation time could be increased to four to six weeks annually, taken as a single block and staggered throughout the year. Rejuvenated rail systems and comfortable buses might attract many vacationers with packaged tours, ski vacations, etc. Three-day weekends, which create enormous jams on highways, can be eliminated by abolishing the recent shift of most holidays to Monday. Such changes would be hard on some recreational businesses, but it could stimulate local entertainment and sports facilities in urban areas, and the shifts could be made gradually.

Companies could find other ways to conduct business than by making many employees travel constantly or transfer to new areas frequently. There would be important benefits to families and communities as well as substantial energy savings. A telephone conference call is a lot cheaper in all ways than a business meeting in another city—though perhaps not as much fun.

All these proposed changes are entirely possible; undoubtedly you can think of others. And none of them would reduce our standard of living. In many ways, the quality of our lives would be enhanced. Who would miss commuting?

Of course, it is easy to outline the directions we could and should take. But whether this nation can decide that the changes are necessary and start making them is quite another question. If the present trends continue, the utilities will fight changing their rate schedules, the building industry will fight any changes (except relaxation) in building codes, businesses will find it "too expensive and inconvenient" to remodel their skyscrapers and factories, the travel and recreation industries will fight any reduction of three-day weekends and will push for special fuel dispensations, the railroad executives will balk at increasing passenger service, the highway lobby will battle any attempt to end the highway program, truckers will join them and oppose expanding rail freight, and labor unions will fight any proposal that seems to endanger their jobs or even the jobs of other unions, no matter what other new job opportunities might thereby be opened up, and so on.

If these trends are followed, you will have a sure sign that America is going to blow it on the energy front. And we think America *will* blow it, which means that the only energy-saving programs you can count on will be your own. But they will be important to you, not just because you will be helping your country solve its problems but because you will be saving money and gaining independence. Uncoordinated individual efforts are not going to see society through *any* of the coming waves of crises, but those who are preparing for them are likely to suffer the least.


## What You Can Do


There are a great many things the average citizen can do to reduce his or her own energy consumption.[7] The first thing is to believe that the energy crunch is *real* and that it is *permanent*, even if generous supplies should be available for a time. It is essential to start behaving *now* as though energy were a scarce and precious commodity—because it is, even if most people don't realize it. If you begin making adjustments before energy prices skyrocket, you will be way ahead of the game, both financially and in the ability to maintain your comfort on less energy. The shortages and price-hikes of the early 1970s were only the beginning.

**Home.** The obvious place to begin is at home. The greatest single use of energy in most homes is for heating, followed by hot-water heaters and air-conditioning.

The best way to reduce energy use in heating and air-conditioning is simply to change your thermostat settings. If you have already done this, you may have noticed a corresponding reduction in your heating bills. A setting of six degrees lower than you have been using in winter and (if you have air-conditioning) six degrees warmer in summer will save substantial amounts of energy. Once you get used to it, you may even find it more comfortable. Thermostats with two settings, which would automatically turn off the furnace at night in mild weather, would conserve even more energy.

The next most helpful way to reduce heating and cooling energy use is by insulation. Nationwide, the average energy savings for heating due to raising insulation standards from the minimum permitted before 1971 to the optimum would be 42 percent.[8] In a colder-than-average climate, obviously, they would be even greater. The savings in power for air-conditioning would be around 20 percent.

If you are building or buying a new house, therefore, be sure that it is very well insulated. If you live in an older house, you can still install additional insulation. (Many new companies have sprung up in addition to older ones that will do this service for you. Be sure the one you choose has enough experience to know what it is doing.) If you are competent at this kind of work, you can do it yourself and save money, but be sure you are aware of the hazards and know how to protect yourself against injury. Insulating is a relatively large investment, but it will add to the value of your house and lower your heating and cooling bills. Extra insulation should be put under the roof, in all outside walls, and under the floor if you have only a crawl-space or unheated basement.

Insulation should be supplemented by weatherstripping and caulking around windows and doors, plus storm windows and storm doors if winters are severe in your area. Extra insulation can be provided by keeping curtains or shades drawn at night or during storms and opening them on sunny days to let the sun help warm your house. Finally, make sure that your furnace is clean and in good working order, close off any rooms that are not in use, and close the fireplace damper when it is not needed.

If you have spare time and a bent for plumbing, you may wish to emulate the man in East Newport, New York, who installed a steampipe system in his fireplace to heat his entire home. (Standard fireplaces are very inefficient heaters.) He still had his furnace as a supplement, but claimed he only used ten dollars' worth of fuel in the first winter.[9]

Another way of emancipating yourself from the furnace is to get a solar heating unit, which reportedly will soon be available for homes.[10] Solar units can also fill in for your water heater. In most areas you would still need your furnace as a supplement in an extended period of bad weather, but your fuel consumption should be a small fraction of what it used to be. It's worth finding out whether the climate where you live and the design of your house would be suitable. Solar heaters are already available for swimming pools. If you have or are planning to build a pool, you should certainly try to get a solar heater. It may cost more to install, but remember, there are no fuel bills.

All the insulating and weatherstripping will, of course, help to keep your house cool in summer. If you don't have air-conditioning, but it is your ambition to get it, consider these alternatives. Plant fast-growing shady trees and large shrubs around your house, especially on the east, and west, and south sides. (Evergreens on the north may give some protection from winter winds.) You can also plant ivy to cover the walls. If the climate is more severe in summer than in winter, paint the house white or some pale color and have a light-colored roof. Put awnings over windows in summer. Get a window or attic exhaust fan— they use much less power than air-conditioners. Close windows, doors, and curtains during the day, open them at night, and use the fan to bring in cool night air. A well-insulated house should stay comfortable through the day, unless nights are also hot. Use a minimum of electric lights and heat-generating appliances during the day in hot weather. Eat cold meals. Do laundry, ironing, and dishwashing in the evening. This will not only help keep your house cool, it will reduce the load on the electrical power system at peak hours, helping to forestall blackouts or brownouts.

If you must have air-conditioning, get the most efficient air-conditioner you can (there is a lot of variation) [11] and use it as sparingly as possible. Close off unused rooms. Turn off the air-conditioning at night unless it's still very warm outside, and don't turn it on until the house is uncomfortably warm. Don't leave it on when you are not home. If it is mainly high humidity that is bothering you, see if the fan alone is enough to keep you comfortable. As with furnaces, keep your air-conditioner clean and working well.

Water heaters are second only to home heating as consumers of energy. One of the greatest wasters of heat (not to mention water) is a leaky hot water faucet. It's astonishing how much can go down the drain in a year, so fix leaks at once. Dishwashing by hand with running water is another heat waster. Don't set the temperature control on your water heater too high, and turn it down low when you're away on a trip (the same goes for the house thermostat). Use warm or cold water rather than hot when washing clothes whenever practical.

Many appliances are also relatively greedy power-consumers, as are incandescent lights. Table 7 shows the relative amounts of electricity consumed by various appliances with average household use. As with heating and cooling, substantial energy savings can be made by being careful and conservative. Obviously, lights and appliances (radio, TV, etc.) should never be left on when they're not needed. When buying new appliances, look for energy efficiency. Here are some other suggestions for reducing power consumption:

Replace light bulbs with ones of lower wattage.
Use candlelight for dinner and social occasions.
Turn off unneeded lights when watching television.
Never do less than a full load in washer or dryer.

Reduce time 10 or 15 percent for drying; you'll find the
   difference is slight and your clothes may last longer.
Remove clothes from the dryer as soon as it stops;
   you'll need to do a lot less ironing.
If possible, dry clothes outdoors.
If you have a natural-gas yard lamp or fireplace starter,
   call the utility and have it disconnected.
Unplug instant-on television sets when they are not
   in use.

## TABLE 7

### Energy Consumption by Home Appliances and Lighting

| Appliances | Annual Energy Consumption (kilowatt-hours) |
| --- | --- |
| Air-conditioner | 2000 |
| Electric blanket | 150 |
| Can opener | 0.3 |
| Clock | 17 |
| Clothes dryer | 1200 |
| Coffee maker | 100 |
| Dishwasher (with heater) | 350 |
| Fan (attic) | 270 |
| Fan (furnace) | 480 |
| Fluorescent light (3 fix.) | 260 |
| Food freezer (16 cu. ft.) | 1200 |
| Food mixer | 10 |
| Food waste disposer | 30 |
| Frying pan | 240 |
| Hair dryer | 15 |
| Iron (hand) | 150 |
| Light bulbs (for average house) | 1870 |
| Radio (solid state) | 20 |
| Radio phonograph (solid state) | 40 |
| Range | 1550 |
| Refrigerator (frost-free, 12 cu. ft.) | 750 |
| Sewing machine | 10 |

| Shaver | 0.6 |
| Television (black/white) | 400 |
| Television (color) | 540 |
| Toaster | 40 |
| Vacuum cleaner | 45 |
| Washer (automatic) | 100 |

Source: *Citizen Action Guide*

**Transportation.** There are many things you can do on a permanent basis to reduce your energy consumption for transportation beyond the emergency measures demanded while the gasoline shortage was in effect. At the same time you would encourage needed changes in society.

The first thing you should do is *use public transport whenever possible.* One of the reasons that city bus and commuter train services are poor is that so few people use them. The restricted clientele may also be a reason for high crime rates on municipal transport systems. Most passengers are the elderly poor and teenagers—victims and predators, in effect. There are few middle-class men between the ages of twenty-five and sixty riding buses and subways, whose mere presence would probably have a strong inhibiting effect on crime. If many more people of all ages started using public transport facilities—and complaining when the service was lousy—they might be improved.

Become familiar with bus and train schedules in your area and always consider whether using them rather than the car might be feasible. Don't be afraid to offer constructive suggestions to the bus or train company as to how they could improve their services for you (and thus gain you as a regular customer). Be liberal with encouragement when you think they are doing a good job. When public-transport issues come up in elections or for discussion at the city council, vote for and support expanded services if they are fiscally sound over the long term. Many such issues are defeated because they represent a large initial outlay and contain an element of risk—for instance, purchasing an expensive fleet of buses that may fail to attract customers. Responsibility doesn't end with buying the buses, however. An effort to promote their use and engage the public in deciding routes and schedules might well ensure their success.

An alternative to public transport in many situations is car-pooling. Many large companies have attempted to organize car-pooling services for their employees. If you work for such a company, cooperate in the effort (unless you are already using public transport). If your company has not started such a service and could use one, do a little prodding. Perhaps it only needs someone to bring up the subject.

If you live a ridiculously long distance from your work, no public transport is available, and car-pooling is impractical, you might consider moving closer (or changing jobs). The savings in transport cost (not to mention wear and tear on you) could compensate for the trouble and expense. And when a real energy crunch comes, you will still be able to get to work (assuming there is still work to do).

You can also car-pool for the endless rounds of errands, shopping, and ferrying of youngsters. It's a good way to get acquainted with neighbors, and if things really get tough, you may be glad you did. As much as possible, combine shopping and errands into single trips. If a second car still seems essential to you, consider joint ownership with neighbors or friends who also occasionally need one. If you try this plan, however, be sure to check out the legal technicalities with a lawyer and the insurance situation with your insurance agent.

You can also encourage your family to walk or ride bicycles in place of using the car. People who live within a few miles of their work-places might consider commuting by bicycle. Besides saving gallons of gas over time, they would be helping to protect themselves against heart attacks.[12] In rush hours, a bicycle can often get there faster than a car.

If you are a student, don't badger your parents for rides or for use of the car for unnecessary trips. Use public transport or school buses, even if they aren't quite as convenient, or ride your bike. When you must use a car, organize a car-pool with your friends.

**Work.** What you can accomplish at your place of work will of course depend on what your position is and how large the organization is. But even a lowly office boy can put suggestions in the suggestion box. You can—at the very least—cooperate with whatever adjustments to the energy shortage your employer is already making. Wear clothing consistent with changed thermostat settings (keep an extra sweater in your desk drawer if necessary), and don't encourage complainers who are too hot or cold. (Offer your sweater instead.) If you get chilly, move around. (If yours is a completely sedentary job, you should try to get up and walk around for a couple of minutes every hour—it's much better for your circulation. Your boss shouldn't complain unless you disappear for long periods.) You probably won't miss the unnecessary lighting—you may even find it less fatiguing. If some of the lights haven't been turned off or the thermostats reset, ask why not.

If your position warrants it, you can even propose and support relatively large structural or procedural changes, such as adding insulation to the building, putting in windows that can be opened, or other improvements mentioned earlier; or recycling waste as fuel and making use of waste heat in factories.[13] A great deal of energy could be saved in your office or factory by turning the heat off completely at night, starting up again at perhaps six A.M., and by reducing the ratio of fresh air to recirculated air in the heating-cooling system. The Lawrence Berkeley Laboratory has saved five gallons of fuel per employee per week just by doing this.[14] Don't fail to emphasize the money that would be saved with such measures; better yet, do an analysis on your own so you can give precise figures.

Perhaps most important, *don't fight the inevitable!* Don't go down with the sinking ship, bailing frantically until you're under water; find a lifeboat and seek a safer berth. This applies whether you're president of the company, foreman of your factory division, or a member of the stenographer's pool. An executive in a company produc-

ing motor homes should have in a stage of advanced plan-
ping either an all-new, lightweight, partly collapsible home
that can be propelled by an economical engine, or perhaps
one that is designed *not* to be moved, or a plan for converting the factory to produce something else, such as
solar heaters or people-powered vehicles. If none of these
plans is in the works, he had better look for a new job
before the old one disappears out from under him. The
same goes for his employees.

If you're an executive at Boeing, don't try to revive the
SST. Get busy on new types of surface transport instead.
If you're a top executive in an energy-intensive industry,
make an all-out effort to trim your company's energy consumption, and try to make your operations convertible to
at least one other form of energy. It may require a huge
capital outlay; but when the lights go out, you'll be glad
you did. If you're in an oil company, realize that your
job is temporary and be prepared to hold another job
twenty years from now. If you're an executive or white-
collar worker and can't persuade your company to di-
versify into a more viable product or service, look for a
job with another company that seems more likely to meet
the needs of the future.

If you're a labor leader who sees a threat to your job
and those of your union, don't struggle for featherbedding
and guarantees of job security in a dying industry. Instead,
negotiate for retraining programs with guaranteed income
during the transition to new jobs. If your present industry
isn't likely to die, but may be in for shrinkage, encourage
your union to cooperate with management in establishing
the fairest way to reduce the payroll and ease the unemployed into a new line of work.

What are the needs of the future that may offer new
opportunities? And what industries (besides automobile
manufacturing and related activities) are likely to have
less than rosy futures? Which established ones are likely
to do well? Much depends on whether American society,
especially the business community, begins making positive
moves to anticipate and accommodate to the age of

scarcity. If it doesn't, there will be no such thing as a job or a company with a good future.

But assuming the economic structure can be held together, there are several areas that are likely to do reasonably well. Even during depressions and times of severe social turmoil, pople need food, clothing, shelter, and medical care. There may be much less demand for meat and heavily processed foods, but food will still need to be produced, distributed, and sold. Second-hand and cheap clothing may do better than luxury goods. The new-home market may be very slow, but maintenance, repair, and renovation may be brisk. Medical care may be strong on the routine side, while research and heart transplanting may be considerably dampened or even halted. Unless disruption is extreme, schools and vocational training will also continue to be needed. Public transport may (and should) become more important. Such changes might not be altogether bad.

Historically, during depressions, businesses that have done very well were those that provided escape—bars and inexpensive entertainment. Some books and magazines may also be in demand. Services of all kinds are a sector of the economy that has been expanding steadily for decades. Once the period of turmoil has been weathered at least, services may continue to grow.

Heavy industry, on the other hand, may undergo very little further increase. Some types of manufacturing indeed may even collapse abruptly, depending on the availability of raw materials and energy and on the course of events. The most unnecessary, wasteful, and antisocial activities—such as the packaging and bottling industries, some kinds of weapons, aircraft, cheap plastic products, etc.—are likely to be eliminated either in a conventional depression or the real energy crunch. The energy industry itself will certainly undergo profound changes. That industry is probably more aware than most that the future holds inevitable change. Some big oil companies also have coal interests and are heavily involved in the development of nuclear power.

If you're open-minded and have a clear idea of what

the future is likely to hold, you won't have any trouble finding opportunities, although they may require you to learn an entirely new set of skills. You may find such a change in your life a stimulating challenge, especially if you have worked at the same job for many years.

**Where To Live.** A critical personal decision in a time of economic and social turmoil is the choice of where to make one's home. Of course, some people have this decision made for them by economic circumstances, but Americans, as a whole, are still among the world's most mobile people. Aside from not living downwind of a nuclear power plant, what kinds of factors should now be considered in choosing a place to reside?

One of the most important is the location of your friends. There is every likelihood that an increasing amount of pleasure in everyone's life is going to have to come from interpersonal relationships—the pleasant ones you have now should be treasured and enhanced. Remember, if the going gets rough, you won't want to be among strangers. Society in the future is likely to become increasingly decentralized, with growing authority vested in local governments. In such circumstances the advantages of being well-established in an area are manifold, and if you have become actively involved in local government, you will find them even greater. Indeed, the advantages of being locally established have already been enjoyed by many Americans, who as old customers have been given preference at the gas pump and at the meat counter in times of shortage. This may seem unfair in some ways, but it is human nature to help friends before strangers.

There are some circumstances, however, where moving may seem to be the best choice, even though it may mean breaking personal ties. If we don't avoid a breakdown, a suburban house with a backyard garden is going to be a much more pleasant place to live than a city apartment, and a small farm would be even better. The quality of your life then will be directly proportional to how independent you have become of the complex and fragile mechanisms that now provide most Americans with the requisites of life.

Most people, including nearly all of the urban middle class and poor, are not in a position to buy a small place in the sticks and take up farming—even if they would like to. For them (and for us) the choice is stark—either try to change society so that the fragile mechanisms that support us can keep functioning well or face a catastrophic decline in the quality of our lives.

In trying to evaluate your present location, a number of things should be investigated. One is the vulnerability of your local water supply to interruption or contamination in a severe energy crisis or time of civil disorder. Another is your position relative to sources of food. Must most of it now be imported over long distances? Is there suitable land nearby that could be farmed in an emergency? How good is public transportation in your area? Even if there is no general social breakdown, the demise of the automobile as a way of getting to work or to the food store could come with shocking suddenness.

In the US, we have created at least one nearly perfect model of the kind of place *not* to live in during an age of scarcity. It is called Los Angeles.

## How Is Your Self-Sufficiency?

Suppose all efforts to help the US grope its way to a workable future in a world of scarcity prove futile—the majority of people refuse to cooperate with the insufficient few who are moving in the right direction. To prepare for this contingency, not all of your efforts at changing the future should be invested in social and political action. You should also be taking steps to reduce your dependence on the services provided by our complex society and making arrangements to protect yourself and your family against the worst eventuality. Depending on the degree of independence you wish to achieve, these steps will require a more or less complete change in your lifestyle. Protecting yourself against the worst means acquiring the the ability to be entirely self-sufficient for at least a short period of time.

One of the best ways to become independent of the system is to learn as many skills as possible. Many young people today are consciously doing this, perhaps to counteract the feeling of helplessness spawned by such an interdependent society as ours. Mastering a variety of skills will give you more self-confidence, save you money and time, and may prove invaluable in an emergency. You don't have to become an expert on the circuitry of color television sets, but there's no harm in being able to change a tire, replace spark plugs, or change the oil in your car, for instance. It is also useful to know how to do basic carpentry, plumbing, and painting, and to have some familiarity with the inner works of appliances. At the very least, you'll be able to diagnose the trouble if something breaks down or judge whether a worker you hire is doing a competent job, and many times you'll be able to do the job yourself.

Competence in survival skills is also desirable.[15] Could you survive a plane crash or auto breakdown in a remote place for more than a few hours? You should know how to find water and food, keep warm or cool, and find your way back to civilization if there is no expectation of rescue. Talents useful when stranded far from civilization might prove equally useful if society breaks down. One side of the coin of self-sufficiency is to be prepared for such unexpected emergencies. Americans tend not to believe in disasters, natural or otherwise. Consequently, they are forever being caught by surprise—and usually quite unprepared.

Suppose your family was stricken by some event that isolated you in your home for a period of days without gas or electricity. The agent could be a hurricane, a disastrous flood, a severe earthquake, a huge blizzard, or any number of human-induced problems. How would you get along? Would you be out of food the next day? Would you be freezing in winter, without light or any way to cook food? If water pipes were broken or the water was contaminated, would you have nothing to drink? If you had to evacuate on short notice (the dam upstream has burst, or the local nuclear power plant has just had an "impossible" accident), could you do it without leaving everything you need behind? Would you have enough fuel available to go more than thirty miles?

Answering such questions can help you plan for short-term self-sufficiency in the event of a natural disaster, severe shortages in food or essential goods, or serious social breakdown. For what length of time you should prepare to be self-sufficient is up to you. The time will, of course, be dictated by such factors as your lifestyle, where you live, the storage capacity of your home, and what you can afford. Arranging to be independent for a week is relatively easy and involves no significant change in your lifestyle. This is better than no preparation at all, but your position would be considerably strengthened if you were prepared to fend for yourself for a longer period and were able to lend help to friends and neighbors as well. The best choice is relatively complete independence from the system as a lifestyle, but this may not be an option open to you.

There is such a wide variety of contingencies to plan against that maximum flexibility is imperative. Ways of conserving energy have already been discussed, but shortages in many other essentials of life—particularly food—are also likely to occur. Scarcity of one important commodity has a way of bringing on problems in other areas not immediately predictable. The shortage of crude oil and natural gas during the mini-crisis reduced supplies of plastics, synthetic fibers, and fertilizers, all made in part from oil or gas, and also put pressure on supplies of substitute items such as coal, paper, wood, and natural fibers.

Obviously, one key to self-sufficiency is to have supplies on hand of everything you need to survive. There is no need to engage in panic buying whenever scarcity is forecast. Remember the great toilet paper panic of 1973? If you hear that a bread shortage is coming next week, we *don't* recommend rushing to the store to buy ten loaves. We hope, rather, that you already have enough flour, yeast, and powdered milk in your pantry to make your own bread, if necessary.

The trick is to build up your stores of emergency supplies slowly. If you have any storage facilities at all—a reasonably dry basement is ideal, but even a small closet can hold a surprising amount—you can gradually accumulate and put by enough food and supplies to tide your family over during an emergency or to compensate for shortages. The Mormons as a regular practice keep enough supplies on hand for a year. This may not be practical for you, but enough food and water to survive for two to four weeks, plus emergency light and heat sources, is within the reach of all but the poorest. Furthermore, buying ahead is a hedge against inflation. Maintaining stores against future times of shortage is a practice that should be encouraged throughout society. It is a very different thing ethically from attempting to hoard more than your share of a commodity once a shortage develops.

Let's look at the various kinds of supplies you should maintain if at all possible.

## Water

Having potable water available is perhaps the first essential in an emergency. Yet clean water is taken so much for granted that it is easy to forget that the supply can be interrupted. If you have enough warning to turn off your outside faucet when the supply becomes unsafe, remember that a considerable amount of water remains in the system. Your water heater contains 40 to 60 gallons of safe, clean water. The water in your pipes can also be removed by opening a faucet at the top of your house to let air into the pipes and draining it from another faucet on the lowest floor.

To ensure having enough water available in an emergency, it is a painless precaution to fill and keep around the house several jugs of water. (These can also serve in case of fire.) The water can be kept in either glass or plastic. Each has disadvantages—plastic may impart a flavor to the water, but glass is fragile. Old wine or vinegar jugs can be used, or plastic jugs of the sort in which bleach, liquid detergent, or distilled water are often purchased. Filling with very hot water and storing in the dark will discourage the growth of algae. Remember, there can be two kinds of water—one kind for drinking and cooking, one for cleaning, washing, and general hygiene.

If you get warning that some disaster will disrupt your water service in a short time, fill your bathtub, soup kettles, buckets, plastic wastebaskets, pots, and pans with water. Such warning might come with floods or possibly earthquakes, for example. If you have even a small yard, there is no reason not to keep a couple of water-filled trashcans available at all times. This water could at least be used in toilets in emergencies.

As extra insurance if your safe water runs out and you can't boil whatever unsafe water is available, keep some halazone or iodine tablets on hand.[16] These are available at your drug store and come with instructions for using. Water treated with halazone isn't the best tasting, but at least it's safer than untreated water.

## Food

Food stores can be built up gradually by buying perhaps 10 to 20 percent more food than you need each time you visit the supermarket. If you plan carefully, most of the food can be used up and replaced as part of your regular consumption, thus avoiding overlong storage. Even canned and some kinds of dehydrated foods deteriorate over time, so it is wise to date everything as you buy. As much as possible, you should try to store foods that your family now likes and eats often. If they don't like a food now, they won't like it any better in an emergency, even if nothing else is available.

Buying in bulk, of course, will save you money, time, and storage space. This may seem inconsistent with the principle of accumulating gradually, but it really isn't. You can buy a couple of cases of tuna one week and chicken the next, for instance. Case discounts are widely available on canned and some other goods, and those with the house label are usually cheaper, though equally as good as the advertised brands. (Very often some cans from the same batch in a cannery are given house labels, others the labels of more expensive, nationally advertised brands. In few areas are consumers more systematically cheated than in purchasing food.) It's a good idea to invest in some airtight storage containers, such as bins, canisters, or glass apothecary jars, to hold flour, nuts, seeds, rice, dry milk, etc., especially if you live in a humid climate.

Some useful items may not be available at your supermarket. Freeze-dried foods of the type used for hiking trips, for instance, are available at sporting-goods shops and some mail-order outfits (see Appendix II for a list of these). These foods are relatively expensive, but because they keep well (freeze-dried foods generally last longer with less vitamin loss than canned foods) and occupy so little storage space, they are worth it. Some other items—noninstant powdered milk, soy flour, and yogurt culture, for example—are found in health-food stores.

Concentrate on foods that require no elaborate preparation. It's all very well to have ingredients to make bread on hand, but if there is no gas or power, there is no way to bake it. As an alternative, learn how to make tortillas or unleavened Middle-Eastern bread. All you need is a fire and a skillet. If you've had extensive camp cooking experience, you're way ahead of the game.

If you are forced by circumstances to subsist on stored food for a long time, you should give thought to extra nutritional insurance for your family to compensate for the inevitable losses. First in this line come vitamin supplements. Like food, these deteriorate with time, so ideally they should be used and replaced regularly. If the Food and Drug Administration goes through with its present plans, vitamins will soon be available only in relatively low concentrations, except by prescription. Therefore you may wish to store ahead just to have them on hand. There are good vitamin mixtures, however, and poor ones. Generally speaking, though not always, the cheaper ones are not very good. They contain only some of the more well-known (by the public) vitamins and minerals, which are cheap to produce, and omit or skimp on the others. Some mixtures are better balanced.[17]

Vitamin C can and perhaps ought to be purchased separately and stored as extra insurance against colds and other infections. It keeps well as pills if protected from moisture and light; but in stored foods and in cooking, it is one of the first vitamins to be lost. In a pinch, vitamin C can also be dissolved and used as a lemon flavoring to perk up bland stored food.

There is nothing wrong with keeping a stock of food in your freezing compartment or freezer. This may prove to be a hedge against rising prices and short-term shortages. But don't count on it to tide you over an emergency in which power is interrupted. You may instead be faced with the problem of cooking and eating a large amount of food before it spoils. For real emergency supplies, depend on canned and dried foods. Some suggestions on what to store are provided in Appendix II at the end of this book.

## Grow Your Own Food

Are you old enough to remember Victory Gardens? During World War II, millions of Americans in residential and suburban neighborhoods planted vegetables in their backyards to supplement the national food supply. The program was a great success, not only in providing extra food, but also in giving a generation of children firsthand knowledge of where their food came from. The Secretary of Agriculture during World War II estimated that an average thirty-by-fifty-foot Victory Garden could produce five hundred pounds of fresh and five hundred pounds of preservable and storable fruits and vegetables each year. At the peak of Victory Garden activity during the war the Department of Agriculture estimated that half of all domestic fruit and vegetable needs was being supplied by home and farm gardens.

In an era of higher prices and food scarcity, many Americans have revived the idea of the Victory Garden. More Americans than ever before live in suburban areas with backyards, and a great many of them contain vegetable patches. Interest in gaining some independence from the food-distribution system is becoming widespread, and grassroots organizations are springing up to provide training in such things as subsistence farming.[18] In 1973, home gardeners spent 100 million for seeds, and seed-industry spokesmen estimated that there would be a 20 percent increase in 1974. A Gallup Poll in 1973 indicated that 31 million out of 68 million households (43 percent) had vegetable gardens, an increase of 4 percent from the previous year.

Millions of acres of fine farm land have been sacrificed to allow people to live outside the cities. There's no practical way for land to be put back into production and the suburbanites returned to the cities—even though such a move might help solve countless problems—but a little of the balance can be redressed with more backyard gardens. Neighbors could trade produce and advice, activities that could help cement friendships. If you have the space, the time, and the inclination, try it. You'll be doing your budget, your body, and your palate a favor.

## Clothing

When the possibility of a future fabric shortage was mentioned to a friend of ours recently, she said, "I could survive the rest of my life with the clothes I have now. They may get a little shabby, but they'd keep me decently dressed." What she said was true enough, provided there was no other change in her lifestyle. But would her present wardrobe be adequate if her home were no longer heated or air-conditioned and if she had to do much heavier work than she now ordinarily does?

What about your wardrobe? Have you in recent years become a slave to fad fashion, buying mostly inexpensive items that go out of style in six months? Or have you started putting your money in somewhat more costly clothes that will last and look attractive for several years? Curiously enough, even the clothing industry, after several years of promoting "throwaway fashion" in the late 1960s, has returned to durable, timeless "classics." Perhaps because they are already having difficulty obtaining the fabrics they need, designers seem to have seen the handwriting on the wall.

As already mentioned, the energy mini-crisis is partly to blame for the fabric shortage. Many synthetic fibers—nylon, acrylics, polyester, spandex, and vinyls, to name some of the most familiar—not only require large amounts of energy to manufacture, they are made in part from petroleum and coal. Some others—fiberglass, rayon, and the acetates—are not made from fossil fuels, but do require power in manufacturing. These synthetic fibers have been so cheap to produce in the past that they have greatly reduced demand, and thus production, of the natural fibers—wool, cotton, silk, linen, etc. In 1971, demand for wool was so low that the Australian wool industry (a leading industry there) nearly went bankrupt. Since then, the market has reversed itself; wool is scarce, and prices have soared. The story for cotton is similar; high quality cotton is especially hard to find in the US. Part of the problem is that Japan has been stockpiling both cotton and wool in recent years. As synthetic fibers become scarcer and more expensive, the demand for natural fibers will increase further.

The production of natural fibers, moreover, competes for land and resources with production of food. This is especially true of cotton, which grows best in subtropical areas already often short of food. And the clothing industry must compete with other industries for fabrics. Synthetic fibers especially are used in many ways in industrial processes and also for other consumer products such as tires, camping equipment, parachutes, bedding, carpeting, upholstery, curtains, and many plastic products. The outlook, therefore, is that fabrics will become increasingly expensive, and shortages of various products are extremely likely.

This is not to say you should rush right out and buy a lifetime supply of clothes. But when you need replacements or new items, you should look for quality and even be willing to pay slightly more—if you can—for it. (The same principle applies if you shop in flea markets and secondhand shops.) Look for well-made clothes constructed of sturdy fabrics in styles that won't look outlandish five years from now.

In particular, you should try to acquire an extra pool of sturdy clothes and shoes that will stand up well to hard wear. Have clothing on hand that will see you through all seasons comfortably, even if you must go without heat or air-conditioning. In much of the US, this means lots of warm sweaters, jackets, lined trousers, boots, socks, etc., for winter, and light, loose, comfortable garments for summer. For really cold weather, by far the most comfortable fiber is wool, and it will pay you to seek it out. Good-quality wool also lasts very well if properly cared for, and keeps its good looks better than most synthetics. Cotton is the most comfortable fabric in hot weather, although it can be a nuisance to care for. But pure cotton garments are hard to find, except in underwear. Cotton blended with polyester may therefore be an easier and better choice.

As insurance against both coming shortages and rising prices, it wouldn't hurt to stock up a little on things like underwear, socks, sweaters, shirts, etc. Keep in mind that life may not always be as comfortable as it is today, and include such things as ski underwear if you live in an area with severe winters. Last but not least, if you sew (another valuable skill), keep your eyes open for good-quality fabrics and stock up on them when you find them at reasonable prices.

## Shelter

Your home is not only your castle, it may prove to be your fortress and your refuge in an emergency. If you have already insulated your house, you'll be doubly glad if the power to heat it disappears. Without power, you will need substitutes for heat, light, and cooking facilities. Have plenty of wood on hand if you have a fireplace, and if possible have your fireplace modified to make it a more efficient heater. If you don't have a fireplace, consider installing a Franklin stove or one of its modern derivatives. Buy your wood in spring and summer when prices are lower and it is easier to get. It might not be a bad idea, if you have ample storage space, to keep a little coal on hand. It burns hotter than wood, which could be a life-saver in a cold snap. Newspaper can also be used for burning as well as starting. You can soak it in water, roll it into log shapes, and let it dry slowly. The result will burn very much as a log does.

To keep warm, you will have to depend in large part on warm clothing and plenty of blankets or sleeping bags. Since the heating efficiency of a fireplace (unless it is piped for steam) is poor, you may have to confine yourselves to the room it is in and close off the rest of the house. If you now use electric blankets, keep in mind that they are not as warm when power is off. Have plenty of warm blankets on hand. Wool is best—if you can find it—and comforters are good. Who knows, a winter power failure might bring back bundling!

For emergency lighting, you should have flashlights and batteries, plenty of candles, kerosene lamps, and/or camping lanterns. Kerosene lamps can be found in hardware stores and some department stores, lanterns in sporting-goods stores. The problem with these (and camp stoves that operate on white gas) is the danger of storing their highly combustible fuels. Having them in your house is not only dangerous and in some areas illegal, it could result in your insurance being voided. The same applies to storing gasoline for the car. If you decide to store these volatile fuels, keep them in some separate outbuilding or shed, as far from the house as possible. Never pour *any* flammable liquid in the vicinity of an open flame, and remember that an "empty" gasoline can that contains a little gas and a lot of gas fumes is as deadly as a bomb.

Cooking can be done in a fireplace, but you do need heavy stoneware or cast-iron kettles, dutch ovens, and skillets. These can be propped up with an arrangement of stones or bricks. A better solution is to use your charcoal grill or a hibachi. If you have chafing dishes, some foods can be heated in them with Sterno and kept warm with a candle. Both charcoal and Sterno are easy and safe to store. But be sure that any room in which you use a charcoal fuel (or any other fire) *is adequately ventilated, no matter how cold the weather*. Carbon monoxide is lethal. A chemical fire extinguisher or two is a good investment for any house, and as candles, fires, and kerosene lamps are used more, they will become increasingly important.

Be sure that you have good mechanical substitutes for all your appliances—for instance, egg beaters, whisks, can-openers, clothes drying racks, etc. It's hard to imagine a more embarrassing situation than being caught in an extended power-out emergency with a pantry full of food and no operative can-opener!

## Health

If our worst expectations are realized, health care will become much more difficult to obtain. There are some precautions that, funds permitting, you can take to help minimize the effects of further breakdown in the health-delivery system. One is to visit a competent dentist and see that your teeth are in top condition. If possible, long-lasting gold fillings should be used instead of the less expensive standard fillings. Conscientious care of your teeth, following your dentist's advice, will pay dividends in the long run if your dentist disappears.

Similarly, periodic checkups by a physician, hopefully a specialist in internal medicine, are a good idea. Be sure to discuss with your physician which programs of immunization might be desirable for you. Many have relatively short-term effectiveness, but others (e.g., against tetanus, polio, and smallpox) provide protection over much longer periods.

If you have a friendly physician, he or she may be willing to prescribe a "survival kit" of antibiotics and other drugs for emergency use in the absence of medical aid. The usefulness of such a kit will, of course, depend on your medical knowledge, and your physician should give you careful written instructions on what to use under what circumstances. Self-medication by the uninitiated *can be very dangerous,* and should only be attempted *in extremis.* But "in extremis" is what we are talking about.

If you are not put off by jargon, you might wish to purchase a copy of the *Merck Manual,*[19] which is a goldmine of information on the diagnosis and treatment of disease. It is compact, thumb-indexed, and with the help of a small medical dictionary, much of it is understandable to the layman. Even if the world doesn't come to an end, you may find it fascinating reading—especially if you're a hypochondriac. Needless to say, if you are now taking medication regularly, you should consult your physician about the possibility of storing a supply against possible future shortages.

If you are having a medical problem, the *Merck Manual* will also help you to ask intelligent questions of your physician. If he is not willing to answer your questions in plain English, it means he is too dumb or too arrogant (the basics of *any* medical problem can be explained in everyday language). If you are uncertain about his conclusions, ask him to refer you to another physician for a second opinion. Unwillingness to give you straight answers or to let you consult another physician are signs that you should run (not walk) to the nearest exit (exception— if you are poor and your problem is simple, your physician may balk at consultation because it might be a needless expense for you). Remember, while the US has many fine and dedicated doctors, it also has a fair number of hopeless incompetents. If you are about to choose a physician, it is always a good idea to try to find out about his or her reputation first. Call your local medical association and ask them for suggestions. The local hospital may be of some help, as might a friend who is a nurse. At any rate, ask around—don't pick a doctor at random from the telephone book.

As with food, it seems sensible, wherever possible, to increase your stocks of first-aid items.[20] You may want to buy a commercial first-aid kit, if you don't have one already, as well as a first-aid manual if a reasonably comprehensive one does not accompany your kit. In some areas a commercial snakebit kit may also be advisable. Other things you can stock without prescription are a mild disinfectant, bandaging materials, alcohol (for use as an antiseptic); aspirin (buy the cheapest, it's all essentially the same); antibiotic creams (watch expiration dates—value is mostly limited to superficial skin infections); calamine lotion or other nonprescription drugs for rashes, poison ivy, etc.; and antidiarrheal preparations. If you ordinarily need antihistamines, have a supply of those on hand. And if you need birth control pills or other items, be sure to include them. A period of social breakdown is a poor time to become pregnant. If possible, have at least one member of your family take first-aid training.

Above all, look at the bright side. Many of the diseases that now lay Americans low will become less common as the age of scarcity removes many of their causes: smog, high-fat–high-sugar diets, tobacco, lack of exercise, food additives, pesticide pollution, and so on. If adequate diets and elementary public-health measures can be maintained, the age of scarcity might even increase the life expectancy of Americans.

## Self-Protection

A growing problem for law-abiding Americans is how to protect themselves against a rising tide of violent crime. There is every reason to believe that this problem will become worse as other problems mount for our ultra-competitive society. It would be nice to discover that Americans will cooperate and share in times of crisis, but only a fool would plan on it. One need only consider the great debate over whether or not it was proper to shoot your neighbors if they tried to get into your fallout shelter to realize that, if things *really* get bad, dog-eat-dog is likely to be the order of the day. Social breakdown in a society armed to the teeth with firearms would be exciting, to say the least.

It is frequently suggested that violent crimes could be greatly reduced by gun-control laws. In theory this is true, but even so we must all expect to live in a heavily armed society for the rest of our lives. Congress is, and will almost certainly remain, much too lily-livered to enact the kind of tough gun-control legislation that would be required to make a real dent in the problem. The gun lobbies are too well organized, and halfway measures will not do. Simply putting a few more restrictions on firearms would probably have exactly the result often predicted by the National Rifle Association—honest citizens would be harassed and would give up their guns, whereas criminals would remain well armed.

Faced with this dilemma, it would seem at first glance that those who can afford it would be wise to turn their homes into arsenals. But for people who are unfamiliar with firearms and the strict requirements of firearm safety, this could be a lethal mistake. The chances that a home-owner, a member of his or her family, or another innocent person may be killed or badly injured would in most cases far outweigh any possible degree of protection provided by owning a firearm. Even for those who are familiar and at ease with guns, the risks of possession are considerable.

Accidental deaths are frequent; guns are often stolen in burglaries. Law-enforcement agencies in general try to discourage citizens from arming themselves—in our opinion with good reason.

In addition, you should know (as many do not) that there is considerable legal risk involved in using a gun; in most urban areas the circumstances under which you can fire a weapon without commiting a crime are few indeed. If you feel that your circumstances require protection with firearms, you would be well advised to consult an attorney about the legal aspects of their possession and use. You might also (if the attorney concurs) discuss the matter with your local police. Many people own and use guns casually, and many of them eventually pay a high price (more than two thousand people are killed accidentally each year in the US by firearms).[21]

There are other ways of protecting yourself and your home from violence that do not involve the great risks associated with firearms. Putting secure locks on the doors and windows of your home or apartment is an elementary precaution. Helpful advice on this kind of protection can be obtained from your local police department. You might want to have a siren installed that you can sound to alert the neighborhood if someone attempts to break into your home. Commercially available whistles and compressed-air sirens can be carried in pocket or purse as partial protection against attack away from home.

In many circumstances, of course, your security can be enhanced by a dog. Maximum protection is probably provided by trained guard dogs, but they are expensive and may be very dangerous. In addition, in times of food shortage, a dog is one more mouth to feed, a burden that is likely to be most severe at precisely the time protection is most needed.

If firearm-type protection still seems desirable to you, recent developments in so-called "less-lethal" weapons provide an alternative. The chances of serious accident or legal complications with these are much reduced. For instance, weapons are available that use carbon dioxide cartridges to fire "bean-bags" filled with lead shot. Such weapons are not classified as firearms. They provide a considerable deterrent to attack (some *look* very impressive) and can provide a ninety-pound weakling with the rough equivalent of a prize-fighter's knockout punch. They also tend to be less expensive than a good handgun.[22] Although such weapons carry less risk of serious injury or death, *they are weapons, not toys. They should be treated with the same care and respect as a firearm.* If fired at a child or an old person, especially at close range, they could prove deadly. And a hit in a particularly vulnerable spot might kill even a strong man.

We close this brief section on self-protection with a comment on fallout shelters. In our opinion, the probability of finding one useful is very small. The chances of thermonuclear war are far from negligible, but if one occurs, the results will be so catastrophic that the relative advantages of owning fallout shelters will be negligible. Most of the "experts" who have projected the consequences of such a war have done so in the typical style of experts—with blinders on. Those who look at the effects on agriculture assume that the rail system will survive; those who look at the effects on transportation assume that survivors will stay on the job at any remaining refineries that produce diesel fuel. *No* competent consideration has been given to the potential ecological effects of World War III,[23] and little to the social-political-psychological effects on the surviving population.

If you are concerned about the chance of a nuclear holocaust (too few are—most Americans seem to have suppressed the whole idea), you can enhance your safety much more by becoming politically active and pushing our government into getting serious about disarmament than you can by digging a fallout shelter.


## Change Your Lifestyle Now and Avoid the Rush Later

The high-energy, waste-happy, growthmanic way of life is on its way out. This is going to be *the central fact* in everyone's future that must be considered as major personal decisions are made. Questions such as "How many children should I have?" "Should we buy a new house?" "What career should I choose?" and "What part of the country do I want to live in?" can only be answered sensibly if that fact is taken into account.

Clearly, the people who are going to be best able to survive and prosper in the time of crises that we are now entering will be those who have anticipated changes. They will have made their personal adjustments gradually and sensibly, rather than in shocked response to events as they unfold. Many of the kinds of changes in lifestyle that we think will improve the situation of the average person have already been discussed, but a summary statement seems in order. The magic formula to avoid being drowned by the coming social tidal wave is: *get involved in your own future and maximize your independence.*

Unless you are expecting and consciously planning for dramatic changes that are certain to occur in the last decades of the twentieth century, your future prospects are dim. Whatever plans you make, they can hardly help but make things easier for you and your society if they move you away from total dependence on the continued smooth functioning of the tottering industrial system. This means, to one degree or another, "dropping out," at least psychologically if not physically.

For some, "dropping out" may mean moving to a rural area and taking up subsistence farming. It's a tough life, but for those with the requisite skills and determination, it could be a rewarding one. For many others, "dropping out" will consist more of "tuning out" the lies of politicians and advertisers. When an executive or a scientist decides that a relaxed lifestyle, good friends, and a happy sex life are much more important than high salaries, profits, or a Nobel prize, then those individuals will have begun to become independent of the social forces moving us toward destruction.

At first glance, "dropping out" may seem to be against the best interests of society, but to the contrary, it can only help. Every individual who has a farm, garden, or sizable reserve of food will be one less person scrambling for the limited supplies in times of shortage, and thus there can be larger quantities to be divided among the improvident. Everyone who has bought kerosene lamps and a supply of kerosene *well before* the brownouts begin will be one less person in line at the hardware store when the power goes off. Each individual who resists the drive for financial success means less pressure for growth in our berserk economic system, a better chance to preserve an environment that can support us in the future, and one less tension-wracked burden on the overextended medical-care system.

The time has come to face up to the basic imbalances in our society and, through personal and (to whatever degree possible) political action, begin to loosen the tightest bonds of interdependence. When and if the real crunch comes, you will get precious little help from Washington or your state capital. If you are fortunate enough to live with good friends or relatives as neighbors, you may find assistance and cooperation there. And presumably your family will do what it can to help. But the one person you can depend on with complete assurance is *yourself*.

# Notes

1. Robert L. Heilbroner, *An Inquiry into the Human Prospect* (New York: W. W. Norton, 1974).

2. Actual figures on deaths from starvation are impossible to find. National mortality statistics, where kept, do not include a category "death from starvation." Indeed, people do not usually die of starvation, but of diseases such as pneumonia, measles, and diarrhea, which would not be lethal for well-fed individuals. There are some 60 million deaths annually worldwide, and French agronomists R. Dumont and B. Rosier have estimated that between 10 and 20 million of them are the result of starvation (*The Hungry Future,* New York: Praeger, 1969). Alan Berg, ("Nutrition, Development and Population Growth," *Population Bulletin,* vol. 29, [1973], p. 11) estimates that some 15 million children die annually of malnutrition and related diseases. In many areas of Latin America, for instance, for well over half of all deaths of children under five years of age, malnutrition is either the primary cause or an associated cause (Pan American Health Organization, "Inter-American Investigation of Mortality in Child-

hood," First year of investigation, *Provisional Report,* Washington, D.C., 1971). The impact of disease on malnourished children in UDCs can be seen in comparisons of death rates in Guatemalan children with those in the United States. They are roughly 500 times as high for diarrheal diseases and 1000 times higher for measles. (Berg, "Nutrition").

3. For further details see P. R. Ehrlich, A. H. Ehrlich, and J. P. Holdren, *Human Ecology: Problems and Solutions* (San Francisco: W. H. Freeman, 1973). This source provides an overview of the problems of population, resources, and environment.

4. Figures here and in the previous paragraph are based on Lester R. Brown, "Population and Affluence: Growing Pressures on World Food Resources," *Population Bulletin,* vol. 29, no. 2 (1973). For more recent information, see his book, *In the Human Interest* (New York: W. W. Norton, 1974).

5. Alan Berg, "Nutrition."

6. *New York Times,* November 15, 1973.

7. *New York Times,* November 18, 1973.

8. "Ethiopia Says Famine Was Covered Up," *New York Times,* November 18, 1973.

9. Perhaps the most prominent among predictors of disastrous famines were William and Paul Paddock, whose book, *Famine 1975!* (Boston: Little Brown, 1967) was ridiculed by proponents of the green revolution.

10. *Time,* November 8, 1948.

11. For details see P. R. Ehrlich and A. H. Ehrlich, *Population, Resources, Environment: Issues in Human Ecology,* 2nd ed., (San Francisco: W. H. Freeman, 1972),

pp. 237–242. This work gives more detailed information than does *Human Ecology*.

12. Reid A. Bryson, "Climatic Modification by Air Pollution, II," *Report* 9, (1973), University of Wisconsin Institute for Environmental Studies. Reprinted in *The Ecologist,* October, 1973, under the title, "Drought in Sahelia: Who or What Is to Blame?"

13. This is especially true in the area of crop protection where the entire approach has been incompetent. See Ehrlich, Ehrlich, and Holdren, *Human Ecology,* pp. 167–170; P. M. Dolinger, P. R. Ehrlich, W. L. Fitch, and D. E. Breedlove, "Alkaloid and Predation Patterns in Colorado Lupine Populations," *Oecologia,* vol. 13 (1973), pp. 191–204.

14. Ehrlich, Ehrlich, and Holdren, *Human Ecology,* pp. 166–170; P. R. Ehrlich and P. Raven, "Butterflies and Plants: A Study in Coevolution," *Evolution,* vol. 18 (1965), pp. 586–608.

15. *State of Food and Agriculture 1973,* UN Food and Agriculture Organization, Rome. This volume is issued annually and is an excellent source for keeping up with the subject.

16. See Ehrlich and Ehrlich, *Population, Resources, Environment,* for UN's population projections. For further detail, see the UN's annual *Demographic Yearbook.*

17. See, for instance, R. Silberberg, *The Challenge of Climate,* (New York: Meredith Press, 1969), pp. 274–280.

18. Updated each year, available at newsstands as well as bookstores.

19. Updated annually, available from Superintendent of Documents, US Government Printing Office, Washington, D.C. 20402, $5.50 cloth. Also very useful are two volumes

of *Historical Statistics of the United States, Colonial Times to 1957* and *Continuation to 1962 and Revisions,* obtainable from the same source for $8.25 and $1.50, respectively. The latter two, along with any recent volume of the *Statistical Abstract,* will tell you more than you ever wanted to know about the US.

20. Updated annually, available from Publishing Service, United Nations, N.Y., $16.50 in paperback.

## Chapter 2, Pages 15 to 36

1. Quote courtesy of Dr. Peter Newman.

2. The most detailed and recent estimates, made recently by Physicist Amory Lovins and now in press in *Science and Public Affairs,* are also the most pessimistic.

3. P. R. Ehrlich and J. P. Holdren, "Impact of population growth," *Science* 171 (March 26, 1971), pp. 1212–1217. For a detailed discussion of factors contributing to environmental deterioration, see P. R. Ehrlich, A. H. Ehrlich, and J. P. Holdren, *Human Ecology* (San Francisco: W. H. Freeman, 1973), Chapter 7.

4. *The Outlook for Energy Sources,* vol. III of Resources for Freedom, A Report to the President by the President's Materials Policy Commission, W. S. Paley, Chairman, June, 1952.

5. Resources for Freedom, p. 13.

6. M. King Hubbert, *Nuclear Energy and the Fossil Fuels: Drilling and Production Practice.* (American Petroleum Institute, 1956), pp. 7–25.

7. In a fossil-fueled power plant, gas, coal, or oil (high-grade energy) is turned into heat (lower-grade energy) to make steam to turn turbines to generate electricity (high-

grade energy). The electricity is then transmitted to a home where it is turned back into heat (low-grade energy) in a resistive heating element. If gas, coal, or oil is turned directly into heat in the home, two conversions are avoided, and the efficiency increases almost three-fold.

8. We do not include here the systematic misinformation passed on by religious and educational institutions, since in most cases the transmitters believe what they are saying. No such charitable interpretation is possible for the activities of many men in industry and politics. The true attitude of many in the oil industry toward conservation, for instance, is typified by a high executive of Exxon who freely admitted he cared not a hoot about Alaska and called environmentalists opposed to the pipeline "god-damned moose-lovers." He clearly was not up to learning the difference between moose and caribou. (Conversation in New York City with P.R.E., January 27, 1974, Stage Delicatessen.)

9. A concise history of the development of the energy shortage can be found in the *New York Times,* February 10, 1974.

10. John P. Holdren, personal communication.

11. One reason for a shortage of refined petroleum products is that refinery capacity in the US has not increased much recently, because the oil giants could make higher profits by building refineries abroad where labor costs were lower, gasoline prices higher, or environmental restrictions not so severe. In addition, because of import quotas, they could not be sure of a sufficiently long-term flow of *low-cost* crude oil to guarantee them the scale of profits they felt was required to make investment in refineries in the US attractive. That scale can be imagined from the simple fact that the oil companies sell gasoline that costs them an average of four cents a gallon to produce at a wholesale price of twenty-one cents (according to Christopher T. Rand, "The Arabian Fantasy,"

*Harper's,* January, 1974). This shortage of refinery capacity may have contributed to the shortfall in the American supply of petroleum products in the winter of 1973–74. Perhaps more important was the rapid decline in domestic production predicted so long ago by Hubbert. A rapid rise in imports was required to offset this short-fall, but the rise was not sufficient.

For a brief time the gap was intensified by the Arab oil "embargo." This, however, seemed to be more of a public-relations device than a tight embargo. The Saudi Arabians, for instance, raised oil production by a million barrels a day during July and August so that they could later reduce production and still maintain the normal supply. The public largely blamed the oil industry for the shortage during the embargo, but failed to appreciate the industry's role in generating the underlying longer-term shortage.

12. Ralph Nader in late February laid the entire blame on the collusion of the giants of the oil industry in refusing to import more oil, which was available to them, because greater profits could be made by withholding supplies from the US to drive up prices, and by selling to Europe and Japan, where prices were already higher (*Today,* NBC, February 26, 1974). We hear the oil companies lie daily; we've never caught Nader in a falsehood. Guess whom we believe?

Further snafuing of the gasoline supply for profit by smaller companies during the shortage was alleged by a Federal Energy Office official in New York (Fred Ferretti, "Turetsky Asserts Oil Concerns Lie," *New York Times,* March 9, 1974).

The major companies were also accused of manipulating prices and supplies, sometimes in collusion with federal government agencies, in a monopolistic fashion by wit-nesses at Congressional hearings in April, 1974 ("Trust Law Offenses Laid to Oil Groups," *New York Times,* April 10, 1974).

13. *New York Times,* February 3, 1974.

14. We did not get a tape of the show, so the quote is approximate.

15. Assume, in a hypothetical example, that previous profits were $100 million, $95 million domestic and $5 million foreign (the "small base"). The new profits were $185 million, of which $20 million were increased domestic profits. That would mean a foreign profit increase from $5 million to $65 million, or 1200 percent.

16. *Time,* May 6, 1974, p. 69; "Understating of Oil Profits Alleged by Some Analysts," *New York Times,* April 27, 1974.

17. Approximately 16.5 million barrels a day. Since there are forty-two gallons to a barrel, this amounts to 693 million gallons per day, or slightly over three gallons per day for every man, woman, and child in the United States.

18. The petroleum figures in this and the preceding paragraph are from the National Petroleum Council Report, *US Energy Outlook to 1985.*

19. Sierra Club Bulletin, June, 1974, p. 29.

20. *New York Times,* April 16, 1973.

21. Christopher T. Rand, "Arabian Fantasy." (See note 11.)

22. See John P. Holdren, "Energy: Resources and Consumption," in Holdren and P. Herrera, *Energy* (San Francisco: Sierra Club, 1971), p. 35. Holdren's half of this "Battlebook" is the best available brief introduction to energy for the layman.

23. Harry M. Caudill, "Farming and Mining: There Is No Land to Spare," *Atlantic,* September, 1973, pp. 85–103.

24. Congressman Les Aspin of Wisconsin released a study

on January 1, 1974, showing donations totaling this amount from 413 directors, senior officials, and major stockholders of 178 oil companies.

25. See, for example, Representative Richard Bolling's *House Out of Order* (New York: E. P. Dutton, 1965); Drew Pearson and Jack Anderson, *The Case Against Congress* (New York: Simon and Schuster, 1968); Mark Green, et al., *Who Runs Congress?* (New York: Grossman, 1972); Dennis Pirages and Paul R. Ehrlich, *Ark II: Social Response to Environmental Imperatives* (New York: Viking Press, 1974).

26. For more details than are given in Appendix I, see Holdren, *Energy;* David R. Inglis, *Nuclear Energy: Its Physics and its Social Challenge* (Reading, Mass.: Addison-Wesley, 1973); and J. Harte et al., "Radiation," in J. Harte and R. H. Socolow, *Patient Earth* (New York: Holt, Rinehart and Winston, 1971), pp. 295–320.

27. Those interested in further discussion of radiation hazards are referred to Harte et al., "Radiation."

28. The standard unit of radiation exposure is the rad. By definition, a person has been exposed to a rad when each gram of body tissue has absorbed, on the average, 100 ergs of energy (an erg, in turn is about one forty-billionth of the energy in the familiar calorie of nutritionists). About 600 rads delivered rapidly will kill most people. Natural radiation has been estimated to expose the average person to a dose of about 0.115 rad (115 millirads) over a period of a year. For further details, see ibid.

29. John W. Gofman and Arthur R. Tamplin, *Poisoned Power: The Case Against Nuclear Power Plants* (Emmaus, Pa: Rodale Press, 1971).

30. D. F. Ford et al., *The Nuclear Fuel Cycle* (Cambridge, Mass: Union of Concerned Scientists, 1973), p. 83.

31. J. P. Holdren, "Uranium Availability and the Breeder Decision," Environmental Quality Laboratory Memorandum Number 8 (California Institute of Technology, 1974).

32. "Power Technology and the Future," presented at Briefing Conference for State and Local Government Officials on Nuclear Development, Columbia, South Carolina, May 21, 1970.

33. This does not mean, however, that exposure to 0.5 rad annually is one-tenth as dangerous as 5 rads—it may be, or it may be considerably less dangerous. We do not know enough about such things as the way radiation damage is repaired in cells to be able to extrapolate from the damage done by exposure to high levels of radiation to that done at very low levels.

34. Much of the story of this controversy is in Gofman and Tamplin's *Poisoned Power*, the basic accuracy of which has been attested to by personal contacts among physicists and biophysicists, including people within the Lawrence Laboratory.

35. "Report of Working Group 5—Radioactive Pollution of the Environment in the Context of the Energy Problem," Twenty-third Pugwash Conference on Science and World Affairs, *Congressional Record*, October 8, 1973, pp. s.18727–30.

36. Quoted in *The Clear and Present Danger*, A Public Report on Nuclear Power Plants, Environmental Education Group, 1973.

37. In theory, there is more than enough water in the oceans to dilute them to an acceptable level, but unfortunately biological systems would inevitably deconcentrate many of them. P. R. Ehrlich and A. H. Ehrlich, *Population, Resources, Environment*. 2nd ed. (San Francisco: W. H. Freeman, 1972), pp. 195–197.

38. In hearings before a committee of the California State Legislature, Dr. Frank Pittman, Chief of Radio-active Waste Disposal of the AEC, stated that the AEC was planning constant surveillance of the wastes for that period.

39. Ford et al., *Nuclear Fuel Cycle,* p. 27. (See note 30.)

40. Arthur R. Tamplin and John W. Gofman, *"Population Control" Through Nuclear Pollution* (Chicago: Nelson-Hall Co., 1970).

41. A. S. Kubo and D. J. Rose, "Disposal of Nuclear Wastes," *Science* 182 (December, 1973), pp. 1205–1211.

42. Twenty-third Pugwash Conference, "Report of Working Group 5." (See note 35.)

43. Ford et al., *Nuclear Fuel Cycle.*

44. Material in preceding paragraphs mostly from Ford et al., *Nuclear Fuel Cycle,* and *Clear and Present Danger* (See note 36).

45. Ford et al., *Nuclear Fuel Cycle,* p. 86.

46. R. D. Doctor et al., *California's Electric Quandary* (Rand Corp., R-1116-NSF/CSA, September 1972), vol. 3, p. 25.

47. Because the studies were carried out for the AEC by the Brookhaven National Laboratory.

48. Ford et al., *Nuclear Fuel Cycle.*

49. If each one of a million people trapped by traffic jams, for instance, received 350 rads of whole-body radiation, about 500,000 would die and the other 500,000 would be seriously ill from acute radiation exposure.

50. If a million people each received 100 rads of radiation,

there would be about 87,500 extra cancer deaths within twenty-five years; the same number of deaths would occur if 2 million people each received 50 rads of radiation, or 4 million people each received 25 rads of radiation (Source: *Congressional Record,* January 25, 1972, pp. E403–14, Gofman *et al.*).

51. On *Face the Nation,* CBS, December 30, 1973. Her performance on NBC's *Meet the Press* three months later was, if anything, more outrageous. Deceit and obfuscation characterized her answers on problems ranging from the possibilities of self-sufficiency to the safety of reactors. Her statement that the amount of plutonium produced by light-water reactors is insignificant was blatantly incorrect. The whole tenor of her discussion also made it clear that she was blissfully unaware of the environmental consequences of continuing to expand mankind's energy use, regardless of energy source.

52. This quote and the following material are from the *Newsletter* of Senator Mike Gravel (Alaska), September 28, 1973.

53. Information on the Fermi accident from Sheldon Novick, *The Careless Atom* (Boston: Houghton Mifflin, 1969).

54. The official report was somewhat more optimistic, but its most pessimistic weather assumption was far exceeded by actual weather shortly after the accident.

55. Holdren, "Uranium Availability and the Breeder Decision."

56. John McPhee, "The Curve of Binding Energy," *The New Yorker,* December 7, 14, and 21, 1973. Subsequently published as a book (New York: Farrar, Straus and Giroux, 1974); paperback: Ballantine Books, 1975.

57. See McPhee articles (*ibid.*) and Robert Gillette

"Nuclear Safeguards: Holes in the Fence," *Science* 182 (December 14, 1973), pp. 1112–1114.

58. Each of today's burners produces about 500 pounds of plutonium annually; liquid-metal fast breeders will produce 600–1200 pounds (U.S. Atomic Energy Commission, "Potential Nuclear Power Growth Patterns." WASH-1098, USGPO. 1970).

59. See, e.g., David B. Hall, "Adaptability of Fissile Materials to Nuclear Explosives" in *Proceedings of Symposium of Implementing Nuclear Safeguards,* Kansas State University, October 25-27, 1971. (New York: Praeger, 1972); Theodore B. Taylor, "Diversion by Non-Governmental Organizations" in *International Safeguards and Nuclear Industry*. Mason Willrich, ed. (Baltimore: Johns Hopkins Press, 1973). Don't be fooled by AEC statements to the effect that fissile materials from reactors are not "weapons grade." Weapons-grade materials are those pure enough to permit making a bomb with a predictable explosive yield. If you are a terrorist who doesn't care whether you get a half-kiloton or two-kiloton "bang," fissile materials from a reactor will do just fine.

60. Ford, et al., *Nuclear Fuel Cycle.*

61. Holdren and Herrera, *Energy,* p. 106. (See note 22.)

62. At $180 per troy ounce, gold was worth $5,253,000 per ton.

63. This was reported in both *Time* and *Newsweek.*

64. Radio Station KCBS, San Francisco, January 8, 1974.

65. Theodore Taylor, personal communication.

66. McPhee, "Curve of Binding Energy," December 3, 1974. (See note 56.)

67. Temperature itself is a measure of the average motion of particles, atoms, or molecules—the hotter a substance is, the more rapidly its parts are in motion.

68. McPhee, "Curve of Binding Energy," December 14, 1974. (See note 56.)

69. J. P. Holdren, personal communication.

70. Amory B. Lovins, *World Energy Strategies: Facts, Issues, and Options* (London: Earth Resources Research Ltd., 1973).

71. See, for example, Alan L. Hammond, "Solar Energy: A Feasible Source of Power?" Science 172 (May 14, 1971), p. 660; Anonymous, "Solar Power Brought Down to Earth," *New Scientist,* March 30, 1972; Walter E. Morrow, Jr., "Solar Energy: Its Time Is Near," *Technology Review,* December, 1973, pp. 31–43.

72. Statistics on installed capacity from *Statistical Abstract of US, 1972.*

73. Dr. Jerome Weingart, Environmental Quality Laboratory, Cal. Tech., personal communication.

74. Derek P. Gregory, "The Hydrogen Economy," *Scientific American,* January, 1973; W. E. Winsche, K. C. Hoffman, and F. J. Salzano, "Hydrogen: Its Future Role in the Nation's Energy Economy," *Science* 180 (June 29, 1973), pp. 1325–1332. Both of these articles envision nuclear power as the primary source of hydrogen, but solar or geothermal could serve as well.

75. Richard I. Lewis, *The Nuclear Power Rebellion* (New York: Viking, 1972), p. 29.

76. The AEC has also been accused of withholding evidence favorable to the development of solar energy ("Solar Energy Data Ignored by A.E.C., a Senator Asserts," *New York Times,* April 1, 1974, p. 24).

77. *N. Y. Times,* "Solar Energy Data Ignored."

78. Citizens Energy Council, Larry Bogart, Box 285, Allendale, N.J. 07401. The Council will send you names and addresses of over 150 safe-power groups in 34 states and British Columbia. The Council also prints a monthly newspaper, "Nuclear Opponents." Other prominent groups against nuclear power are Friends of the Earth (529 Commercial, San Francisco, California 94111), and Natural Resources Defense Council, 36 West 44th Street, New York, New York 10036). Most environmental groups are more or less actively opposed to nuclear power plants.

79. Lewis, *Nuclear Power Rebellion.* (See note 75.)

### Chapter 3, Pages 37 to 87

1. On *Issues and Answers,* ABC television network, October 4, 1970.

2. *Time,* July 9, 1973, pp. 57–58; *Newsweek,* August 13, 1973, pp. 73–74.

3. *San Francisco Chronicle,* May 29, 1973, p. 26.

4. See, for instance, Walter Laqueur, "The Idea of Europe Runs Out of Gas," *New York Times Magazine,* January 20, 1974, p. 12.

5. Richard Falk, *This Endangered Planet* (New York: Random House, 1971).

6. N. J. Maidenberg, "The Shift in Commodity Power," *New York Times,* January 13, 1974; and reports of commodity markets.

7. E.g., Louis J. Halle, "Does War Have a Future?" *Foreign Affairs,* October, 1973.

8. K. E. F. Watt, *The Titanic Effect* (New York: Dutton, 1974). Also available in paperback from Sinauer Associates, Stamford, Conn.

9. C. Fred Beigston, "The World May Have to Live with Shortages," *New York Times,* January 27, 1974.

10. Quoted in "Raw materials: U.S. Grows More Vulnerable to Third World Cartels," *Science,* 183 (January 18, 1974), p. 186.

11. Data in this paragraph from *New York Times,* December 13, 1973, and January 20, 1974; and Marcus F. Franda, "India and the Energy Crunch," *Fieldstaff Reports,* American Universities Field Staff, Hanover, New Hampshire.

12. Peter R. Kann, "The Agony of India," *Wall Street Journal,* April 16 and 17, 1974. These two articles describe in detail the overwhelming problems India has been facing.

13. Trevor Drieberg, "The Lessons of the Drought," *Ceres,* March-April, 1974, pp. 13–17.

14. Kenneth L. Murray, "India's Wheat Harvest to Fall Below Last Year's, Supply Tight." *Foreign Agriculture.* US Department of Agriculture, May 13, 1974.

15. Bernard Weinraub, "Seven Births Every Minute: Bangladesh's Biggest Long-Range Problem," *New York Times,* February 1, 1974, p. 2.

16. John Dillon, "Asian Food Shortage—World Threat," *Christian Science Monitor,* July 3, 1974, p. 1.

17. Per capita GNP ranges from $60 to $90 in the countries with 90 percent of the people affected (1973 *World Population Data Sheet,* Population Reference Bureau).

18. The Hindustan Aeronautics, Ltd., HF-24 Marut (Wind Spirit). According to *Jane's All the World's Aircraft, 1966–67,* ten production Maruts were flying by 1965.

19. Preparatory Conference for the World Population Conference of 1974, held in Stockholm, September, 1973.

20. For example, *Foreign Agriculture,* USDA Foreign Agriculture Service, and *Ceres,* a monthly journal of the United Nations Food and Agriculture Organization.

21. In 1972 the US alone accounted for the following percentages of the world's exports: Wheat, 33%; corn, 55%; soybeans, 89%; rice, 19%. Export figures from *Statistical Abstract of the US, 1973.*

22. "Vaccination Blitz Battles Smallpox in Bangladesh," *Los Angeles Times,* March 6, 1973; "Cholera's Comeback," *Newsweek,* September 17, 1973; "Cholera on the March," *Time,* September 17, 1973.

23. R. E. Kissling, et al., "Agent of disease contracted from green monkeys," *Science* 160 (1968), pp. 888–890.

24. *UN Statistical Yearbook, 1972.*

## Chapter 4, Pages 117 to 137

1. Quoted by N. Huddle and M. Reich in *The Ecologist,* August 1973.

2. Georg Borgstrom, *The Hungry Planet* (New York: Collier-Macmillan, 1967), p. 318.

3. Japan permits 351 additives while the US only allows 133, and countries with more concern for the health of food consumers permit much fewer—Sweden 78, West

Germany 64, France 32. Source: Jun Ui, ed., *Polluted Japan* (Tokyo: Jushu-Koza, 1972).

4. F. Roy Lockheimer, "Population Review 1970: Japan," *Fieldstaff Reports,* vol. 18, no. 1 (1971), p. 3.

5. *UN Statistical Yearbook, 1971.*

6. Georg Borgstrom, *World Food Resources* (New York: Intext, 1973), p. 225.

7. Borgstrom, *Hungry Planet,* p. 179. (See note 2.)

8. Lockheimer, "Population Review 1970: Japan," p. 3. (See note 4.)

9. *FAO Trade Yearbook, 1968.*

10. Charles F. Gallagher, "Toward Population Redistribution in Japan," *Fieldstaff Reports,* vol. 19, no. 1 (1972), p. 7.

11. Lockheimer, "Population Review 1970: Japan," p. 3.

12. Charles F. Gallagher, personal communication.

13. P. R. Ehrlich and A. H. Ehrlich, *Population, Resources, Environment: Issues in Human Ecology,* 2nd ed. (San Francisco: W. H. Freeman, 1972), Chapter 6.

14. Gallagher, "Toward Population Redistribution in Japan," p. 7. (See note 10.)

15. F. Roy Lockheimer, "Japan's New Population Politics," *Fieldstaff Reports,* vol. 17, no. 5 (1970).

16. See Alan Sweezy, 1970, "Economic meaning of a labor shortage," *Science* 167 (1970), p. 97.

17. An exception is one small reactor that is a safer British gas-cooled design.

18. *Proceedings of the Fourth International Conference on Peaceful Uses of Atomic Energy, Geneva, September 1971.* (Published by UN and the International Atomic Energy Agency, Vienna, 1972).

19. See Ehrlich and Ehrlich, *Population, Resources, Environment,* pp. 37ff, for a discussion of the technical meaning of "replacement reproduction."

20. In that year the astrological signs of fire and horse coincided, something which occurs only every sixty years. Such years are thought by many Japanese to be extremely inauspicious for childbearing. Females born in such years are, for instance, considerably less marriageable than those born in other years. Source: Lockheimer, "Japan's New Population Politics." (See note 15.)

21. Charles F. Gallagher, personal communication.

22. This was the largest award in the four major pollution cases settled so far. In September, 1971, the Showa Denko Company was found responsible for mercury poisoning in Niigata, where there were 330 victims and thirteen deaths. The award was $810,000. In July, 1972, $285,000 in damages were given to victims of "Yokkaichi asthma" (1,054 victims, 76 deaths), a disorder caused by air pollution from six petrochemical companies in Yokkaichi, central Japan. The third settlement was $480,000 for the victims of "Itai, itai" cadmium poisoning (265 victims, 47 deaths), assessed against Mitsui Mining and Smelting Company. Source: *New York Times,* March 21, 1973.

23. Norie Huddle, Michael Reich, and Nahum Stiskin, *Island of Dreams—Environmental Crisis in Japan* (Autumn Press, in press).

24. Ibid.

25. *Time,* July 9, 1973; *New York Times,* July 29, 1973.

26. *Time,* December 24, 1973.

27. *San Francisco Examiner and Chronicle,* December 30, 1973.

28. Ibid.

29. *New York Times,* January 19, 1974.

30. Canaries are more susceptible to odorless poison gases than are human beings. Therefore, until modern gas-detecting methods were developed, miners took canaries with them to warn of dangerous concentrations of gases in the mines.

31. *UN Demographic Yearbook, 1971.*

32. Much of the information in this section is from Thomas G. Sangers, "Brazil: Population, Development and the Dream of Greatness," *Fieldstaff Reports,* (American University Field Staff, 1971).

33. H. J. Maidenberg, "The Giant's Shadow Lengthens," *New York Times,* January 28, 1973.

34. *New York Times,* January 28, 1973; the state is Minas Gerais.

35. *New York Times,* January 20, 1974.

36. Production is not the same as assembly, which means simply putting together vehicles from parts made largely or entirely elsewhere. Moreover, Brazil produced and assembled almost twice as many automobiles as were assembled in all the rest of Latin America. UN statistics for countries that are producers include vehicles that are assembled there. In Latin America, Chile, Colombia, Mexico, Peru, and Venezuela have automobile assembly plants, but no production.

37. *New York Times,* January 28, 1973.

38. *1973 World Population Data Sheet,* Population Reference Bureau.

39. *New York Times,* July 28, 1973.

40. James P. Grant, "Development: The End of Trickle Down," *Foreign Policy,* no. 12 (Fall, 1973).

41. Ibid.

42. Borgstrom, *Hungry Planet,* 2nd ed., p. 363.

43. *Time,* September 13, 1971.

44. See, for instance, Mary McNeil, "Lateritic Soils," *Scientific American,* November 1964; reprinted in *Global Ecology.*

45. H. Sioli, "Recent Human Activities in the Brazilian Amazon Region and Their Ecological Effects," in B. J. Meggers, E. S. Ayensu, and W. D. Duckworth, eds., *Tropical Forest Ecosystems in Africa and South America: A Comparative Review* (Washington, D.C.: Smithsonian Institution Press, 1973), pp. 321–334; see also B. J. Meggers's article in the same volume. The best general review of the ecological barriers to high-yield agriculture in the tropics is Daniel H. Janzen, "The Unexploited Tropics," *The Bulletin of the Ecological Society of America,* September, 1970, pp. 4–7.

46. *Time,* September 13, 1971.

47. Quoted by Affonso Henreques in "The Awakening Amazon Giant," *Americas,* February, 1972.

48. Ibid.

49. *Time,* September 13, 1971.

50. *Time,* September 13, 1971.

51. McNeill, "Lateritic Soils." (See note 44.)

52. B. J. Meggers, *Amazonia, Man and Culture in a Counterfeit Paradise* (Chicago: Aldine Atherton, 1971), p. 154. Those interested in the human ecology of the Amazon Basin should consult this fine, brief paperback.

53. *New York Times,* March 11, 1973.

54. A discussion of the indispensible free services provided to mankind by natural ecosystems can be found in P. R. Ehrlich, A. H. Ehrlich, and J. P. Holdren, *Human Ecology: Problems and Solutions* (San Francisco: W. H. Freeman, 1973).

55. *Reports on Population/Family Planning,* Population Council, no. 2, September 1973.

56. Instituto Brasileiro de Geografia e Estatistica: *Series Estatisticas Retrospectivas, 1970,* and *Annuario Estatistico de Brazil, 1972.*

57. Ehrlich, Ehrlich, and Holdren, *Human Ecology.*

## Chapter 5, Pages 139 to 183

1. From *Whole Grains, A Book of Quotations,* by Art Spiegelman and Bob Schneider, reprinted in *Intellectual Digest,* March, 1974.

2. David Halberstam, *The Best and the Brightest* (Greenwich, Ct.: Fawcett-Crest, 1973); and Neil Sheehan et al., *The Pentagon Papers* (New York: Bantam Books, 1971).

2a. Richard J. Whalen, *Catch a Falling Flag* (Boston: Houghton-Mifflin).

3. Superbly summarized in Richard Harris, "The New Justice," *The New Yorker*, March 25, 1972.

4. Dennis Pirages and Paul Ehrlich, *Ark II: Social Response to Environmental Imperatives* (New York: Viking Press, 1974).

5. *CBS News*, March 14, 1974.

6. Pirages and Ehrlich, *Ark II*. See bibliography for entry into the extensive literature on governmental reform.

7. In recent years, polls have shown politicians to be very low in public esteem relative to those in other occupations, and that a large portion of the population disapproves of the way they do their jobs (e.g., Gallup Poll reported in the *New York Times*, April 28, 1974, that only 30% of Americans approved of the way Congress was handling its job, while 47% disapproved).

8. Michael Barone et al., *Almanac of American Politics* (Boston: Gambit, 1974).

9. Write to 324 C Street, S.E., Washington, D.C. 20003 for the League of Conservation Voters; for Common Cause, write 2030 M Street, N.W., Washington, D.C. 20036.

10. Pirages and Ehrlich, *Ark II*. (See note 4.)

11. *Daedalus*, Fall, 1973, p. 117.

12. For further details, see P. R. Ehrlich and A. H. Ehrlich, *Population, Resources, Environment*, 2nd ed. (San Francisco: W. H. Freeman, 1972), pp. 62–64.

13. For further discussion of this and related economic problems, see Herman E. Daly, ed., *Toward a Steady-State Economy* (San Francisco: W. H. Freeman, 1973). The ability of the GNP to grow is a fundamental element

of current economic models, and thus all of these models require revision.

14. K. E. F. Watt, *The Titanic Effect* (Stamford, Ct.: Sinauer, 1974), pp. 74–77.

15. Watt, *The Titanic Effect*.

16. For details on the German inflation see Gustav Stolper's *German Economy 1870–1940: Issues and Trends* (New York: Reynal and Hitchcock, 1940).

17. Both US banks and savings and loan institutions are insured for less than 2 percent of their insured deposits by the Federal Deposit Insurance Corporation (FDIC) and the Federal Savings and Loan Insurance Corporation (SLIC). Check their annual reports for the most recent information.

18. See Milton Friedman, "The Poor Man's Welfare Payment to the Middle Class," *Washington Monthly,* May, 1972. One place where the ideas of archconservative but smart economist Friedman makes sense is in the area of welfare reform, where his basic notion might be summarized as "the hell with bureaucratic programs, give the poor *money*." His views on Social Security are shared by, among others, ultraliberal newspaper columnist Nicholas von Hoffman; see p. 14 of the same issue of the *Monthly*.

19. For an ultrasimplified but very amusing discussion of monetary matters, see Harry Browne's book *You Can Profit from a Monetary Crisis* (New York: Macmillan, 1974). His attack on governmental handling of economics is devastating, but he fails to recognize the fundamental environmental constraints that make total laissez-faire unwise. You will learn a lot while you try to pick holes in his arguments. At the other end of the spectrum, the best thinking of "mainstream" economics (with a reasonably fair shake for heterodoxy) can be found in Professor Paul Samuelson's superb text, *Economics,* 9th ed. (New York: McGraw-Hill, 1973).

20. Pirages and Ehrlich, *Ark II.*

21. *US News and World Report,* July 2, 1973. For more details on pension abuses, see Ralph Nader and Kate Blackwell's book, *You and Your Pension,* (New York: Grossman, 1973).

22. Browne, *You Can Profit from a Monetary Crisis.*

### Chapter 6, Pages 185 to 216

1. Howard T. Odum, *Environment, Power, and Society* (New York: Wiley, 1971).

2. P. R. Ehrlich and A. H. Ehrlich, *Population, Resources, Environment,* 2nd ed. (San Francisco: W. H. Freeman, 1972).

3. *San Francisco Chronicle,* May 29, 1973, p. 26.

4. For example, in 1971 the world (excluding China) produced 353 million metric tons (mmt) of wheat; of that, the US produced 44.6 mmt and exported 17.2 mmt (*U.N. Statistical Yearbook, 1972*).

5. 47.7 million metric tons 1972 world soybean production; 34.9 mmt US production; 12 mmt exported (*Foreign Agriculture,* USDA, February 5, 1973; and *World Agriculture Production and Trade,* USDA, March, 1973).

6. David Weisbrod, "What Happens When America Runs Out of Leftovers," *Washington Monthly,* July-August, 1973, pp. 66–71.

7. Lester Brown, "The Need for a Food Reserve," *Wall Street Journal,* October 10, 1973.

8. Ehrlich and Ehrlich, *Population, Resources, Environment.*

9. Joseph Albright, "Some Deal," *New York Times Magazine,* November 25, 1973.

10. Data for this section are taken primarily from four sources: The Federation of American Scientists' *Special Newsletter on World Food Production,* Sept. 1973; Lester R. Brown, "Population and Affluence: Growing Pressures on World Food Resources," *Population Bulletin,* vol. 29, no. 2, 1973; Frances Moore Lappé, *Diet for a Small Planet,* (New York: Ballantine Books, 1971); and The President's Science Advisory Committee, *Report on the World Food Problem,* vol. II (Washington, D.C.: US Government Printing Office, 1967).

11. N. W. Pirie, *Food Resources, Conventional and Novel* (Baltimore: Penguin Books, 1969).

12. President's Science Advisory Committee, *Report on the World Food Problem.*

13. Lappé, *Diet,* quoting "Major Uses of Land and Water in the US, Summary for 1959," *Agricultural Economic Report No. 13,* Farm Economics Division, Economic Research Service, USDA, p. 2.

14. Eric Hirst ("Living off the Fuels of the Land," *Natural History,* December, 1973, pp. 21–22) estimates six times, J. S. and C. E. Steinhart ("Energy Use in the U.S. Food System," *Science,* vol. 184, April 19, 1974, pp. 307–316) estimate nine times. The latter study may have included elements of the system omitted by Hirst.

15. David Pimentel et al., "Food Production and the Energy Crisis," *Science* 182 (November 2, 1973) pp. 443–449.

16. Malcolm Slesser, "How Many Can We Feed?" *The Ecologist,* June, 1973, pp. 216–220.

17. Pimentel et al., "Food Production"; Steinhart and Steinhart, "Energy Use." (See notes 15 and 14.)

18. John Kenneth Galbraith, *A China Passage* (New York: Signet, 1973). Galbraith thought it quaint that "superstitious Chinese peasants" still prefer natural wastes to modern fertilizers.

19. "What Does It Take to Solve the Sludge Crisis?" *Rodale's Environment Action Bulletin,* vol. 5, no. 10 (March 9, 1974).

20. Pimentel et al., "Food Production"; Steinhart and Steinhart, "Energy Use" (see notes 15 and 14); Paul Ehrlich and Peter Raven, "Butterflies and Plants," *Scientific American,* June, 1967; and P. M. Dolinger, et al., "Alkaloid and Predation Patterns in Colorado Lupine Populations," *Oecologia,* vol. 13 (1973).

21. *Patterns of Energy Consumption in the United States,* Report prepared for the Office of Science and Technology, Executive Office of the President, by Stanford Research Institute, Stanford, Calif., Jan. 1972.

22. *U.S. News and World Report,* January 19, 1970, pp. 24–26.

23. A relatively detailed analysis of what various nutrients do for you can be found in Ehrlich and Ehrlich, *Population, Resources, Environment,* Appendix 3, pp. 464–469. A simplified method of measuring food values is described in Michael Jacobson, *Nutrition Scoreboard: Your Guide to Better Eating,* Center for Science in the Public Interest (1779 Church Street NW, Washington, D.C. 20036), 1973.

24. Roger J. Williams, *Nutrition Against Disease* (New York: Bantam Books, 1973).

25. For detailed analysis, see Lappé, *Diet.* This book also includes recipes for using high-quality protein combinations.

26. Ibid., Ballantine Books, 1971.

27. For an enlightening discussion of the complex nutritional factors in cardiovascular disease as far as they are known, see Williams, *Nutrition Against Disease*.

28. James S. Turner, *The Chemical Feast* (New York: Grossman, 1970). The information on cheating FDA scientists appeared in *Science*, vol. 180 (June 8, 1973), p. 1038.

29. One individual who doesn't quite fit either category is Adelle Davis, whose popular books on nutrition can be very helpful to the layman interested in nutrition. The best-known of these is *Let's Eat Right to Keep Fit* (New York: Signet, 1970), but her book on cooking to minimize loss of nutrients, *Let's Cook it Right* (New York: Signet, 1970) is also very useful. Mrs. Davis's basic information is sound, but she has on occasion aroused the ire of professional nutritionists by making poorly substantiated claims for the value of some nutrients and by recommending what they consider potentially dangerous doses, especially for vitamins A and D.

30. Williams, *Nutrition Against Disease*. (See note 24.)

31. *Newsweek,* September 18, 1972, p. 71.

## Chapter 7, Pages 217 to 257

1. *Geschichte und Nächtereisen* (Vienna: 1926), p. 32.

2. Cited in L. J. Peter, *The Peter Prescription* (New York: Bantam, 1973), p. 235.

3. *Time,* April 15, 1974.

4. Eric Hirst and John C. Moyers, "Efficiency of Energy Use in the United States," *Science* 179 (March 30, 1974), pp. 1299–1304.

5. For further discussion, see Dennis Pirages and Paul R. Ehrlich, *Ark II: Social Response to Environmental Imperatives,* (New York: Viking, 1974).

6. Hirst and Moyers, "Efficiency of Energy Use."

7. *Citizen Action Guide to Energy Conservation,* Citizen's Advisory Committee on Environmental Quality, 1973, is a useful compendium on the subject. It is available at $1.75 from the Superintendent of Documents, US Government Printing Office, Washington, D.C. 20402.

8. Hirst and Moyers, "Efficiency of Energy Use."

9. *San Francisco Chronicle,* Sunday Punch section, January 13, 1974.

10. Dr. Jerome Weingart, Environmental Quality Lab., Caltech, personal communication.

11. *Citizen Action Guide to Energy Conservation* includes a section on determining the efficiency of air-conditioning units.

12. Kenneth H. Cooper, *Aerobics,* (New York: Bantam Books, 1968).

13. *Citizen Action Guide,* section on conservation in industry.

14. John P. Holdren, personal communication.

15. Bradford Angier, *Survival with Style* (New York: Vintage Books, 1974). This is a goldmine of information on survival skills.

16. See Angier, *Survival with Style,* for additional details on water purification.

17. Adelle Davis, *Let's Eat Right to Keep Fit* (New York: Signet, 1970). While some of Adelle Davis's claims for the value of many nutrients should be taken with a grain of salt, she is generally sound on information of this sort.

18. One example is The Self Reliance Institute, a new organization headquartered in Palo Alto, California (*Palo Alto Times,* March 29, 1974). The Institute plans to teach many skills that would be helpful for gaining independence from "the system." According to Paul Growald of the Institute, their program includes systematic, proven methods for food production, preservation, and storage; home heating and maintenance; medical self-reliance; and economic survival. The Institute's first courses teach techniques for growing as many vegetables and small animals (particularly rabbits) as possible with the limits of time, space, and light available to most city and suburban people. The teachers are Dr. William Olkowski of the University of California Agricultural Experiment Station and his wife Helga. The Institute's goal is to return self-reliance to North American lifestyles and to reduce dependence on large institutions. We encourage you to start your own schools for self-reliance or to organize your friends and learn practical survival skills on your own. If you are interested, you can write to the Self Reliance Institute, P.O. Box 11176, Palo Alto, California 94306 (include a stamped, self-addressed envelope).

19. *The Merck Manual,* 17th ed., (Rahway, N. J.: Merck and Co., 1972).

20. See Angier, *Survival with Style,* for several helpful suggestions for a first aid kit. His discussion is based on short wilderness trips, but many of the recommendations are also applicable to home emergencies when medical care is not readily available.

21. *Statistical Abstract of the US, 1973.*

22. One firm supplying less-lethal weapons is MB Associates, Box 238, San Ramon, California 94583.

23. For further details see P. R. Ehrlich and A. H. Ehrlich, *Population, Resources, Environment,* 2nd ed. (San Francisco: W. H. Freeman, 1972), pp. 243-245.

# Appendixes

## Appendix I—Fire From a Nuclear Burner

There are two basic ways in which nuclear energy may be made available to generate power: fission and fusion. In fission, the atomic nuclei of very heavy elements, such as uranium and plutonium, are *split*, producing nuclei of medium weight, among other fragments, and releasing surplus energy. In fusion, two very light nuclei are *forced together* so that they fuse into a medium-weight nucleus, and surplus energy is also released.

Whenever free protons and neutrons combine into an atomic nucleus, they lose a small portion of their mass, which is converted into energy. The more energy released, the more tightly the nucleus is bound together—thus, the name "binding energy." As one goes through the elements from lighter to heavier, the curve of binding energy per nucleon (proton or neutron) in the nucleus first climbs and then drops. It is highest in elements like copper, with atomic weights around 60 (hydrogen has a weight of about 1.0, helium 4.0, uranium 238, plutonium 239). Whenever medium-weight nuclei with high binding energy are created from either lighter or heavier nuclei with lower binding energy, some mass is transformed into energy (as described in Einstein's famous formula $E = mc^2$). Thus surplus energy can be produced either by fission of heavy nuclei or fusion of light nuclei.

This surplus energy may be used to heat water to make steam, which is then used to drive turbines, just as it would be in a fossil-fuel fired power plant. A standard nuclear power plant, which uses the fission process, may be thought of as a power plant that "burns" heavy elements; hence, these are often referred to as "burners." Fusion power, which is still in the early stages of development, will not be discussed in detail here.

The trick to running a fission power plant is to keep a controlled "chain reaction" going. When an atomic nucleus of the appropriate type is fissioned, some of the fragments produced are neutrons. Neutrons traveling at appropriate speeds may hit other nuclei and cause them to fission. This process may be repeated so that a chain of such reactions occurs, each releasing neutrons and creating heat. The only kind of atoms found in nature with nuclei capable of sustaining a chain reaction is a variety (isotope) of uranium called uranium 235 ($U^{235}$).

The nuclei of all atoms of an element contain the same number of positively charged particles (protons), but two atoms of the same element may differ in the number of uncharged particles (neutrons). All hydrogen atoms have one proton, and most have no neutrons. But occasional atoms of hydrogen have a proton and neutron, weigh almost twice as much as common hydrogen (they are sometimes called "heavy hydrogen"), and represent another isotope of hydrogen, deuterium (or $H^2$). A third isotope of hydrogen, tritium ($H^3$), has one proton and two neutrons. Atomic weights are either an average of various isotopes in the proportion in which they occur naturally, or, in the case of transuranium artificial elements, the weight of the most stable isotope.

Isotopes of an element may differ from each other in more than mass. For instance, while $U^{235}$ is capable of sustaining a chain reaction, the uranium isotope with three more neutrons, $U^{238}$, is not. The kinds of atoms capable of sustaining such reactions are termed "fissile." Two manmade isotopes, uranium 233 ($U^{233}$) and plutonium 239 ($Pu^{239}$) are also fissile. Natural uranium as mined is more than 99 percent the isotope uranium 238, which is not fissile.

At any given time, some of the multitudes of nuclei in

a chunk of $U^{235}$ will be giving off radiation, changing into new kinds of lighter nuclei. Much less frequently, a $U^{235}$ nucleus will fission, releasing both neutrons and radiation. In either case, it is said to be undergoing "radioactive decay." Radiation (in the context of radioactivity) is a general term covering high-energy waves or particles. It is of great interest to us because, when an object is exposed to radiation, some or all of that energy may be absorbed by the target, with various effects (such as the initiation of a cancer by causing a change in the genetic material in a human cell). Three principal kinds of radiation are given off by radioactive substances: the nuclei of helium atoms, electrons and positrons (the positively charged analog of electrons), and very high-energy electromagnetic radiation. Before their exact nature was understood, these were named alpha rays, beta rays, and gamma rays, respectively. X-ray is the term often used to describe electromagnetic radiation, which has less energy than gamma rays, but at least several hundred times the energy of the most familiar form of electromagnetic radiation, visible light. Neutrons released from the nuclei of atoms are also considered a form of radiation, as are various less-frequently encountered subatomic particles. Thus nuclear decay can produce a wide variety of products.

Although no one can say exactly when a given nucleus will decay, when a huge number are present (as in any visible bit of the element—remember, atoms are extremely small), the proportion of nuclei decaying per unit time can be measured. For any isotope undergoing radioactive decay, this proportion is constant. Since, when a nucleus of, say, $U^{235}$ has fissioned, it is no longer $U^{235}$, we can think of any chunk of $U^{235}$ as continually destroying itself. (Most radioactive isotopes decay without fissioning simply by giving off radiation and changing to other isotopes in the process.)

Physicists have calculated the time it takes for the breakdown of one-half of any given number of nuclei of an isotope that will decay spontaneously; this is known as the "half-life" of that isotope. The half-life of uranium

235 is over 700 million years. Thus, if a chunk of pure uranium 235 were kept for some 1.4 billion years, at the end of that time about one-fourth of what was left would still be uranium 235, and the rest would be lead, as it turns out. Strontium 90 is an isotope of medium weight produced in nuclear reactors. Its unstable nuclei undergo radioactive decay, but it does not fission. Strontium-90 has a half-life of about 28 years. After 280 years, less than one-thousandth of the original amount remains. Some isotopes have half-lives measured in tiny fractions of a second, and they essentially disappear immediately. The half-lives of radioactive isotopes determine how long atomic wastes must be carefully segregated from the environment. A rule of thumb is twenty half-lives, after which less than one-millionth of the original amount remains.

When one wishes to build an atomic bomb or a nuclear power plant, the first job is to get sufficient fissile material. For an atomic bomb, one must assemble what is known as a "critical mass." This means enough fissile material, sufficiently pure and tightly enough packed so at least one neutron emitted from each fission will cause another fission. (Other fates of neutrons include absorption in nonfissile U238 or impurities, or escape into the surroundings.) The essential problem, then, is to provide enough nuclear targets to assure an eventual "hit" as each neutron travels along, or to jam the nuclei together to make the probability of a hit per unit of travel great enough. Technically, the term "critical" refers to the situation in which each fission causes *exactly* one more fission, leading to a constant reaction rate. A bomb requires a rapidly increasing reaction rate, which follows when each fission causes appreciably more than one additional fission. Any situation in which the reaction rate is increasing is called "super-critical"; reactors being brought gradually up to full power are slightly supercritical, bombs are highly supercritical.

Under normal conditions (that is, if it is not surrounded by neutron-reflecting material or compressed), a critical mass of $U^{235}$ is slightly less than fifty pounds. In designing an A-bomb made from $U^{235}$ then, the problem is either to bring together two chunks of $U^{235}$, each less than a critical mass (subcritical), in order to assemble a super-critical mass, or to compress a subcritical ball of $U^{235}$ to a density that makes it supercritical. In either case, the idea is to create the uncontrolled, rapidly escalating chain reaction known as an atomic explosion.

In one type of atomic bomb, a conventional explosive is used to shoot a subcritical cylinder of $U^{235}$ into a cylindrical hole in a subcritical sphere of $U^{235}$, thus instantly producing a supercritical mass. (The critical mass is often less than fifty pounds because a neutron reflector is employed.) In another type of atomic bomb, a nearly-critical mass of $U^{235}$ is surrounded by conventional explosives, which, when triggered, compress it into a super-critical mass. In either case, if the assembly of the critical mass is not rapid enough, the result is a small explosion known as a "fizzle." The chain reaction blows the critical mass apart before it can go far enough to generate a full-scale atomic blast.

One can think of a nuclear power station as being at the opposite end of the chain reaction from the bomb. The idea is to produce a controlled chain reaction, one which neither dies out nor "fizzles." A large amount of heat is generated over a long period of time, not in a tiny fraction of a second as in a nuclear bomb. Burner-reactor design is such that the rapid critical-mass assembly necessary to produce a large atomic-bomb-type explosion is virtually impossible.

In a typical burner, the reactor uses as "fuel" slender rods of uranium covered with a thin sheath (cladding) of a special metal alloy. The uranium has been "enriched" so that there is a higher percentage of $U^{235}$ relative to $U^{238}$ than is found in naturally occurring uranium. Bundles of thousands of these rods (fuel elements), interspersed with movable rods of a neutron-absorbing material like cadmium or boron, are bathed in flowing water. The water serves two functions. First, it is a moderator; that is, it functions to slow down neutrons so they will be more readily "captured" by $U^{235}$ nuclei, which in turn will split. Second, the water serves as a coolant, carrying away the heat created by the chain reaction. The coolant accomplishes two things. It cools the rods so that the reactor does not melt and destroy itself, and it carries the heat to a heat exchanger, where it is turned into steam to spin turbines and run generators. Remember, the production of heat is the purpose of the reactor. This heat production can be considered a replacement for the heat produced by coal, oil, or gas burners in a conventional fossil-fuel power plant.

Gradually, the fuel elements in an operating reactor change as the chain reaction proceeds. Nuclei of fissile material disappear as they fission to be replaced with fission products. These products absorb neutrons and thus tend to dampen the chain reaction. After a year or so an element must be replaced, and the element is sent to a reprocessing plant where the remaining fissile material, leftover $U^{235}$ and newly created $Pu^{239}$, are separated for reuse, and the radioactive fission products (wastes) are sent to storage.

The movable rods of neutron-absorbing material in a reactor are equivalent to the valve on the oil or gas jet of a conventional power plant boiler. They serve to control the rate of the chain reaction by making fewer neutrons available. The further the control rods are slid in between the fuel elements, the slower will be the chain reaction. The more they are withdrawn, the faster the reaction. In many reactors, the control rods also serve as the main safety device. In case of a problem, they can be quickly inserted all the way to shut down ("scram") the reactor. There are several different kinds of burner reactors, characterized by various combinations of substances used as moderator (e.g., water, heavy water, graphite) and as coolant (e.g., water, helium, $CO_2$, organic liquids). But they all have cores with the same basic components: fuel elements, control rods, coolant, and moderator.

For every fission, two to three neutrons are produced, but only one neutron per fission is needed to sustain the chain reaction. Some of the excess neutrons are absorbed in uranium 238 and initiate a sequence of nuclear reactions in which the $U^{238}$ is transformed into fissile plutonium 239. In the terminology of nuclear engineering, $U^{238}$ is called "fertile" material, and the process of transforming it into plutonium by means of neutron capture is called "conversion." In an alternative conversion process, fertile thorium 232 absorbs a neutron and is transformed after a sequence of reactions to fissile uranium 233. Typical burner reactors are actually moderately efficient converters; they produce an average of 0.4 to 0.6 new fissile nuclei (via neutron capture by fertile materials) for each fissile nucleus consumed. The great importance of this process is that the two naturally occurring fertile isotopes, uranium 238 and thorium 232, are much more abundant than is the naturally occurring fissile isotope uranium 235.

It is possible to build reactors that produce *more than one* new fissile nucleus from fertile material for each fissile nucleus consumed. Such a reactor is called a breeder. The type of breeder reactor that is presently most highly developed is the LMFBR (for Liquid Metal-cooled Fast-neutron Breeder Reactor). The core of an LMFBR is quite different in design from standard commercial burners. It lacks a moderator, since fast neutrons are more efficient at "breeding" $U^{238}$ into $Pu^{239}$. To sustain a fast-neutron chain reaction, a more highly enriched fuel is required, since there is a lower probability of a given neutron–$U^{235}$ collision causing a fission. An LMFBR core of the same power-generating capacity is much smaller (has a higher "power density") than a burner core. To carry away the enormous amount of heat produced in a small volume, a very efficient transfer medium is required. A further stringent requirement is that the coolant not slow neutrons. The molten sodium metal used in LMFBRs meets these requirements (sodium melts at about the boiling temperature of water).

Liquid sodium is very tricky stuff to handle, as it burns fiercely when exposed to air or water. In a demonstration LMFBR of one-third the proposed commercial size, liquid sodium flows through a core roughly two cubic yards in

volume at a rate of some five cubic yards per second.*
When it comes out of the core, the molten sodium has
been heated to about 1000° Fahrenheit and is highly radioactive. Designing a successful LMFBR consequently presents a considerable challenge to nuclear engineers.

But the rewards would be great. A world powered by
safe breeder reactors would, for practical purposes, never
have to worry about running out of fuel. The kicker lies
in that word "safe."

## Appendix II—Food Storage for Self-sufficiency

The Mormons recommend 300 pounds of grain, 100
pounds each of powdered milk and sugar, and 5 pounds
of salt to support a person for a year at 2400 calories per
day. This is a pretty bare minimum, and of course they
supplement it with a variety of canned and dried foods.
If you have any Mormon friends, or if there is a Church
of Latter-day Saints in your neighborhood, they would
probably be willing to help you organize your food plans.
They also might help you obtain bulk foods at low prices
through their outlets.

Grain, of course, can be stored in a variety of ways:
flour, cornmeal, cooked and dry cereals, and whole grain.
Whole grain keeps best, but would require a grinder, preferably one that can be hand operated. Cereals that require no cooking are preferable to the cooked variety in
an emergency situation, but your family's tastes should
determine the choice. Of uncooked cereals, granola is a
good choice, especially for children who can tolerate the
extra calories. Wheat germ is a useful addition to supplement other foods. It provides high quality protein, iron,
B vitamins, vitamin E, and essential fatty acids. Wheat
germ should not be kept too long and should be stored in
airtight containers in a cool place. Another useful supplement, if you find it palatable, is brewer's yeast, a con-

* According to physicist Amory B. Lovins ("The Case Against
the Fast Breeder Reactor,") *Bulletin of the Atomic Scientists,*
March 1973, pp. 29–35).

centrated source of high-quality protein and B vitamins.

Milk can be stored either as canned condensed milk, or dried milk. Condensed milk requires more space and costs a little more, but if your family prefers it, you should have it. Skimmed milk is now available condensed. It may be wise to have both dried and condensed milk. Non-instant dry milk may be harder to dissolve, but it keeps longer, costs less, and is only about half as bulky. If you don't like drinking reconstituted milk, it can be added to other foods. If you have yogurt culture on hand, you can make yogurt too, which will add some variety to your food. Yogurt is a good substitute for sour cream, especially if made from whole milk. If there is no refrigeration, it will also keep better than reconstituted milk. Milk, in one form or another, is essential for both children and adults, but some adults do not tolerate milk well in its natural form. For these people, the alternative forms such as yogurt and cheese will probably be tolerated and should be provided. Unfortunately, the only kinds of cheese that keep for any length of time without refrigeration are processed cheeses, such as Cheese-Whiz in a jar, and Parmesan cheese.

We would be inclined to recommend much less sugar than the Mormons do. Canned fruits are usually loaded with sugar (save the syrup; it does contain some vitamins), and dried fruits (apricots, prunes, raisins, etc.) are also full of concentrated sugar and also provide iron, vitamin A (especially apricots), and some B vitamins. Honey, molasses, preserves, and brown sugar can also be substituted for much of the sugar and can be used to flavor other dishes or put in sandwiches. All of them provide additional vitamins and minerals that white sugar lacks. The fruits we especially recommend in your canned collection are mandarin oranges, grapefruit, tomatoes, berries (vitamin C), apricots (vitamin A and iron), peaches, and applesauce (some vitamins A and C, generally beneficial). A word of caution: canned fruits should not be stored longer than eighteen months, especially if the temperature is above 68°. As mentioned earlier, freeze-dried fruits last much longer. Sugar and starch are also provided by some vegetables, especially carrots and yams (good for vitamin A), peas and beans (B vitamins, iron, other minerals, and substantial protein).

Many vegetables provide relatively little in the way of calories but a lot of vitamins and minerals: asparagus, broccoli, chard, spinach, and kale (vitamins A and C, minerals); sauerkraut, brussels sprouts, and cauliflower (vitamin C). As with fruits, vegetable juices in the cans should be carefully saved. Cook vegetables in the juice, add what's left over to soups.

Dried beans and peas keep as well as canned ones if they are kept dry in sealed containers that exclude pests. Although they are more trouble to prepare, vitamins may be better preserved, and beans offer the option of sprouting. Beansprouts are rich in vitamins and minerals, and, in the absence of refrigeration or access to fresh produce, they can provide a welcome crisp, fresh addition to your meals.

Fresh potatoes and onions can be kept for several months in a cool, dry, dark place. The canned or dried varieties add very little nourishment, but fresh potatoes, especially baked in their skins, provide significant amounts of vitamin C and iron. The value of onions is chiefly in the zest they add to other foods.

One of the problems in living on stored food is obtaining essential fatty acids and vitamin E. For this reason, we suggest that you have a supply of various nuts and peanut butter. If your grain is whole grain, that will provide some insurance, especially if you also use wheat germ. For cooking, you can use olive oil, which seems to keep well at room temperature and comes in tins; but it provides little of the essential fatty acids or vitamin E. Neither do butter or margarine. (These do exist in canned versions, but may be very hard to find.) Lard contains some fatty acids, but vegetable oils are the best sources, although the least stable, especially after opening. They should be purchased in small containers, not in bulk. Oil with preservatives keeps best, but may lack vitamin E. Probably the best solution is to have a variety of the above fat sources. Any oil that becomes rancid should immediately be discarded. The same applies to any grains, nuts, or peanut butter that show any sign of mold—the toxin produced by a common mold in nuts and grains is extremely carcinogenic (cancer-inducing).

Some form of animal protein—meat, poultry, fish—is essential; it can be stored either canned or dehydrated. Nearly everyone eats some kinds of canned fish regularly —for instance, tuna and salmon. Most people can afford to stash a few cases of tuna in their cellars as a hedge against meat shortages. This would be a good start for your protein stores. Other good choices (in canned form) are sardines, boned chicken and turkey, Spam, corned beef, deviled ham, and liverwurst. All these can be used regularly in sandwiches and salads; most also can be used in casseroles and soups. The liverwurst is especially valuable for iron and B vitamins. Some canned meats and fish will keep for up to twenty years, particularly tuna. Some more expensive items, but still useful if you like them and can afford them, are smoked and canned oysters, shrimp, clams, anchovies, and crabmeat. Even a few of these can add variety to your limited diet.

Most Americans are unaware of the keeping qualities of eggs. Without refrigeration, they will remain edible for two weeks or more; if hard-boiled or coated with vaseline or grease, they can be kept for several months. Powdered eggs are also available, but are less palatable and hard to find (try the camping outlets). It must be remembered that eggs are a protein bargain and very useful in cooking and baking.

Don't overlook the meal-in-a-can possibilities—corned-beef hash, beef stew, pork and beans (but the amount of pork is minuscule and the bean protein should be supplemented), etc. Some of these are quite inexpensive, and children, especially, like them. Soups, particularly those containing a lot of meat, beans, lentils or peas, can provide the basis of a nourishing meal; others are useful for making your own soups, stews, and casseroles. Most canned soups and mixtures also keep well.

The suggestion has been made that a combination of a short-term (two weeks or so) emergency store of canned

goods and water be kept for acute emergencies such as
natural disasters, plus a long-term (a year or more) store
of long-keeping foods such as canned meats and freeze-
dried foods for disruptions of long duration.* This plan
would allow the greatest flexibility. Freeze-dried foods last
from ten to twenty years, perhaps more, and occupy the
least space. Nutrient loss also appears to be minimal. The
only severe disadvantage is that there must be an adequate
supply of water available. The easiest way to obtain them
is by mail-order. A list of suppliers can be found at the
end of this Appendix.

Last, but not least, consider flavorings and baking essentials such as yeast, baking soda, and baking powder.
Salt is essential, but how much you need will depend partly
on your tastes and partly on what foods you have stored.
Canned vegetables, meats, soups, and mixtures generally
contain large amounts of salt. If you are subsisting on these
foods to a great extent, you won't need a great deal more
salt. On the other hand, if you are subsisting chiefly on
grains, dried pulses, nuts, dehydrated foods, and relatively
few canned foods, you'll need more. Be sure the salt you
get is iodized.

Other flavorings are mostly to add enjoyment to what is
otherwise a rather bland diet. Some of them also contribute small amounts of vitamins and minerals. You
might wish to keep on hand catsup, mustard, pickles,
chutney, chili and cocktail sauces (these should be in
small containers and used up quickly after opening if there
is no refrigeration), tabasco and Worcestershire sauces,
reconstituted lemon and lime juices or Tang (which also
provide vitamin C), vanilla and other extracts, and your
favorite herbs and spices. Finally, you will want to have
coffee and/or tea, if you're used to drinking them. Neither
contributes any nutrition, but both are stimulants. Both
are also imported and might be hard to find at times in
the future.

You may also wish to have a supply of alcoholic bev-
erages on hand. Brandy, particularly, is useful for medic-

* Dorris Herrick "Setting Food By," *CoEvolution Quarterly,*
Summer 1974.

inal purposes. In addition, people's desire for alcohol seems to rise in troubled times, and bottles of wine or liquor might be useful as items to trade if the need arises.

If you happen to live in a rural area or have a backyard garden, your problems of obtaining fresh foods and your worries about vitamins will be alleviated, at least in summer. If you can, pickle or preserve some of your produce yourself, you could save money and probably vitamins, too.

**Storable Food.** These companies carry food products for storage; prices quoted are for one year's supply for one person.

Perma-Pak, Inc. . . . . . . . . . . . . .$378.55 (FOB Salt Lake City)
40 East 2430 South
Salt Lake City, Utah 84115

Deseret Supply Company . . . . . $400 (Honeybee Primary D Unit)
410-418 N. Fifth Street
Redlands, California 92373

Pioneer Foods . . . . . . . . . . . . . .$425 (FOB Des Moines, shipping
215 East Third Street            charge $20 to either coast)
Des Moines, Iowa 50309

Lanello Reserves . . . . . . . . . . .$375 (400 lbs. FOB Santa Bar-
2112 Santa Barbara           bara)
Santa Barbara, California

Sam-Andy Dehydrated Foods . . $335 (180 lbs. supplement for
525 South Rancho           basics of flour and sugar, one
Colton, California 94324      person for twenty months)

Bernard Food Industries, Inc. . Does not carry a "year's supply"
222—S. 24th                package per se; customer may
San Jose, California 95103    choose supply from product
                                     lists; orders of over $200 are
                                     shipped prepaid

FSP Foods . . . . . . . . . . . . . . . .Units at $360 and $475 (400 lbs.
6200 Hollis St.                FOB Emeryville)
Emeryville, California 94608

from *CoEvolution Quarterly*, Summer 1974.

# Reading Lists

The following is a list of publications which can help you either to understand and keep track of world events that will affect your personal future or to become less dependent on the fragile social and economic system that now supports you.

## General Information

*The New York Times,* 229 West 43 Street, New York, N.Y. 10036. Essential for day-by-day monitoring of events.

*The Washington Post,* 1515 L Street, N.W., Washington, D.C., 20005. Less useful than above for world events, but useful if you're interested in more detailed political coverage.

*Time,* Rockefeller Center, New York, N.Y., 10020; or *Newsweek,* 444 Madison Avenue, New York, N.Y., 10022. Very useful for monitoring and summaries of events that take place over days or weeks. Business pages are also good for economic news if you know how to interpret it.

*Wall Street Journal,* 30 Broad Street, New York, N.Y., 10004. Good for economics if that's your thing. Also often carries excellent in-depth stories of important foreign events, for instance, India's perpetual crisis, the famines in sub-Saharan Africa, etc.

*Ceres,* Via delle Terme di Caracalla, 00100 Rome, Italy. A monthly publication of FAO, this carries regular information on food production around the world.

*Statistical Abstract of the US,* Updated annually, available from Superintendent of Documents, US Government Printing Office, Washington, D.C. 20402, $4.50 cloth; also most useful are two volumes of the *Historical Statistics of the United States, Colonial Times to 1957* and *Continuation to 1962 and Revisions,* obtainable from the same source for $8.25 and $1.50 respectively.

*UN Statistical Yearbook,* available from Unipub, Inc., P.O. Box 433, Murray Hill Station, New York, N.Y., 10016. $16.50. Published annually. A goldmine of information of all sorts.

*State of Food and Agriculture,* Food and Agriculture Organization of the United Nations, available through Unipub, Inc. (see above). $10.00. Published annually in the fall. Because it often takes months to get to the US, it pays to watch for newspaper coverage when it is released. *The New York Times* always carries a report. The *SOFA Report,* as it is called, is essential for following the food situation in detail.

*Population, Resources, Environment,* Paul R. Ehrlich and Anne H. Ehrlich, 2nd edition, W. H. Freeman and Co., 660 Market Street, San Francisco, California, 94104. 1972. $9.50. This is a detailed treatment of the crises now facing mankind. Extensive bibliographies.

*Energy,* by John P. Holdren and Philip Herrera, Sierra Club Battlebooks, 529 Commercial Street, San Francisco, California, 94111. 1971. $2.95. Slightly out of date, but still the best general treatment for laymen.

*Human Ecology,* by P. R. Ehrlich, A. H. Ehrlich, and J. P. Holdren. W. H. Freeman and Company, 660 Market Street, San Francisco, California, 94104. 1973.

An abbreviated and updated version of *Population, Resources, Environment.*

*Population Bomb,* by P. R. Ehrlich. Ballantine Books, 201 East 50th Street, New York, N.Y. 10022. Rev. ed., 1971. 95¢. A layman's introduction to our present predicament.

*Ark II: Social Response to Environmental Imperatives,* Dennis C. Pirages and Paul R. Ehrlich. Viking Press, 625 Madison Avenue, N.Y., 10022. 1974. In-depth discussion of the kinds of social change necessary if an interdependent society is to continue to work.

*How To Be A Survivor,* by P. R. Ehrlich and R. L. Harriman. Ballantine Books, 201 East 50th Street, New York, N.Y., 10022. 1971. $1.25. A brief, popular introduction to the topics dealt with in *Ark II.*

## Food and Nutrition

*Diet for a Small Planet,* by Frances Moore Lappé. Ballantine Books. 1971. $1.25. Includes facts on the US food system and tells you how to maintain a high protein diet without eating meat. Recipes included.

*Let's Eat Right to Keep Fit,* by Adelle Davis. Signet. 1970. $1.50. Although it contains errors, it is still the best popular guide to nutrition.

*Putting Food By,* by Ruth Hertzberg, Beatrice Vaughn, and Janet Greene. Stephen Greene Press. 1973. $3.95. A guide for canning, freezing, drying, and preserving food. Some recipes included.

*The Food Conspiracy Cookbook,* by Lois Wickstrom. 101 Productions, San Francisco, Calif. 1974. $3.95. Tells how to save money by forming a neighborhood buying club. Based on the experiences of the Berkeley Food Conspiracy. Includes many recipes.

*The Supermarket Handbook, Access to Whole Foods,* by Nikki and David Goldbeck. Harper and Row. 1973. $7.95. How to get the most nutrition from your supermarket for the least money. Includes many recipes and a lot of nutritional information.

## Self-Sufficiency Publications

*The CoEvolution Quarterly* (Supplement to the *Whole Earth Catalog*), Stewart Brand, ed. $6/yr from 558 Santa Cruz, Menlo Park, California 94025. Includes extensive articles on food storage, land use, alternate technology, community organizing, etc.

*Mother Earth News,* John Shuttleworth, ed. $8/yr (bimonthly) from Box 70, Hendersonville, North Carolina, 28739. Excellent coverage of everything relating to "homesteading"—farming, building construction, alternate technology, communes, etc.

*Organic Gardening and Farming,* Robert Rodale, ed. $6.85/yr (monthly) from 33 Minor Street, Emmaus, Pennsylvania, 18049. The best grow-your-own-food publication.

*Finding and Buying Your Place in the Country,* by Les Scher. 368 pp. Macmillan. 1974. $4.95. Best guide to buying country land.

*Grow It,* by Richard W. Langer. 365 pp. Avon. 1973. $4.95. Complete small-farm guide, from vegetables to livestock.

*The Updated Last Whole Earth Catalog,* Stewart Brand, ed. 448 pp. Random House. $5; and *Whole Earth*

*Epilog,* Stewart Brand, ed. 320 pp. Penguin Books. 1971, 1974. $4. How to create your own civilization.

*The Book of Survival,* by Anthony Greenback, 223 pp. New American Library. 1967. 95¢. What to do in burning buildings, colliding cars, crowds, blizzards, hold-ups, etc.

*Living Poor with Style,* by Ernest Callenbach. 600 pp. Straight Arrow. 1972. 95¢. How to live better when money buys less and there's less to buy.

*Survival with Style,* by Bradford Angier. Vintage Books. 1974. A goldmine of information on survival skills.

*One Acre and Security: How to Live off the Earth without Ruining it,* by Bradford Angier. Vintage Books. 1973. $2.45. Useful advice for those who want to be completely self-sufficient.

*Five Acres and Independence, a Practical Guide to the Selection and Management of the Small Farm,* by M. G. Kains. Dover Publications. 1973. $2.50. This book was originally published in 1935, but much of the advice it contains remains pertinent and timely.

*The Basic Book of Organic Gardening,* edited by Robert Rodale. Ballantine Books. 1971. $1.25.

*Passport to Survival,* by Esther Dickey. Random House. 1969. $4.95. A guide to storing food against disaster or times of trouble. Includes some recipes and survival advice on other subjects besides food: i.e., first aid, safe water, wilderness emergencies, etc.

*Zero Population Growth* (ZPG) is a non-profit, grass-roots, political action organization concerned about resolving many of the problems discussed in this book. ZPG believes that the environmental and social impacts of individual actions can be reduced and the quality of life can be sustained if the United States population size is stabilized and per capita consumption of resources and energy is thoughtfully reduced.

---

## MEMBERSHIP BLANK

Name _____

Address _____

City and State _____ Zip _____

- ☐ $15.00—General Membership
- ☐ $22.50—Family Membership
- ☐ $50.00—Donor Membership
- ☐ $100.00—Contributing Membership
- ☐ $500.00—Patron

Return to: Zero Population Growth, Inc.
1346 Connecticut Avenue N.W.
Washington, D.C. 20036

Membership automatically includes a year's subscription to the ZPG National Reporter.

*FRIENDS OF THE EARTH*, founded in 1969 by David Brower, is a nonprofit membership organization streamlined for legislative activity in the United States and abroad aimed at restoring the environment misused by man and at preserving remaining wilderness where the life force continues to flow freely.

*FRIENDS OF THE EARTH* lobbies, publishes, and litigates in pursuit of its objectives.

*FRIENDS OF THE EARTH*, in order to lobby without restrictions, does not wish to be tax-deductible. For that reason, we need and invite your participation.

Addresses:

**FRIENDS OF THE EARTH**
529 Commercial Street
San Francisco, Calif. 94111

620 C Street, S.E.
Washington, D.C. 20003

------------------------------------------------------------

## FRIENDS OF THE EARTH

☐ I enclose $_____ for membership.

    $15 Regular
    $25 Supporting
    $50 Contributing
    $1000 Life

☐ I wish to participate actively from time to time. My special interests are:

_____

_____

☐ My own field is: _____
☐ I enclose $_____ as a contribution.

NAME _____

ADDRESS _____

CITY _____ STATE _____ ZIP _____